Policy Convergence in the UK and Germany

Policy convergence and policy learning have emerged as central themes in the study of public policy in recent years.

This book complements the rich literature on theoretical aspects as well as individual case studies by undertaking a systematic comparison of policy convergence between two specific countries, the UK and Germany. Both are member-states of the EU and face similar policy challenges across a number of policy sectors; as such, both are ideally suited to such a comparison. In particular, in the late 1990s, the social-democratic governments of both countries explicitly sought to develop common solutions under the heading of the 'Third Way'. By including analyses of not only of institutions but also of key areas of domestic and foreign policy, this volume makes a unique contribution to the study of public policy in two of the EU's key member-states.

This book was previously published as a special issue of *German Politics*

Simon Green is Senior Lecturer in German and European Politics at the European Research Institute and Deputy Director of the Institute for German Studies, University of Birmingham.

Edward Turner is a doctoral candidate at the Institute for German Studies, University of Birmingham.

Policy Convergence in the UK and Germany

Beyond the Third Way?

Edited by
SIMON GREEN and EDWARD TURNER

LONDON AND NEW YORK

First published 2008 by Routledge
2 Park Square, Milton Park, Abingdon, Oxfordshire OX14 4RN

Simultaneously published in the USA and Canada
by Routledge
711 Third Avenue, New York, NY 10017

First issued in paperback 2016

Routledge is an imprint of the Taylor & Francis Group, an informa business

©2008 Edited by Simon Green and Edward Turner

Typeset in Times-Roman by Techset Composition, Salisbury, UK

All rights reserved. No part of this book may be reprinted or reproduced or utilised in any form or by any electronic, mechanical, or other means, now known or hereafter invented, including photocopying and recording, or in any information storage or retrieval system, without permission in writing from the publishers.

British Library Cataloguing in Publication Data
A catalogue record for this book is available from the British Library

ISBN 13: 978-1-138-99503-1 (pbk)
ISBN 13: 978-0-415-44580-1 (hbk)

Contents

1. Understanding Policy Convergence in Britain and Germany: Towards a Framework for Analysis **Edward Turner and Simon Green** 1

2. Germany, Britain and William Paterson **Peter Pulzer** 22

3. Different Road Maps, Similar Paths? Social Democratic Politics in the UK and Germany **Dan Hough and James Sloam** 26

4. Germany, Britain and the European Union: Convergence through Policy Transfer? **Simon Bulmer** 39

5. Balancing Territorial Politics and Social Citizenship in Germany and Britain: Constraints in Public Opinion **Charlie Jeffery** 58

6. Same Challenges, Diverging Responses: Germany, the UK and European Security **Kerry Longhurst and Alister Miskimmon** 79

7. Divergent Traditions, Converging Responses: Immigration and Integration Policy in the UK and Germany **Simon Green** 95

8. Convergence in Employment-Related Public Policies? A British–German Comparison **Lothar Funk** 116

9. The Unmovable Elephant: Germany and the UK's Competitiveness Jungle **Rebecca Harding** 137

10. Health Policy: Obstacles to Policy Convergence in Britain and Germany **Nils C. Bandelow** 150

11. Environmental Policy in the United Kingdom and Germany **Charles Lees** 164

12. Conclusions **Edward C. Page** 184

Index *191*

Understanding Policy Convergence in Britain and Germany

EDWARD TURNER and SIMON GREEN

INTRODUCTION: THE NOTION OF POLICY CONVERGENCE IN BRITAIN AND GERMANY

This collection of essays analyses the extent to which public policy has converged in the United Kingdom and Germany since the late 1990s. It examines the pressures for convergence, both endogenous and exogenous, and the outcomes over a range of different policy areas, discussing both the policy choices which have been made, and whether convergence can be seen, and also, as far as is possible, the pressures underlying those choices.

The two countries are ideally suited to such a comparison, constituting as they do important examples of modern industrial nations; what is more, both face parallel, if not necessarily equal, challenges on a range of issues. They are characterised by uneven geographic distribution of economic activity, with the eastern Länder and areas such as the North-East of England similarly depressed. Both have grappled, albeit for very different reasons, with their public finances throughout most of the 1990s and beyond, which has periodically circumscribed the policies each government could actually implement. Internationally, both are trading nations, with corresponding exposure to international economic conditions and capital flows. Both are members of NATO and traditional 'Atlanticists' in their definition of security policy. Structurally, both are facing adverse demographic developments, with ageing populations and reduced birth rates predicted to lead to a halving of support ratios by 2050, and corresponding impacts for welfare and pensions.[1] Both are major destinations for migration and asylum seekers. Perhaps most importantly, both are member states of the EU, which *ipso facto*, through the adoption of common legislation in the form of EU Directives and Regulations, has led to at least some form of convergence; moreover, membership of the EU promotes *negotiated* and *voluntary* convergence, for instance via the open method of co-ordination. What is more, the culture of co-operation under the auspices of EU membership by definition makes cross-national policy learning and convergence in any case more likely.[2]

Certainly, the UK and Germany are by no means the only sources for cross-national policy learning. Indeed, both countries have frequently looked to solutions adopted elsewhere, for instance in the United States and the Netherlands. But what is perhaps most fascinating about looking at policy convergence in a UK–German comparison is the political dimension. In the late 1990s, and after sometimes long periods in opposition, centre-left parties found themselves in government again across the developed world, including in the UK and Germany, where New Labour and the SPD won resounding victories in the 1997 and 1998 elections respectively. Seizing this moment, US President Bill Clinton and the new UK Prime Minister Tony Blair took the lead in attempting to give cross-national coherence to this development, by formulating what was heralded as a new kind of social-democratic political agenda. This agenda broadly fell under the label of the 'Third Way' and was famously championed by the sociologist Anthony Giddens.[3] Under this rubric, policy convergence and cross-national policy learning were integral elements of Third Way politics, as political parties looked to kindred spirits abroad for inspiration.

From the outset, the UK and Germany were seen as leaders in this process. Under Tony Blair, Labour in the UK had explicitly distanced itself from its traditional socialist roots, while the new German Chancellor Gerhard Schröder had successfully conjured up the image of a new centre ground in German politics (*die neue Mitte*) during the 1998 federal election campaign. And so it seemed only natural that, less than one year after the SPD swept to power in Germany, the two leaders should present their now infamous document on the 'Third Way' in early 1999. In the context of this comparison, the paper itself in fact emphasised the need for a bilateral UK–German approach to policy solution. As the two leaders argued:

> We face the same challenges – to promote employment and prosperity, to offer every individual the opportunity to fulfil their unique potential, to combat social exclusion and poverty, to reconcile material progress with environmental sustainability and our responsibility to future generations, to tackle common problems that threaten the cohesion of society such as crime and drugs, and to make Europe a more effective force for good in the world ... We need to strengthen our policies by benchmarking our experiences in Britain and Germany, but also with like-minded counterparts in Europe and the rest of the world. We must learn from each other and measure our own performance against best practice and experience in other countries.[4]

Almost ten years on, of course, the Third Way project, which some initial partners, such as the French *Parti Socialiste* under Lionel Jospin, had always viewed with considerable suspicion, has all but disappeared from public view. But at the same time, the issue of cross-national policy learning remains very much *au courant* in politics: governing parties regularly point to the performance of other countries to showcase the success of their own policies, while opposition parties regularly look abroad when seeking inspiration for new policy ideas. Often, such initiatives have come as a response to the pressures of globalisation or Europeanisation (to be discussed further below). In other words, there are clearly endogenous and exogenous pressures towards the convergence of public policies: the question is, do they actually produce convergence? This is the central question which this volume seeks to address.

For despite all these common pressures, the starting points for this process in each country are clearly quite different: divergent models of the welfare state, with Germany relying on social insurance, the UK on tax funding; contrasting political systems, with the UK's generally centralised and remarkably unrestricted and Germany's requiring major political decisions to be approved by a variety of veto players; Britain an oft-cited example of a liberal market economy, Germany close to the paradigm of a co-ordinated market economy; the one committed to an active role in the world, the other reluctant to commit troops abroad, constrained by the weight of history and the Franco-German axis.[5] This throws up enticing possibilities for comparison – when these common pressures for convergence are refracted through the prisms of divergent histories and institutional settings, will similar policies be pursued? And might we expect policy outcomes to shift closer together?

In this context, it is important to differentiate between macro- and micro-level outcomes. As Table 1 shows, it is very clear that, at the macro-level of policy outcomes, there is little clear evidence of systematic convergence. Apart from some parallel slight decline in levels of economic growth in very recent years, and quite similar levels of inflation, we see a trend towards growing public expenditure in the UK while public expenditure in Germany declines; similar divergence in the levels of the national debt, with Germany's national debt growing and the UK's declining (albeit with a slight increase in 2005); trends in unemployment point in opposite directions, with unemployment stagnating or on the rise in Germany while declining in the UK; and trends in net migration fluctuate from year to year, but with little identifiable pattern between changes in the two countries. But then, given the number of factors which affect such macro-level indicators, their convergence is always likely to be the exception rather than the rule. Of greater interest in the context of this collection is the question of micro- or sectoral-level convergence, where there might well be an *a priori* expectation to see similar policy challenges being addressed in similar ways.

DEFINING POLICY CONVERGENCE

The notion of 'policy convergence' has, in recent years, firmly established itself in the epistemological repertoire of comparative politics. An important starting point was Colin Bennett's 1991 discussion of the issue. He suggests that policy convergence can mean one of five things: a convergence of policy goals, policy content, policy instruments, policy outcomes or 'policy style'.[6] The point is also well made that convergence is essentially *temporal*, rather than *spatial*, in that it means countries are moving from different positions towards one common point: 'Convergence should ... be seen as a process of "becoming" rather than a condition of "being" more alike'.[7]

However, the term must be approached with some care, as it clearly competes with a range of other terms used to describe different aspects of the broader question of the adoption of similar policies in different countries, most especially *policy transfer*, *policy diffusion* and *isomorphism*. Of these, policy transfer is of course easily the best known and most influential and was first catalogued by David Dolowitz and

TABLE 1
KEY INDICATORS IN BRITAIN AND GERMANY, 1998–2005

	Germany								UK							
	1998	1999	2000	2001	2002	2003	2004	2005	1998	1999	2000	2001	2002	2003	2004	2005
Net migration in '000s	47.0	202.1	167.8	274.8	218.8	142.2	81.8	n/a	97.4	137.5	143.7	151.0	157.6	177.8	201.8	n/a
Ratio of government expenditure to GDP	48.0	48.1	45.1	47.6	48.1	48.4	46.9	46.7	40.2	39.6	39.8	40.8	41.5	43.2	43.9	45.5
General government gross debt in % of GDP	60.9	61.2	60.2	59.6	60.3	63.8	65.5	67.7	47.7	45.1	42.0	38.7	37.6	39.0	40.8	42.8
Real GDP growth rate	2.0	2.0	3.2	1.2	0.1	−0.2	1.6	0.9	3.2	3.0	4.0	2.2	2.0	2.5	3.1	1.8
Inflation	0.6	0.6	1.4	1.9	1.4	1.0	1.8	1.9	1.6	1.3	0.8	1.2	1.3	1.4	1.3	1.9
Unemployment	8.8	7.9	7.2	7.4	8.2	9.0	9.5	9.5	6.1	5.9	5.4	5.0	5.1	4.9	4.7	4.7

Source: Eurostat, available at http://epp.eurostat.cec.eu.int (accessed 22 May 2006).

David Marsh, who famously defined it as 'the process by which actors borrow policies developed in one setting to develop programmes and policies within another'.[8]

In making the distinction between these terms for definitional purposes, we draw directly on Christoph Knill's recent and authoritative discussion of the issue.[9] In fact, Knill, in developing his typology, acknowledges that there is a considerable degree of overlap between the various terms, and that their application is not necessarily mutually exclusive (Table 2).

Building on this, he develops a more precise definition of the term 'policy convergence' as follows: policy convergence can be defined as any increase in the similarity between one or more characteristics of a certain policy (e.g. policy objectives, policy instruments, policy settings), across a given set of political jurisdictions (supranational institutions, states, regions, local authorities) over a given period of time. Policy convergence thus describes the end result of a process of policy change over time towards some common point, regardless of the causal process.[10]

Knill's definition evidently conceives of policy convergence as an umbrella term, to encompass all the categories listed in Table 2. Thus, policy convergence can, under certain circumstances, incorporate the processes of transfer and diffusion.[11] Equally, a discussion of policy convergence, or indeed isomorphism, may identify policy transfer or policy diffusion as independent variables. Indeed, the distinction between studies drawing on policy convergence and those drawing on isomorphism is also not hard and fast.[12] But such a broad approach suits the purposes of this study perfectly, where the aim is to undertake a systematic analysis of the question of policy convergence in two major European nation states, the United Kingdom and Germany.

In considering this very question, the comparison is in fact timely and fills a quite significant gap in the literature, as a recent survey of the research on policy convergence shows.[13] In particular, amongst the 74 studies considered, the variation in the choice of topics was striking (Table 3).

The bulk of these 74 studies considered over ten cases each, rather than a detailed discussion of only a few. The findings were diverse, even within the same broad policy area. Around half the studies found evidence of convergence, whereas only 15 found evidence of divergence, and the remainder found limited convergence, either within only some of the countries under examination, or only in certain periods of the timeframe under study.[14] Crucially, the United Kingdom and Germany were compared in just seven of the small-*n* studies surveyed; in the fields of telecommunication,

TABLE 2
POLICY CONVERGENCE AND RELATED CONCEPTS

	Policy convergence	Isomorphism	Policy transfer	Policy diffusion
Analytical focus	Effects	Effects	Process	Process
Empirical focus	Policy characteristics	Organisational structures	Policy characteristics	Policy characteristics
Dependent variable	Similarity change	Similarity change	Transfer content, transfer process	Adoption pattern

Source: C. Knill, 'Introduction: Cross-national Policy Convergence: Concepts, Approaches, and Explanatory Factors', *Journal of European Public Policy* 12/5 (2005), pp.764–74, here p.768.

TABLE 3
POLICY AREAS IN 'CONVERGENCE' LITERATURE

Policy area	Number of studies undertaken
Social policy (including employment and labour market policy)	15
Fiscal policy	12
Environmental policy	12
Trade policy	5
Banking regulation	4
Telecommunication	4
Health policy	4
Monetary policy	3
Migration policy	3
Organisational practices and infrastructure	3
Competition policy	2
Justice and data protection policy	2
Agricultural policy	2
Education policy	1
Foreign policy	1

Source: Derived from S. Heichel, J. Pape and T. Sommerer, 'Is There Convergence in Convergence Research? An Overview of Empirical Studies on Policy Convergence', *Journal of European Public Policy* 12/5 (2005), pp.817–40, here pp.820–23.

electricity and media, convergence was noted, while in the field of banking regulation, competition policy and justice and data protection policy, evidence for convergence was either lacking or patchy.

There is, then, a significant gap in the literature on 'policy convergence' (as defined above) in discussions of Britain and Germany. Previous studies have generally focused only on very few areas of policy, and in a number of those areas (such as social and labour market policy) the studies have focused on a large number of country cases. In consequence, there is real value in undertaking a detailed comparison of convergence (or otherwise) both across a wide range of policy areas and in these two countries. This is the specific gap that this set of contributions seeks to fill. Six of the case studies, on security, migration, multi-level governance, health policy and productivity growth, draw on the discussions held within a series of high-level bilateral policy seminars, organised by the Anglo-German Foundation for the Study of Industrial Society and the Institute for German Studies at the University of Birmingham during 2003–5.[15] By bringing together representatives of think tanks, civil servants, politicians and academics, these seminars were able to explore such issues with a wider range of actors, and in rather more depth, than would be possible in a large-n study based simply on quantitative data.

This collection therefore aims to examine both common pressures for convergence, and the ways in which the two countries have responded – to incorporate both why convergence is anticipated, and how it is, or is not, in fact taking place. The case studies presented here consider a range of policy areas, including domestic policy but also foreign policy, which are only seldom viewed under this analytical framework (see Table 3). In doing so, the focus is explicitly on the period between 1997/98 and 2005, when the UK has been governed by the Labour Party, and also encompassing the period of office of the SPD–Green coalition in Germany. Although the Schröder–Blair paper alluded to above probably represents the high-water mark in explicit, top-level co-operation between the two governments, the specific comparison of social-democratic responses to these policy pressures additionally provides an insight into the scope for achieving political change which parties of the centre-left enjoy, as well as highlighting areas of divergence amongst social-democratic policy choices.

The remainder of this introduction will, firstly, review the different factors which lead to, and mechanisms which generate, change comprising 'policy convergence'. Secondly, the phenomena of 'globalisation' and 'Europeanisation' will be briefly considered in relation to these previously outlined pressures and mechanisms. We argue that, rather than being analytically distinct, they are in fact combinations of different factors leading to convergence. Thirdly, we will consider some of the obstacles to such convergence, and will hypothesise that significant cross-national variations might be expected to persist, in spite of undoubted pressures to convergence in some sectors and across some time periods. In particular, three arguments will be discussed: the 'Varieties of Capitalism' literature which suggests that significant differences between economies will persist, as there is more than one path to economic success, refuting the neo-liberal model that prophesies convergence along Anglo-American lines. Secondly, the suggestion that the impact of 'globalisation' in fact varies across different nation states, or that it is simply overplayed, will be considered. Thirdly, institutional perspectives will be considered: the argument that, while there may be cross-national pressures of convergence, these are shaped through the lens of national institutions, leading to different policies and indeed different outcomes of those policies.

FACTORS PROMOTING POLICY CONVERGENCE

In the literature, a number of discrete pressures which lead to policy convergence (in its broadest sense) can be distinguished, as well as a number of distinct mechanisms which achieve it.[16]

Political Pressures or Demands: 'Forced Policy Transfer'
Clearly, one of the most obvious ways in which policy can converge is if an outside agent forces a policy to effect policy change. There are a number of different terms reflecting 'forced' policy transfer, for instance, 'direct coercive transfer', identified by Dolowitz and Marsh.[17] They rightly suggest that there are different degrees of coercion which can be deployed by other actors (be they other nation states, or supranational organisations), and so view the degree of coercion involved in policy transfer as a continuum, with 'lesson-drawing' at one end, and 'complete imposition' at the other. An alternative interpretation is put forward by DiMaggio and Powell, who view their model of *coercive isomorphism* as stemming from 'both formal and informal pressures exerted on organizations by other organisations upon which they are dependent'.[18]

In the case of forced policy transfer, the mechanism promoting convergence is 'imposition' and it assumes that one political actor can require the other to comply. There are a number of examples of one nation state forcing another to change, for instance, after a defeat in a war, as with the numerous impositions upon West Germany after the Second World War; the attitude of the Soviet Union towards some of its Warsaw Pact allies within certain policy domains; or indeed the current situation in Iraq. But at the same time, this is an extreme form of policy transfer, and in the context of this collection, we are of course primarily concerned with the latter end of Dolowitz and Marsh's continuum.

Political Pressures or Demands: 'Conditional Policy Transfer'

Secondly, it seems useful to distinguish between 'forced' and 'conditional' policy transfer. Simply put, in conditions of the former, policy-makers in the country concerned have *no* choice but to comply with demands for convergence, while in the latter, conditions are imposed upon a country by the outside agent. For instance, as Coate and Morris note, 'the World Bank carries out extensive policy conditionality: developing country policy makers agree to a program of economic policy reform in exchange for grants and concessionary finance'.[19] A further distinction is usefully drawn by Karen Smith between positive and negative conditionality: positive conditionality promises benefits as a reward for convergence, while negative conditionality implies sanctions, such as reducing, suspending or terminating benefits if a country does not converge.[20] In either event, an asymmetry in power between the two political units is required.

Although discussion of 'conditionality' has been most prominent in relations between EU accession countries and the European Union itself,[21] it is also of relevance to existing member states, most notably through the Stability and Growth Pact, which was set up to curb excessive budget deficits of members of the Eurozone. Equally, certain EU funding streams may impose elements of positive conditionality – for instance, applicants for cohesion funds have to respect the 'polluter pays' principle.[22] It is worth noting that 'conditional policy transfer' covers a wide range of phenomena, from World Bank loans which a developing country is barely in a position to refuse, through to potential grant aid to a local authority for an infrastructural project: the link is that a common policy is created through the introduction of an incentive or disincentive, by a more powerful actor to a weaker one.

Obligations through International Laws

A third pressure for convergence stems from the development of obligations as a result of international law. As Holzinger and Knill note, 'harmonisation refers to a specific outcome of international co-operation, namely to constellations in which national governments are legally required to adopt similar policies and programmes as part of their obligations as members of international institutions'.[23] Policies will converge not only due to actual rulings and sanctions under international law, but also through the anticipation of the reaction of those international institutions.

There are numerous examples of these which are pertinent to modern industrial nations such as Britain and Germany. Most importantly, as will be discussed below, is the impact of the European Union and its predecessor institutions: the pooling of sovereignty to the EU, driven by the potential benefits of co-operation, has led to the creation of a body of European legislation, and the European Court of Justice which can enforce compliance.[24] Other examples of such compliance are the body of international law enshrined in treaties, such as the UN Charter, the Geneva Convention, and the European Convention on Human Rights.

In all of these cases, it would be misleading to identify these mechanisms with the degree of coercion associated with, for instance, the imposition of new policies or institutions by an occupying power after an invasion. Unlike domestic law, where citizens are not generally in a position to 'opt out' of the nation state's legal framework, members of international organisations are at liberty to opt out of international legal frameworks; the costs of this may in practice be high (for instance, neither Britain nor Germany can seriously contemplate withdrawal from the EU), or nation states may be sanguine about so doing (witness the UK's decision to derogate from Article 5 of the European Convention on Human Rights, which it did under provisions contained in the ECHR's own Article 15).

Competitive Pressure

Fourthly, competitive pressures, deriving both from globalisation and growing economic integration amongst countries, are held by Drezner to give rise to 'regulatory competition':

> One view [of convergence pressures stemming from 'globalisation'] is that the primary pressure for convergence is economic: the pressure to modify regulatory policies comes from the threat of mobile capital to exit, causing nonconverging states to lose their competitiveness in the global economy.... The most prominent of these convergence theories is the 'Race to the bottom' (RTB) hypothesis, ... which assumes that the pressure for convergence comes from the mobility of trade and capital flows, and that the size of these flows overwhelms the ability of the state to act contrary to market forces.[25]

This has been the subject of lively debate, not only, as might be expected, in the areas of social and labour market regulation,[26] but also, for instance, in the parallel adoption of particular legal models, or particular models of corporate law.[27] In general, convergence is allegedly likely to be on an Anglo-American model of the liberal market economy (LME), with a move away from the co-ordinated market economies (CMEs).

Under this analysis, the UK's model is likely to be relatively unchallenged (or indeed face increasing liberalising pressures), while the distinctive 'German model' – or at least its 'co-ordinated' features – will be eroded. Two key elements of the model, in particular, will come under challenge: firstly, the institutions of labour market co-ordination, with bipartite works councils at the level of the firm, as well as collective wage bargaining would be undone. Secondly, the distinctive German banking sector, and the *Hausbank* model, under which German banks would invest in firms for the long term and play an active role in those firms' corporate governance, would come under threat.[28] While most definitions of the German model focus on political economy, other important aspects of German society since the Second World War will also come under pressure to converge. For instance, the relatively generous systems of social insurance, 50 per cent of which are financed by employers' contributions, will theoretically become unviable as the high non-wage labour costs threaten competitiveness.[29] Moreover, high levels of labour market regulation, and restrictions on the ability to 'hire and fire', become difficult to sustain.

In an engaging recent discussion, Andreas Busch identifies five key ways in which the German model is argued (by others – Busch views this analysis critically) to have either declined or failed, each of which can be related to these 'competitive pressures'.[30] Firstly, there is a greater emphasis on shareholder value, and firms are less protected from hostile takeover. Secondly, there has been a substantial weakening of associational strength on both employer and trade union sides. Thirdly, the German banking sector has moved away from the *Hausbank* model towards a focus on investment banking – there is a greater emphasis on shareholder value and short-term returns, and the banks have largely pulled out of corporate governance arrangements. Fourth, political reforms underpinned this development, with legislation, ironically since 1998 and the election of the SPD–Green government, weakening the power of the German banking sector and removing disincentives to the sale of corporate investments. Finally, corporate law is shifting, with a move towards shareholder interests.

An influential recent discussion of institutional change by Wolfgang Streeck and Kathleen Thelen has broadly supported these points: 'The dominant trend in advanced political economies ... is liberalisation: the steady expansion of market relations in areas that under the postwar settlement of democratic capitalism were reserved to collective political decisionmaking'.[31] They argue that, while rapid liberalisation will occur only occasionally and in special circumstances (such as the Thatcher governments in the UK), gradual liberalisation is inevitable as a result of the greater incentives to competition, rather than co-ordination. Specifically, actors are readier to leave co-ordinated institutional arrangements, than they are to engage in the creation and maintenance of such institutional arrangements.

These approaches are not without their critics, as will be discussed below. It is also worth noting that the same logic of regulatory competition arising from competitive pressure has led, in one analysis, to an entirely different conclusion: a 'race to the top'. The argument, most forcefully advanced by David Vogel, is that if a large and powerful jurisdiction sets strict standards of regulation and makes access to its market conditional on meeting them, then in order to access that market foreign producers will need to meet those standards.[32] Once such producers have accepted these jurisdictions, they will at least accept, and quite possibly encourage, their adoption in their home jurisdictions, which will give them a comparative advantage over competitors.

'Problem Pressures'

Clearly, at times governments face challenges which they know are faced by other governments too: these might be considered 'problem pressures'. Several potential reactions to this exist, which fit into the 'policy learning' paradigm. Holzinger and Knill distinguish between 'lesson-drawing' and 'transnational problem-solving', holding that the former is inspired by 'problem pressure', while the latter stems from 'parallel problem pressure'. The distinction is that, in the case of 'problem pressure', 'lesson-drawing is based on a voluntaristic process whereby government A learns from government B's solution to a common problem what to do ... or not to do'.[33] Transnational problem-solving occurs when 'convergence is not the result of bilateral transfer. Rather, it is driven by the joint development of common problem perceptions and solutions to similar domestic problems and their subsequent adoption at the domestic level'.[34]

This dichotomy seems mistaken for two reasons: firstly, it is not clear that 'parallel problem pressure' will necessarily result in transnational co-operation to achieve a solution. Secondly, 'lesson-drawing' may involve elements of international co-operation and collaboration, but without a quest for a common solution.[35] The line between lesson-drawing and collaboration is too murky to justify a strict dichotomy.

Several examples of this 'problem pressure' will be discussed later in this volume. For instance, as Lothar Funk notes in the field of labour market policy, the Minister-President of Hesse, Roland Koch, was extremely keen to draw on the 'Wisconsin model' of 'workfare' for his own policy initiatives.[36] In addition, in the field of health-care policy, the sharing of expertise cross-nationally is particularly widespread. It is also worth noting that lesson-drawing may be negative, as well as positive (and, indeed, the process of searching for a common solution might in the end lead to the decision not to converge). Later in this volume, for instance, Nils Bandelow points out that Germany is often cited as a negative example in the UK's National Health Service plan from the year 2000, with its insurance system held to be inefficient and unfair. Conversely, in Germany, public discussion sometimes revolves around *Englische Verhältnisse* ('English circumstances') in health care provision, which in this case is used as a metaphor for perceived inadequate levels of funding and standards of care.[37]

Problem pressures may, however, not result in any sort of lesson-drawing at all, but rather may lead political actors independently to arrive at the same conclusion: 'Just as individuals open their umbrellas simultaneously during a rainstorm, governments may decide to change their policies in the presence of tax evasion, environmental pressures ... or an ageing population'.[38] In consequence, lesson-drawing is but a sub-set of policy convergence. As Lenschow *et al.* note, the extent of convergence, based on these common pressures, will depend on the extent of similarity between the countries, specifically the similarity of culture, institutions and economy.[39]

Here, rather than thinking of distinct categories (as is at least implicit in some of the literature), it may be useful to consider the extent of international co-operation as a continuum, as illustrated in Figure 1, with independent problem-solving at one end, through 'desk-based' lesson-drawing, lesson-drawing with discussion and co-operation, through to collaboration in the search for joint solutions.

Desire for Conformity

Sixthly, Holzinger and Knill identify three reasons why a desire to achieve conformity, which then manifests itself in policy emulation, may arise.[40] Firstly, 'herding' might occur: the very fact that a policy has been chosen by a number of followers sends a

FIGURE 1
A CONTINUUM OF INTERNATIONAL CO-OPERATION IN POLICY CONVERGENCE

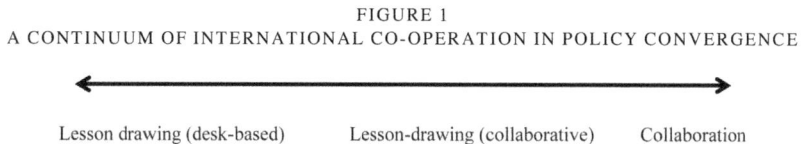

Lesson drawing (desk-based)   Lesson-drawing (collaborative)   Collaboration

signal that it is a policy worth following, even without substantive information on the benefits of the policy. Secondly, drawing on the notion of *normative isomorphism* in the work of DiMaggio and Powell, the social legitimacy of an organisation might be increased by drawing on established practices.[41] Thirdly, *mimetic isomorphism* can occur – it reflects the desire of actors not to be 'left behind'. Finally, there might be more 'rational' underpinnings, they argue, for such emulation: if a policy solution is urgently required, the use of an 'off-the-shelf' solution, taken from another polity, will allow far swifter implementation, and the costs of acquiring information are lower.

Dolowitz *et al.* certainly see evidence of this in the UK's relationship with the US, arguing that, 'faced with an increasingly complex and quickly changing policy environment, governments look for ready-made policy solutions; to put it another way, there is considerable pressure to look for a "quick fix"'.[42] They also note the seemingly ubiquitous influence of the Wisconsin model of workfare, this time in exercising great influence on the UK government's New Deal. Tim Haughton presents a similar argument about the influence of 'Third Way' discourse on the Slovak politician Robert Fico, after a trip to the United Kingdom.[43]

Legitimacy Pressure

Lastly, Holzinger and Knill identify 'legitimacy pressure', which manifests itself in the propensity of international organisations to promote particular policy models; policy convergence 'is driven by the active role of international institutions that are promoting the spread of distinctive policy approaches they consider particularly promising'.[44] This definition can usefully be extended to situations where no particular model is explicitly promoted, but where performance indicators or 'benchmarking' and league tables set certain national standards.

This is distinct from 'conditional' policy transfer from such organisations, as there is no sanction involved should a country fail to comply, although again there is no hard-and-fast distinction. Holzinger and Knill are somewhat vague in what in fact leads to this 'legitimacy pressure', suggesting a need for countries at the lower end of internationally comparative league tables to improve their performance as a result of 'international scrutiny'. At the same time, low ranking could lead, for instance, to domestic political pressure (as has been the case following the Germany's poor performance in the Organisation for Economic Co-operation and Development (OECD)'s Programme for International Student Assessment (PISA) study of levels of education attainment), or could affect investment decisions.

THE IMPACT OF 'GLOBALISATION' AND 'EUROPEANISATION'

So far, this introduction has focused on some of the main pressures underpinning, and mechanisms delivering, policy convergence. It can be observed that all seven of the factors discussed above relate in some way to the twin processes of globalisation and Europeanisation. Thus, demands ensuing from other international actors (such as the European Union or the IMF) will have increased as these actors have grown stronger, with these demands themselves results of growing inter-dependence and the benefits to be achieved by co-operation. A growth of international law is also identified with globalisation, and as such the demands emanating from it will increase.

In particular, competitive pressure will grow as a result of globalisation: the greater mobility of capital will raise pressure to achieve shareholder value, and the growth in international trade also intensifies competitive pressure. 'Problem pressure' is related in part to globalisation, as the growing economic interdependence of nations suggests they will be subject to similar pressures. The 'desire for conformity' is increased, in part through the growing availability of alternative models (both because they are more likely to be considered suitable, due to a convergence of policy pressures, and because of greater 'accessibility' due to far greater levels of global communication), in part through the increasing time pressure in policy-making. Finally, 'legitimacy pressures' will grow, in particular that stimulated by international organisations and their research: the rise in power of, for instance, the OECD, the World Bank, and the European Union leads to greater levels of international comparison, and thus more pressure for convergence.

If, then, we accept that globalisation is a process, not an event, and that it reflects the *growing* economic interdependence of national economies, then across all these different pressures we might anticipate growing levels of convergence. At the same time, if no or only limited convergence can be identified, this should certainly lead to a questioning of the extent to which globalisation might be held to constrain the 'possibility' of domestic politics.

Perhaps even more than globalisation, Europeanisation is held to lead to policy convergence, but through a variety of different mechanisms, again including those discussed above. Like 'globalisation', 'Europeanisation' has a variety of different uses, some five of which are identified by Olsen.[45] Firstly, it can involve changes in external boundaries: specifically, the growing degree to which Europe as a continent becomes a single political space (most notably through enlargement). Secondly, it involves the development of institutions at the European level. Thirdly, it involves the 'central penetration of national systems of government ... [implying] adapting national and sub-national systems of governance to a European political centre and Europe-wide norms'.[46] Fourth, it can involve the export of European forms of politics and governance beyond the European territory. Fifth, it may reflect a 'political unification project'.

It is clear that each of these will, in some way, lead to convergence. However, again in the interests of clarity it may be helpful to disaggregate the term Europeanisation, instead specifying explicitly the type of convergence and the mechanisms involved. This is shown in Table 4.

Bulmer and Padgett argue that different types of transfer will result depending on the type of 'Europeanisation' present: where hierarchical governance exists, the more coercive types of transfer will result. Where 'negotiation' exists, as the EU seeks to agree common norms or rules, policy transfer will occur by negotiation. Where member states retain sovereignty, there is nonetheless the possibility of transfer by 'facilitated unilateralism'.[47]

The impact and process of globalisation and Europeanisation on the UK and Germany is discussed in greater detail in the contribution by Simon Bulmer, but suffice it to say that both phenomena provide a valuable additional dimension to the types of convergence outlined above. Of these, Europeanisation is arguably the most directly important in that it provides both agency and structure to the

TABLE 4
EUROPEANISATION AND TYPES AND MECHANISMS OF CONVERGENCE

'Type' of Europeanisation	Type(s) of convergence promoted	Mechanisms of convergence promoted
Changes in external boundaries	• Demands through EU on new member states • Legal obligations • Competitive pressure (notably on 'previous members') • Problem pressure • Desire for conformity • Legitimacy pressure • Harmonisation leads to increasingly similar problem pressures	• 'Conditional' policy transfer • EU legal obligation • Regulatory competition through growth in trade amongst member states • Lesson-drawing • Transnational problem-solving in EU arena • Policy promotion via EU
Developing institutions at the European level	• Legal obligations	• Increasing availability of EU as arena for transnational problem-solving and international harmonisation
Central penetration of national systems of governance	• Growing demands on member states through 'deepening' of union • Legal obligations • Competitive pressure • Problem pressure • Desire for conformity • Legitimacy pressure • Harmonisation leads to increasingly similar problem pressures	• 'Conditional' policy transfer • EU legal obligation • Regulatory competition through growth in trade amongst member states • Lesson-drawing • Transnational problem-solving in EU arena • Policy-promotion via EU
Exporting forms of political organisation	• Competitive pressure on non-members (especially 'race-to-the-top') • Desire for conformity • Legitimacy pressure	• Regulatory competition • Emulation of EU paradigm • International policy promotion by EU (e.g. to potential member states)
Political unification project	*Dependent on the nature of the project*	*Dependent on the nature of the project*

process of policy convergence: not only is the EU by itself a source of convergence, but its institutions, including the Council of Ministers and the European Court of Justice, act as a highly significant forum for the promotion of policy transfer and convergence.[48]

WHY CONVERGENCE MAY NOT HAPPEN

Notwithstanding these pressures, it is equally clear that policy convergence across different countries, time periods and policy areas has at most been patchy.[49] Indeed, there are some very significant differences in the approach, aims and methods of policy reform between countries, and in this case between the UK and Germany.

This section will consider three differing yet complementary reasons why convergence might not occur as anticipated.

'Varieties of Capitalism'

Over the past 15 years, a significant body of literature in the 'Varieties of Capitalism' school has developed.[50] As Wood notes, 'The central focus of the "varieties of capitalism" literature is the persistence of differences in the organisation of national political economies'. This applies not only in the organisation of economic activity, but also in other areas of public policy: again, as Wood argues, 'the core features of different world of welfare capitalism remain firmly in place ... convergence has been equally unforthcoming in the case of policies towards organised labour'.[51]

Specifically, the 'Varieties of Capitalism' literature compares liberal market economies and co-ordinated market economies and argues that the different components of each of the systems (finance, industrial relations, training and inter-firm relations) are inter-related, giving the system a 'comparative institutional advantage'.[52] As a result, 'the business communities of CMEs will not automatically support deregulation, since many firms may want to retain competitive advantages that depend on high levels of regulation'.[53]

The implication of this is that there need not be convergence upon the Anglo-American economic model due to 'competitive pressures' – rather, there may be more than one equilibrium which an industrial economy can reach, and where a shift in any sub-system will prove detrimental to the system as a whole. The consequence, for instance for Germany, is that change to any of its inter-related sub-systems (corporate finance, industrial relations, firm relations and training) would prove costly, due to their complementarity.[54]

Differing Impact of 'Globalisation' across Different Countries

The 'Varieties of Capitalism' approach also challenges the conventional view of the impact of 'globalisation'. While it agrees that LMEs will probably support deregulation, this will be a positively dangerous path for CMEs to follow, and both sides of industry will instead rally round to safeguard their particular regulatory regime.[55] This challenges the view that a common pressure will necessarily lead to a common solution – rather, different solutions may rationally result. Continuing an analogy used earlier in this introduction, just as two people may put up an umbrella when it starts to rain, so one person may put up an umbrella, while another one, passing a shelter, will simply step inside.

Geoffrey Garrett draws similar conclusions in his study of the possibility of 'politics' in the global economy, and that convergence on a neoliberal paradigm is neither inevitable nor necessarily desirable: 'Macroeconomic outcomes in the era of global markets have been as good or better in countries where powerful left-wing parties are allied with broad and centrally organized labour movements ("social democratic corporatism") as they have where the left and labour are weaker'.[56] There are two main arguments for this: firstly, investment in skills in the workforce are attractive to capital, increasing prospective future returns; secondly, according to Hay, 'social democratic policies are not without other benefits for capital – ... for instance, social protection of labour is effectively exchanged ... for predictable patterns of wage setting ..., co-operation between capital and labour, low levels of social strife and higher levels of economic growth'.[57] As a consequence, confronted with globalisation, while there are pressures to be competitive, in the sense of making the economy attractive to capital, there is more than one way of achieving it, and 'social democratic corporatism' is, along with the liberal market economy, a plausible response to globalisation. As Garrett states,

> Those who argue that national autonomy in the economic sphere – and social democratic alternatives to the free market in particular – are outmoded relics of a different age greatly exaggerate the constraining effects of market integration ... Even in the global economy, and despite the fanfare to the contrary, citizens still have a real choice to make about how to govern the market.[58]

Other authors have questioned the extent of globalisation altogether. For instance, Hirst and Thompson argue that, 'If we look at merchandise trade flows between the main economic blocs expressed as a proportion of the originating country or bloc GDP, then, for the most part, quite low percentages of GDP seem to have been traded in 1998'.[59] Comparing five different trade blocs, they find that, while the degree of integration between Western European countries is significant, international trade flows are not as great as might be expected. They conclude that 'there are good and interesting reasons for our continuing to take the issues of borders seriously in economics, despite the fashionable insistence that they are no longer significant in an age of globalization'.[60]

National Institutional Resilience

Thirdly, there is no 'binary' relationship between a pressure for convergence and a particular output. Rather, these pressures for convergence are channelled through the prism of existing institutions. Even allowing for the fact that institutional settings may make different responses to the same phenomenon rational, as discussed above, even where such a response might, in 'utilitarian' terms, be desirable, it might not be possible.

In cases where 'conditional policy transfer' might be expected, due to the presence of external pressures or demands, national institutions must still be willing, and able, to accept the conditions imposed. In the case of legal obligations through international law, again it can be seen that responses to international law are distinctly mixed, and it remains possible for actors, notably larger actors, to ignore international law, notably in the absence of any effective sanctions. In the case of competitive pressure, not only may national partisan politics lead to the possibility of different responses, as Garrett argues, but also the presence of domestic veto players will clearly make a difference to potential outcomes: it may not prove possible, for instance, to reduce the non-wage labour costs associated with the welfare state, even if it might be a sensible thing to do.[61] For instance, the number of veto players (such as coalition government, bicameralism, federalism, a strong constitutional court, weak party cohesion) will directly affect the likelihood of policy change being enacted. Differently put, the presence of additional veto players – contributing to the 'openness' of a political system (the extent to which it can be subject to outside influence) makes policy change less likely, and stability more likely. Again, this may strengthen the hypothesis that, in a CME, a different equilibrium may be possible: according to Wood, the sustenance of co-ordination structures is reliant upon 'credible restraint on the power of government to undermine these governance structures'.[62]

This is also the case for parallel problem pressures, desires for conformity, and 'legitimacy pressure': in each case, while these are undoubtedly stimuli for convergence, the stimulus needs to be taken up by domestic political actors. Again, to take an example cited above: the PISA study of educational standards might have been expected to lead to calls in Germany to converge on a particular paradigm of education policy. Not so: rather, the response to the 2003 study was nakedly partisan, with politicians of the CDU/CSU arguing that it strengthened the case for early selection and Land-level administration, and SPD politicians making much the opposite point.[63]

Finally, and on a related point, institutional 'stickiness' stems not only from the presence of veto points, but also from the possibility of 'path dependence', as 'initial social outcomes concerning institutional, organisational, or policy design – even suboptimal ones – can become self-reinforcing over time'.[64] As the late Vincent Wright pithily put it, 'the biggest decision-maker in any political system is the past'.[65] For instance, in the case of a welfare state, the presence of a large number of beneficiaries of a particular type of transfer will make it extremely difficult to remove that transfer, leading to the rather paradoxical conclusion that welfare retrenchment may be hardest to achieve in precisely those welfare states where the exogenous pressures for convergence are greatest.[66] More generally, of course, cross-national variations in public opinion can exert an endogenous influence upon the extent of policies pursued. For instance, Padgett explicitly and convincingly links voters' preferences on welfare issues to the lack of reform in the German economy.[67]

Nation States: Retaining the Power of Agency

In a useful contribution, Hurrell and Menon offer an important antidote to the literature on globalisation. They point out that 'states themselves are not passive players. Globalisation has been driven not by some unstoppable impersonal logic of technological innovation, but by specific sets of state policies'.[68] The corollary to this is that the impact of globalisation upon states will vary, depending on the extent to which those states wield power in international institutions. International institutions, such as the World Trade Organization (WTO), the Group of 8 (G8) and the OECD, are not an autonomous, even alien force, but are influenced by nation states; moreover, the ground rules of globalisation can be influenced through the externalisation of national rules, or the construction of 'transnational coalitions'.[69] So, not only do national-level institutions mediate the impact of external changes, but they also help to shape those external changes – in a way, then, which will lead to those forces having a different impact upon different states.

CONCLUSION AND PREVIEW

The aim of the preceding discussion has been to contextualise the overarching goal of this collection, namely to analyse empirically the extent of and reasons for policy convergence in the UK and Germany. We have argued that significant pressures towards convergence do exist in the form of globalisation, Europeanisation and endogenous pressures such as demographics and party politics. At the same time, we have noted that the extent to which these feed into *actual* convergence may be somewhat less and will depend largely on how these pressures for convergence are refracted through the national prism of history, cultural assumptions and institutions. Indeed, given that, the policy responses adopted might even be expected to diverge.[70] The relationships we are seeking to analyse in this volume are heuristically illustrated in Figure 2.

The following contributions will examine these relationships in more detail and in a range of instances. Each essay will therefore consider the pressures for convergence, the extent to which common policy solutions are being adopted, as well as the source – be it exogenous or endogenous – of policy change in the area concerned. The contributions themselves are structured into two main groups. First, the studies by Dan Hough and James Sloam, and Simon Bulmer provide an analysis of the institutional context of policy convergence, by looking at party politics, Europeanisation respectively. Charlie Jeffery's contribution examines British and German public opinion on the balance between equity and diversity in public policy provision, and considers the shifting dynamics in our two cases.

These are followed by six policy case studies encompassing security (Kerry Longhurst and Alister Miskimmon), migration (Simon Green), labour markets (Lothar Funk), productivity (Rebecca Harding), health policy (Nils Bandelow) and environmental policy (Charles Lees). The six thus cover a wide range of policy areas, from high politics fields (migration and security) to low politics fields (health care and labour markets), from welfare (health care) to economics (productivity and labour markets), from highly symbolic issues (migration) to the effects of globalisation (environment). As such, the case studies are ideally suited to illustrating the extent to

FIGURE 2
TOWARDS A HEURISTIC UNDERSTANDING OF CONVERGENCE PROCESSES IN THE UK AND GERMANY

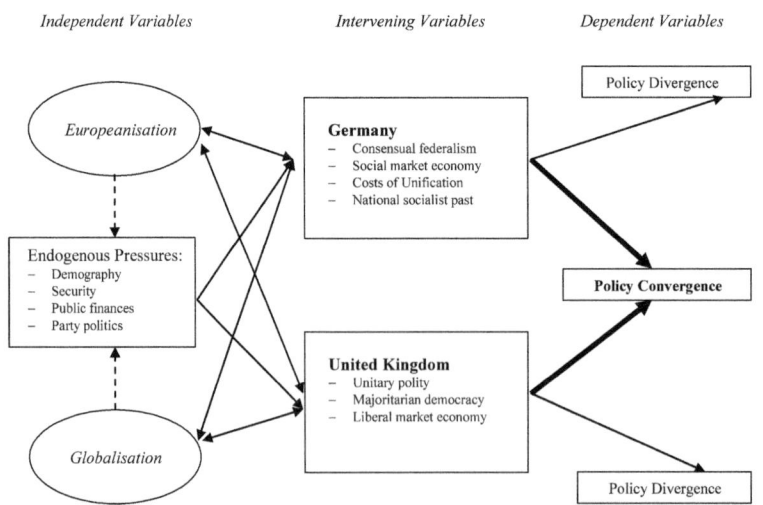

which policy convergence occurs in practice as well as the reasons why. These various threads are brought together in the conclusion by Ralf Dahrendorf.

In summary, there are clear forces for convergence between Britain and Germany. Both exogenous factors, such as the processes of Europeanisation and globalisation, as well as endogenous ones, such as the simultaneous elections of centre-left governments, can be expected to push each country in the same direction. However, if we consider these external pressures, in particular, as being light shining through a prism, made up of each country's institutional, historical, and cultural make-up, they will be distorted, and at times pushed along divergent paths. The extent to which these two 'big beasts' of Europe in fact converge or diverge, and through it the make-up of this prism, will be elucidated by this volume.

NOTES

The authors are grateful for comments on an earlier draft of this paper from Simon Bulmer, Andreas Busch, Anneliese Dodds, Dan Hough, Anand Menon, and Thomas Poguntke, and for assistance in data collation from Nicola Corkin. They accept full responsibility for any errors.

1. United Nations Population Division, *Replacement Migration: Is It a Solution to Declining and Ageing Populations?* (New York: UN, 2000), available at: http://www.un.org/esa/population/publications/migration/migration.htm (accessed 1 Dec. 2005). See also S. Green, 'Immigration in the UK and Germany: A Panacea for Declining Labour Forces?', in L. Funk and S. Green (eds.), *New Aspects of Labour Market Policy* (Berlin: Verlag für Wissenschaft und Forschung, 2002).
2. S. Bulmer and S. Padgett, 'Policy Transfer in the European Union: An Institutionalist Perspective', *British Journal of Political Science* 35/1 (2005), pp.103–26.
3. See A. Giddens, *The Third Way: Renewal of Social Democracy* (Oxford: Polity Press, 2000); A. Giddens, *The Third Way and its Critics* (Oxford: Polity Press, 2000)
4. T. Blair and G. Schröder, *Europe: The Third Way* (London: The Labour Party, 1999). For further discussion, see L. Funk (ed.), *The Economics and Politics of the Third Way* (Münster: LIT-Verlag, 1999).
5. The UK and Germany are thus often juxtaposed in seminal comparative studies. Classic examples include G. Esping-Andersen, *The Three Worlds of Welfare Capitalism* (Princeton, NJ: Princeton University Press, 1990); A. Lijphart, *Democracies: Patterns of Majoritarian and Consensus Government in Twenty-one Countries* (New Haven, CT: Yale University Press, 1984); G. Tsebelis, *Veto Players: How Political Institutions Work* (Princeton, NJ: Princeton University Press, 2002); M. Albert, *Capitalism against Capitalism* (London: Whurr, 1993).
6. C. Bennett, 'Review Article: What Is Policy Convergence and What Causes It?', *British Journal of Political Science* 21 (1991), pp.215–33, here p.218.
7. Bennett, 'Review Article', p.219.
8. See D. Dolowitz and D. Marsh, 'Who Learns What and From Whom? A Review of the Policy Transfer Literature', *Political Studies* 44 (1996), pp.343–7, here p.357; also D. Dolowitz and D. Marsh, 'Learning from Abroad: The Role of Policy Transfer in Contemporary Policy-Making', *Governance* 13 (2000), pp.5–4.
9. C. Knill, 'Introduction: Cross-national policy convergence: concepts, approaches, and explanatory factors', *Journal of European Public Policy* 12/5 (2005), pp.764–74.
10. Ibid., p.768.
11. Ibid., p.767.
12. For instance, Mary Bowerman draws on isomorphism in her study of the Business Excellence Model in Local Government: '"Isomorphism without Legitimacy?" The Business Excellence Model in Local Government', *Public Money and Management* 22/2 (2002), pp.47–52; while Mike Geddes' study 'Neoliberalism and Local Governance – Cross-national Perspectives and Speculations', *Policy Studies* 26/3–4 (2005), pp.359–77, uses a policy convergence model to discuss a not dissimilar hypothesis.
13. Derived from S. Heichel, J. Pape and T. Sommerer, 'Is there Convergence in Convergence Research? An Overview of Empirical Studies on Policy Convergence', *Journal of European Public Policy* 12/5 (2005), pp.817–40, here pp.820–23.
14. Ibid., p.824.

15. Project e1441, *The Search for Solutions: Policy Learning in the UK and Germany*, available at http://www.igs.bham.ac.uk/searchforsolutions/. The authors would like to express their gratitude to the Anglo-German Foundation and subsidiary sponsors for their generous support of this research.
16. K. Holzinger and C. Knill, 'Causes and Conditions of Cross-national Policy Convergence', *Journal of European Public Policy* 12/5 (2005), pp.775–96. In the foregoing section, their categories are adapted somewhat, focusing on the stimuli of convergence, rather than the actual mechanisms which achieve it.
17. Dolowitz and Marsh, 'Learning from Abroad'.
18. P. DiMaggio and W. Powell, 'The Iron Cage Revisited. Institutionalized Isomorphism and Collective Rationality in Organizational Fields', in W. Powell and P. DiMaggio (eds.), *The New Institutionalism in Organizational Analysis* (Chicago: Chicago University Press, 1991), pp.63–82, cited in Holzinger and Knill, 'Causes and Conditions of Cross-national Policy Convergence', pp.779–80.
19. S. Coate and S. Morris, 'Policy Conditionality', *PIER Working Paper 97-013*, July 1996.
20. K. Smith, 'The Use of Political Conditionality in the EU's Relations with Third Countries: How Effective?', *European Foreign Affairs Review* 3/2 (1998), pp. 253–274.
21. See for instance M. Vachudová, *Europe Undivided: Democracy, Leverage and Integration after Communism* (Oxford: Oxford University Press, 2005); W. Jacoby, *The Enlargement of the European Union and NATO: Ordering from the Menu in Central Europe* (Cambridge: Cambridge University Press, 2004); H. Grabbe, 'EU Conditionality and the Acquis Communautaire', *International Political Science Review* 23/3 (2002), pp.249–68.
22. Available at http://europa.eu.int/scadplus/leg/en/lvb/l60018.htm (accessed 23 Nov. 2005).
23. Holzinger and Knill, 'Causes and Conditions of Cross-national Policy Convergence', p.782.
24. For a discussion of this process, see A. Stone Sweet and W. Sandholtz, 'Integration, Supranational Governance and the Institutionalization of the European Polity', in W. Sandholtz and A. Stone Sweet, *European Integration and Supranational Governance* (Oxford: Oxford University Press, 1998), pp.1–26.
25. D. Drezner, 'Globalization and Policy Convergence', *International Studies Review* 3 (2001), pp.53–78, at p.57.
26. For a review of this debate, see C. Hay, 'Common Trajectories, Variable Paces, Divergent Outcomes? Models of European Capitalism under Conditions of Complex Economic Interdependence', *Review of International Political Economy* 11/2 (2004), pp.231–62.
27. D. Kelemen, 'Suing for Europe: Adversarial Legalism and European Governance', *Comparative Political Studies* 39/1 (2006), pp.101–27
28. A. Busch, 'Globalisation and National Varieties of Capitalism: The Contested Viability of the "German Model"', *German Politics* 14/2 (2005), pp.125–39, at p.126.
29. W. Streeck and C. Trampusch, 'Economic Reform and the Political Economy of the German Welfare State', *German Politics* 14/2 (2005), pp.174–95.
30. Ibid., pp.129–30.
31. W. Streeck and K. Thelen: 'Introduction: Institutional Change in Advanced Political Economies', in W. Streeck and K. Thelen, *Beyond Continuity: Institutional Changed in Advanced Political Economies* (Oxford: Oxford University Press, 2003), pp.1–39, at p.30.
32. D. Vogel, *Trading Up: Consumer and Environmental Regulation in a Global Economy* (Cambridge, MA: Harvard University Press, 1995), discussed in R. Kelemen and E. Sibbett, 'The Globalization of American Law', *International Organization* 58/1 (2004), pp.103–36, here pp.107–8.
33. Holzinger and Knill, 'Causes and Conditions of Cross-national Policy Convergence', p.783.
34. Ibid., pp.783–4.
35. See, for instance, the discussion of UK/US policy transfer, with significant emphasis on collaboration: D. Dolowitz, S. Greenwold and D. Marsh, 'Policy Transfer: Something Old, Something New, Something Borrowed, But Why Red, White And Blue?', *Parliamentary Affairs* 52/4 (1999), pp.719–30.
36. For instance, see Koch's article 'Sozialhilfe, eine zweite Change – Kein Lebensstil', available at http://www.roland-koch.de/akzente_im_fokus_sozialhilfe.php (accessed 1 Feb. 2006).
37. For instance, J. Flintrop, 'Krankenhäuser: Englische Verhältnisse', *Deutsches Ärtzeblatt* 99, 6 Dec. 2002, available at http://www.aerzteblatt.de/v4/archiv/artikel.asp?id=34705 (accessed 2 Jan. 2006).
38. Holzinger and Knill, 'Causes and Conditions of Cross-national Policy Convergence', pp. 786.
39. A. Lenschow, D. Liefferink and S. Veenman, 'When the Birds Sing. A Framework for Analysing Domestic Factors behind Policy Convergence', *Journal of European Public Policy* 12/5 (2005), pp.797–816.
40. Holzinger and Knill, 'Causes and Conditions of Cross-national Policy Convergence', pp.784–5.
41. P. Dimaggio and W. Powell: 'The Iron Cage Revisted: Institutionalism and Collective Nationality in Organizational Fields', *American Sociological Review* 4812 (1983), pp. 147–60.
42. Dolowitz *et al.*, 'Policy Transfer', p.729.

43. Fico spent some hours discussing his political vision with British academics, without mentioning the 'Third Way' once. A few days later he announced that the 'Third Way' would underpin his party's policies. Haughton suggests that the language, rather than necessarily the substance of policy, was emulated. Tim Haughton, 'What's Left in Slovakia?', European Research Institute Seminar, University of Birmingham, 16 Nov. 2005.
44. Holzinger and Knill, 'Causes and Conditions of Cross-national Policy Convergence', p.785.
45. J. Olsen, 'The Many Faces of Europeanization', *Journal of Common Market Studies* 40/5 (2002), pp.921–52.
46. Ibid., p.924.
47. Bulmer and Padgett, 'Policy Transfer in the European Union', p.104.
48. Ibid.
49. C. Hay, 'What's Globalisation Got to Do with It? Economic Interdependence and the Future of European Welfare States', *Government and Opposition* 41/1 (2006), pp.1–22.
50. The literature is wide-ranging, in particular drawing on the work of David Soskice from 1990 onwards, but it is brought together in the edited volume by P. Hall and D. Soskice, *Varieties of Capitalism: The Institutional Foundations of Comparative Advantage* (Oxford/New York: Oxford University Press, 2001).
51. S. Wood, 'Business, Government, and Patterns of Labour Market Policy in Britain and the Federal Republic of Germany', in Hall and Soskice (eds.), *Varieties of Capitalism*, pp. 247–74, at p.247.
52. Busch, 'Globalisation and National Varieties of Capitalism', p.131.
53. P. Hall and D. Soskice, 'Introduction', in Hall and Soskice (eds.), *Varieties of Capitalism*, pp.1–70, at p.63. For an alternative analysis, see Matthew Allen, *Varieties of Capitalism Paradigm: Explaining Germany's Comparative Advantage?* (London: Palgrave, 2006)
54. Busch, 'Globalisation and National Varieties of Capitalism', pp.131–3.
55. Hall and Soskice, 'Introduction', pp.56–9.
56. G. Garrett, *Partisan Politics in the Global Economy* (Cambridge: Cambridge University Press, 1998), p.1.
57. C. Hay, 'Globalization, Social Democracy and the Persistence of Partisan Politics: A Commentary on Garrett', *Review of International Political Economy* 7/1 (2002), pp.138–52, here p.142.
58. Garrett, *Partisan Politics in the Global Economy*, pp.24–5.
59. P. Hirst and G. Thompson, 'The Future of Globalization', *Cooperation and Conflict* 38/3 (2002), pp.247–65; also Hay, 'What's Globalisation Got to Do with It?'.
60. Hirst and Thompson, 'The Future of Globalization', p.263.
61. Streeck and Trampusch, 'Economic Reform and the Political Economy of the German Welfare State'.
62. Wood, 'Business, Government, and Patterns of Labour Market Policy in Britain and the Federal Republic of Germany', p.258.
63. See, for instance: 'Bund-Länder Gezerre: Es lebe die Kleinstaaterei', *Der Spiegel*, 26 Feb. 2003.
64. P. Pierson, 'Coping with Permanent Austerity: Welfare State Restructuring in Affluent Democracies', in P. Pierson (ed.), *The New Politics of the Welfare State* (Oxford: Oxford University Press, 2001), pp.410–56, at p.414.
65. Cited in A. Menon, 'Conclusion', in J. Hayward and A. Menon, *Governing Europe* (Oxford: Oxford University Press, 2003), pp.411–432, here p.421.
66. Pierson, 'Coping with Permanent Austerity', p.416.
67. S. Padgett, 'Welfare Bias in the Party System: A Neo-Downsian Explanation for Gridlock in Economic Reform', *German Politics* 13/2 (2004), pp.360–83.
68. A. Hurrell and A. Menon, 'International Relations, International Institutions and the European State', in Hayward and Menon (eds.), *Governing Europe*, pp.395–412, here p.403.
69. Ibid., pp.404–5.
70. An excellent example of such a study is A. Busch, *Staat und Globalisierung. Das Politikfeld Bankenregulierung im internationalen Vergleich* (Wiesbaden: Westdeutscher Verlag, 2003).

Germany, Britain and William Paterson

PETER PULZER

Few names are more intimately connected with German studies in Britain and the wider world than that of William Paterson. In a teaching and publishing career stretching over nearly 40 years he has covered almost the whole range of political institutions and policy areas. His interests have covered industrial policy, environmental policy and political parties.[1] But the one topic to which he has returned again and again and on which he has stamped his firmest mark is that of foreign policy, whether of the old Federal Republic or of the post-unification 'Berlin' republic. Within that topic it is Germany's European policy that he has emphasised most, providing a running commentary on its evolution over the decades, with several glances at the peculiarities of Anglo-German relations.

Paterson's starting point in these studies is now so familiar that it is easy to forget how original it was. It is that of German 'semisovereignty' or 'tamed power', to use the formulations popularised by Peter Katzenstein, though with a somewhat different emphasis.[2] While for Katzenstein the causes of Germany's semisovereignty were predominantly exogenous–'Semisovereignty is an external condition of West German politics'[3]–Paterson placed more emphasis on endogenous factors, not least on the domestic dimensions of foreign policy-making. True, in the beginning was the Cold War: early German politics was 'defined by [its] realities', but from the partial restoration of sovereignty in 1955 onwards the policy-makers of the Federal Republic increasingly had choices and exercised them.[4] To realise these, Paterson argued, a number of preconditions had to be satisfied. The first was domestic political stability and the securing of liberal-democratic norms: 'The political miracle of the Federal Republic ... [has] been if anything a greater achievement than the earlier economic miracle'.[5] Precisely because the Federal Republic was a 'new state', compared not only with Britain or France, but even with Italy, it was not only obliged to discard a lot of historical baggage, but was happy to do so. Whatever Germany engaged in either before or after 1989 bore little resemblance to any Bismarckian *Machtpolitik*, or indeed to any 'historically determined perception of national interest'.[6] The main exception to this rule that Paterson rather underplays was the Francophilia of Konrad Adenauer which can be traced back to the end of the First World War.[7] One can, however, agree that the actions of Germany's policy-makers from 1949 onwards were determined not by inherited preconceptions, but by the world as they found it, a world – or at least a Europe – that they increasingly helped to fashion.

The world that confronted German policy-makers had two components. The first was that of the Cold War, of a divided Germany and a divided Europe. It was also one in which there was a historically-derived distrust of German power and hegemonic ambitions. What evolved in response to these challenges Paterson named 'reflexive multilateralism', an instinctive avoidance of national self-assertion and an instinctive preference for working in supra-national and inter-state arenas.[8] The second component was the divided sovereignty of the West German state, a deliberate attempt at the taming of power. This meant that German policy-makers accustomed themselves to the politics of incrementalism and to shared decision-making, with inputs from the Länder, the social partners, the Federal Constitutional Court and the Bundesbank, so that in many ways the European dimension of politics resembled the institutional pluralism of Germany – for better or worse.[9] This world was not, of course, static. Not only did European institutions evolve, more often than not under German impetus, but so did the domestic configurations.[10] As Paterson points out, a powerful Chancellor can transcend semisovereignty, a process he has analysed in detail with special emphasis on Helmut Kohl.[11] The parties and therefore the legislature also play their role,[12] though Paterson is careful to point out that the integrative character of the *Volksparteien* inhibits polarisation on European issues.[13]

While relations with France, though not always smooth, have maintained a consistent priority in German thinking, those with Britain have frequently been problematic. One might have thought that the trajectories of two medium-sized welfarist industrial economies with a common interest in an Atlanticist orientation would run in parallel. But, as the terms 'ambivalence' and 'misunderstanding' which feature as subtitles in Paterson's contributions to this topic show, that was not to be.[14] On the one hand there has been no lack of reciprocal institutional influence. One has only to think of British input into German trade unions and broadcasting in the immediate post-war years and more recent German models for the admittedly asymmetrical federalism of the British state, the partial electoral reform that accompanied it and the independence of the Bank of England. Despite the sluggish performance of the German economy in the twenty-first century, the 'Rhenish' model of the social market economy still has its admirers on the British liberal Left.[15] On the other hand, there have been plenty of dissonances, which have been no respecters of party associations, whether on the Left or on the Right. Few relationships between European Conservative leaders have been more embittered than that between Margaret Thatcher and Helmut Kohl. The relations between the Labour Party and the Social Democratic Party (SPD) have also been less than happy. Immediately after the war the SPD assumed that the Labour government would act as its patron, a profound misunderstanding of Britain's role in the Allied Control Council. But there were also specific divergences. British post-war policy was to ally with the United States, that of the SPD to preserve German unity through neutrality. The cultural gap between the two parties, hinted at by Paterson, is given greater importance by one of the senior British advisers at the time, who had himself voted Labour in 1945. Lt.-Col. Annan, later Provost of King's College, Cambridge and Vice-Chancellor of the University of London, found Kurt Schumacher's 'unbridled nationalism ... alarming'. As for the SPD's conference delegates, their 'speeches were as stratospheric as the combined ages of the speakers were astronomical'.[16] Again and again the two parties failed to synchronise their programmes or their actions, whether in the immediate post-war period, at the time of the SPD's Bad Godesberg turn, or in the attempt at programmatic convergence in the Schröder–Blair paper of 1999.[17] Even the most Anglophile of West German Chancellors, Helmut Schmidt, suffered his frustrations: there was no chance of winning either a Labour or a Conservative government to his vision of Europe's future.[18]

The unification of Germany has brought about new questions. If Bonn was not Weimar, will Berlin not be Bonn? Or will Berlin become Weimar, as some fear? Certainly German power is tamed in a different way at the beginning of the twenty-first century. Reverting to Katzenstein's categories, Paterson concludes that 'semi-sovereignty is no longer an external condition German politics ... It will, however, remain semi-sovereign in its internal face'.[19] One could amplify this change by stressing two factors. While the constraints of the victor powers on German sovereignty have disappeared, the voluntarily adopted constraints of post-Maastricht Europe have actually diminished the ability of a German state to act autonomously. As for domestic politics, a federal structure expanded to 16 Länder and a more kaleidoscopic party constellation have made effective government more difficult. Paterson has little patience with those German publicists, like Hans-Peter Schwarz or Arnulf Baring, who saw in a united Germany a return to a pre-1914 order, in which a revived German power would hold a balance between East and West. Too much had happened since 1945 and 1989 to make such a prospect either desirable or feasible. Yet even those who rejected this vision – Paterson included – did not immediately realise that in the new Europe Germany, though larger, would also be weaker and above all that public enthusiasm for further European integration was on the wane.[20] As 'the congruence between German interests and the European level is not so comfortable as before', some German political leaders, including Gerhard Schröder and, one might add, Angela Merkel, favour some 'renationalisation' of decision-making.[21] As the future organisation of Europe remains uncertain following the French and Dutch rejections of the Constitutional Treaty, we shall need informed and insightful guidance more than ever. It is a safe assumption that retirement will not deter Paterson from continuing to offer us these and will, indeed, give him a second (or is it a tenth?) wind.

If Paterson's contribution to German studies had been restricted to the written and the spoken word, that alone would have been enough to earn him the recognition and gratitude of the profession. But it is his organisational achievements that are at least as significant. He was one of the moving spirits behind the foundation of the Association for the Study of German Politics in 1974 and of its house journal, *German Politics*, of which he was one of the original editors. Both the ASGP and the journal have become the leading organs of their kind outside Germany. The crowning glory of his career, after directing the Europa Institute at the University of Edinburgh, was to establish and direct the Institute for German Studies at Birmingham from 1994 onwards. The award of the OBE and of the *Bundesverdienstkreuz* for his services in this connection speak for themselves as testimonies to his achievements.

NOTES

1. With A. Thomas (eds.), *Social Democratic Parties in Western Europe* (London: Croom Helm, 1977); with S. Padgett, *A History of Social Democracy in Post-war Europe* (London: Longman, 1981); with A. Thomas (eds.), *The Future of Social Democracy: Problems and Prospects of Social Democratic Parties in Europe* (Oxford: Oxford University Press, 1986); with R. Gillespie (eds.), *Rethinking Social Democracy in Europe* (London: Frank Cass, 1993); with W. Grant and C. Whitston, *Government and the Chemical Industry: A Comparative Study of Britain and West Germany* (Oxford: Oxford University Press, 1988); 'Environmental Politics', in G. Smith, W. Paterson and P. Merkl (eds.), *Developments in West German Politics* (Basingstoke: Macmillan, 1989), pp.267–89.

2. P. Katzenstein, *Policy and Politics in West Germany: The Growth of a Semisovereign State* (Philadelphia: Temple University Press, 1987); P. Katzenstein (ed.), *Tamed Power: Germany in Europe* (Ithaca, NY: Cornell University Press, 1997).
3. Katzenstein, *Policy and Politics*, p.9.
4. S. Green and W. Paterson (eds.), *Governance in Contemporary Germany: The Semisovereign State Revisited* (Cambridge: Cambridge University Press, 2005), p.6.
5. W. Paterson and D. Southern, *Governing Germany* (Oxford: Basil Blackwell, 1991), p.4.
6. Ibid., p.258.
7. P. Pulzer, 'Nationalism and Internationalism in European Christian Democracy', in M. Gehler and W. Kaiser (eds.), *Christian Democracy in Europe since 1945* (London: Routledge, 2004), pp.19–20.
8. Green and Paterson (eds.), *Governance in Contemporary Germany*, p.270.
9. Ibid., pp.278–9.
10. Ibid., p.278.
11. Ibid., p.277; W. Paterson, 'Helmut Kohl, "The Vision Thing" and Escaping the Semi-Sovereignty Trap', *German Politics* 7/1 (1998), pp.17–36. For a detailed chronological account see also W. Paterson, 'The Chancellor and Foreign Policy', in S. Padgett (ed.), *Adenauer to Kohl: The Development of the German Chancellorship* (London: Hurst & Co., 1994), pp.127–56.
12. S. Bulmer and W. Paterson, *The Federal Republic of Germany and the European Community* (London: Allen & Unwin, 1987), pp.123–84.
13. W. Paterson, 'Britain and the Berlin Republic: Between Ambivalence and Emulation', *German Politics* 10/2 (2001), p.214.
14. Ibid.; W. Paterson, 'Between Mutual Support and Misunderstanding: The British Labour Party and the SPD', in H. Tewes and J. Wright (eds.), *Liberalism, Anti-Semitism and Democracy: Essays in Honour of Peter Pulzer* (Oxford: Oxford University Press, 2001), p.232.
15. W. Hutton, *The State We're In: A Declaration of Interdependence. Why America Should Join the World* (London: Cape, 1995).
16. N. Annan, *Changing Enemies: The Defeat and Regeneration of Germany* (London: HarperCollins, 1995), pp.177–8.
17. Paterson, 'Between Mutual Support and Misunderstanding', pp.232–45.
18. Paterson and Southern, *Governing Germany*, p.264.
19. W. Paterson, 'Beyond Semi-Sovereignty: The New Germany in the New Europe', *German Politics* 5/2 (1996), p.183.
20. W. Paterson, 'Germany and Europe', in S. Padgett, W. Paterson and G. Smith (eds.), *Developments in German Politics 3* (Basingstoke: Palgrave, 2003), p.208.
21. Ibid., p.215.

Different Road Maps, Similar Paths? Social Democratic Politics in the UK and Germany

DAN HOUGH and JAMES SLOAM

INTRODUCTION

Parties that win elections – particularly if they win them frequently and convincingly – are never short of admirers. Some of these will be interested in the campaign techniques and marketing strategies that have brought electoral success rather more than the ideological and programmatic package that has been sold; others, frequently on the other side of national borders, will look enthusiastically and openly for programmatic lessons that they themselves can learn in order to be more successful in their own election campaigns; a final group of parties may seek to mix the two, learning how to 'sell' policies that are in themselves more 'sellable' than the ones that they already possess. Willingness to learn from other actors is, however, one thing; actually being able to adopt or adapt policies, strategies or techniques can be quite another. There are many possible hindrances to political parties in their attempts to draw direct lessons from similar actors in other ostensibly similar contexts. Firstly, parties themselves remain heterogeneous actors comprising wings and factions that can have very different perceptions of what lessons should be drawn, from whom and from where. Secondly, rarely do parties in continental Europe govern alone, hence the wants, needs and sensitivities of coalition partners or other prospective legislative veto-players will need to be taken into consideration and, thirdly and most noticeably, the uniqueness of national opportunity structures can ensure that successful policies in one context may have an altogether different set of effects if implanted into another. This can make even attempting to import 'alien' policies a hazardous and frustrating task.[1] All of these potential barriers can very rapidly crush any willingness to implement new, and frequently controversial, ideas from abroad.

One party that prompted more than its fair share of admirers in the mid- to late 1990s was the revived and revitalised British Labour Party under the leadership of Tony Blair. Labour's success prompted much discussion of social democracy's apparent transformation into a modern, forward-thinking progressive agenda for the future. By the end of the 1990s centre-left governments were in power across most of Europe (as well as in a number of states beyond) and the 'Third Way' experiment that was being led by the Clinton and Blair administrations was attracting both scholarly attention and the eyes of politicians eager to know more about this new winning electoral formula.

Yet it did not take long for this allegedly unstoppable force to hit its own metaphorical iceberg in the political equivalent of the north Atlantic – the chastening reality of practical politics. The post-Clinton (New) Democrats were marginally defeated in the US (2000), and the centre-left in a number of key European states – Italy (2001), France (2002), the Netherlands (2002) – were ousted rather more unceremoniously from power. The short-lived ideational dominance of social democratic thinkers began to be questioned as critics argued that the Third Way was nothing more than an apparently vacuous and hollow marketing gimmick. Social democratic politicians across the democratic world subsequently discarded the term from their speeches and programmes. The era of Third Way politics seemed to have disappeared almost as quickly as it had arrived.

This contribution does not seek to engage with the fundamentals of what any such project might (have) be(en). It is clear that there remains very little consensus as to what such nebulous ideas mean in practice and the Third Way is still both hotly contested and consistently ill-defined.[2] Some authors claim that there are a number of Third Way models that parties could adapt to the societal and political context within which they act.[3] Others claim that all centre-left parties are developing their own specific Third Way agenda, even if they have long since ceased to call it that.[4] These arguments are discussed in much detail elsewhere.[5] What this discussion does do is engage with the practical consequences and difficulties that parties – in this case the German Social Democratic Party (SPD) and the British Labour Party – have in developing and transporting common agendas and common strategies over national borders. Initial positive moves in this direction – shaped in Third Way discourse – were quickly put on ice as the willingness of Gerhard Schröder's SPD to learn from the electoral and political successes of Labour proved very difficult to implement in practice. Disadvantageous national and institutional (party) opportunity structures and an unwillingness to genuinely swallow the medicine of radical economic reform soon prompted Schröder to backtrack from his initial Blairite ideas. Only post-2002 did the SPD–Green government adopt policies that even vaguely resembled those of its British counterpart, and even then the pressure of poor economic performance in Germany was the main catalyst for the creation of the SPD–Green government's controversial 'Agenda 2010' reform programme.[6] This piece analyses these reforms within the context of policy learning from external sources and broader pressures for policy convergence, illustrating that while 'choosing from the menu' is possible, and at times advisable, the final meal is rarely as was initially intended. We begin by explaining how political parties learn lessons from other parties and outline under what circumstances policy learning is most likely to take place. We highlight the difficulties not just of ideological misfit but also, crucially, institutional incompatibility – something that had a differential effect on the ability of the Labour and SPD leaderships to impose their agendas on their own parties. We continue by stressing that the opportunity structures of government create a high degree of conditionality as the national and European levels shape a party in power's room for manoeuvre. The European context, in particular, leads to common challenges which make policy convergence more likely. We finish by surveying the empirical evidence from SPD and Labour Party programmes over the last ten years to see if there is any evidence of a convergence of ideas and rhetoric even though the public discourse of coherent a Third Way project has long since been shelved.

POLITICAL PARTIES, POLICY TRANSFER AND POLICY CONVERGENCE

One such tool for analysing these questions, as is illustrated in the introduction to this collection, is the analytical framework developed around ideas of policy transfer, lesson-drawing and policy convergence. The generic term 'policy transfer' envelops a host of concepts describing the process of moving policies, programmes, ideas or institutions across time and space. Studies of this temporal and spatial transfer of policy knowledge present us with many varied forms, from voluntary lesson-drawing[7] through policy learning[8] to coercive policy pushing.[9] At its simplest, policy transfer is 'a dynamic whereby knowledge about policies, administrative arrangements, or institutions is used across time or space in the development of policies, administrative arrangements and institutions elsewhere'.[10] The most well-known and coherent framework for analysis remains that devised by Dolowitz and Marsh, although they clearly encourage other analysts to expand, amend and review their model.[11] Dolowitz and Marsh's model was created principally to promote more focused thinking about linkages and values existing between the various activities put forward to describe aspects of the policy transfer process (whether voluntary or coercive), and it has acted as a springboard for more detailed, empirically-grounded investigations of individual cases of hypothesised policy transfer.[12]

Yet just because policies appear to have converged across space this does not necessarily mean that overt (or indeed covert) policy transfer has taken place. It may have done, but we cannot – at first sight at least – be sure. In order to be certain of policy-makers' aims we need to look closely not just at outcomes but also at processes, as convergence may occur in spite of the aims of the actors involved, perhaps more by luck than judgement or even without the actors actually being aware of it. Convergence, as was illustrated in the introduction, is therefore a much broader term, perhaps more operationalisable, and certainly more measurable, if only as one is dealing with a series of definites (i.e. outcomes of the policy process) rather than hypotheticals (i.e. what policy-makers may or may not have wished to happen). An understanding of the dynamics of process coupled with the reasons for the eventual outcome of policy development should therefore be the real aim of the game. Knowing why, and on whose impetus, policy converges is important as it tells us plenty about how policy-making actually occurs in the real world. And, as has long been clear to connoisseurs of the policy transfer literature in particular, real-world case studies testing just these models and explanatory frameworks have been notoriously few and far between.

PUTTING SOCIAL DEMOCRACY INTO CONTEXT

In the case of social democratic party politics through the 1990s, the most obvious objects of emulation were the policies and programmes of the social democratic parties that did win elections. In theory, social democratic parties were likely to confront their own programmatic failure by looking to other similar (successful) actors for inspiration. Labour's success in 1997 therefore came at a most opportune moment. Transferring external ideas into policies that are suitable for given local circumstances is, however, a task fraught with difficulty, and it is clear that a degree of political support for developing and pushing through transferred policies is necessary if it is to be done successfully.[13] For the purposes of understanding how Labour and the SPD have eventually found themselves converging in policy terms the concept of policy transfer is clearly less useful than the broader idea of policy learning, which better portrays the part self-determined, part exogenously imposed routes of adaptation taken by western European social democratic movements in general and the SPD in particular.[14]

Whilst all of the contextual detail for the SPD and Labour Party cannot be covered here, these contexts are indeed crucial for setting out opportunity structures. These can be conceptualised on three levels.[15] On the institutional level, the circumstances of individual parties are ever-changing in terms of who they are competing with for votes (influencing their political strategy), levels of leadership autonomy (different forms of party organisation), and relationships with their core supporters (identity). In terms of the national context, policy alternatives must be adapted to both national socio-economic structures (such as the state's industrial profile, levels of state ownership and so forth) and indigenous political systems (for example the nature of government coalitions). The national context is especially relevant when a party is openly looking to import policies whilst concurrently being in government.[16] The international context is also a consideration when policy-making meets policy implementation in government. Elsewhere in this volume Simon Bulmer explains the importance of Europeanisation for the policy-making processes in the UK and Germany, and frameworks created and shaped by the EU's institutions have both constrained SPD and Labour policy (for example, the development of the Internal Market, the creation of the Growth and Stability Pact and so forth) and increased the logic of social democratic collaboration.

Both parties have developed more hierarchical leadership structures over the course of the 1990s, whether by formal organisational change (Labour) or as a consequence of the need for leadership autonomy in fast-moving media democracies (SPD and Labour). This autonomy was enhanced by the emergence of two charismatic party leaders, Tony Blair and Gerhard Schröder. In terms of political campaigning, the SPD borrowed heavily from the successful examples of the US Democratic Party and the British Labour Party. Labour's Campaigns and Communications Directorate provided a model for the SPD's 'Kampa' in the 1998 federal election campaign, particularly with regard to its efforts to control the news agenda through media events and the portrayal of its leader as a 'doer' and a winner.[17] The leadership in government enjoys a particularly strong position in relation to the party. As a result of the leaders' independent power base and the resources at their disposal, the party as whole plays a more reactive role in government policy. The opposition–government paradigm is therefore central to the evolution of party programmes, since parties in government must pay more attention to implementation of policies in practice.

For Labour, the institutional constraints are relatively loose. The Labour Party under the leadership of Neil Kinnock and John Smith in the 1980s and 1990s neutralised the threat from vested interests (in particular, the trade unions) – a process that was continued in programmatic terms by the symbolic revision of Clause IV under Tony Blair. Top-down leadership structures in the party and in government have therefore allowed higher levels of leadership autonomy than is the case for the SPD. In fact, the main institutional constraints for the current Labour Party have emanated from differences within the party leadership itself – in particular, between Tony Blair and Gordon Brown – over ideological and strategic considerations, manifesting themselves in differences over issues such as pensions and education reform. This has opened the channels to policy transfer from abroad in a number of areas. Although much policy learning has been attributed to Labour's attraction to the US Democratic Party and US politics in general (for example, in the adoption of its 'welfare to work' programme), the party has nevertheless sought to meet its commitment to bring British public services up to EU standards. However, whilst leadership autonomy opens paths for policy transfer, the need for policy learning is lessened by strategic and programmatic certainty.

The SPD leadership, by comparison, faces far greater institutional constraints. First, the SPD has a flatter organisational structure than the Labour Party both horizontally (across Germany's federal structures) and vertically (given the continuing importance of the party conference). Although the party leadership has sought to streamline the decision-making process in practice, programmatic change has often been difficult to achieve due to the existence of several institutional veto players. The Berlin Basic Programme took most of the 1980s to draft, and – by the time it was agreed – was rapidly overtaken by events (mainly as a result of German reunification). Since the late 1990s the SPD has subsequently been engaged in an ongoing programmatic review. More specifically, Schröder, Bodo Hombach and other proponents of the *Neue Mitte* (New Centre) found it difficult to adopt UK/US Third Way-style policies (even after the departure of Oskar Lafontaine from office in 1999) because of opposition from within the party and because the German state had not gone through the radical process of change set in motion by Margaret Thatcher in the UK. Even with the departure of the traditional left's talisman a mere six months into the SPD–Green government's term of office, the term '*Neue Mitte*' was nonetheless jettisoned from the party's vocabulary as the main body of the party reined the leadership back in. This explains the internal uproar caused by the Blair–Schröder paper later that year. Even after the SPD was drawn back to Third Way-style policies by severe national economic problems (explored below), the opposition of sections of the party to the Government's Agenda 2010 was a large factor motivating Chancellor Schröder's decision to precipitate federal elections in 2005. Yet, as the SPD began, after 2002, to face more strategic uncertainties, its search for new programmatic alternatives became more active.

A key purpose of party programmes is to build alliances and to enable parties to elections. The success of social democratic parties at the polls in the late 1990s was characterised by their ability to mobilise broad coalitions of voters, whilst maintaining support within traditional constituencies. This was the electoral purpose of New Labour and the *Neue Mitte*. Perceptions of a move to the centre have nevertheless involved certain risks.[18] In strategic terms, the SPD has, again, faced greater challenges. The SPD has had to struggle against serious competition – initially from the New Left but latterly also from more overtly socialist groupings – whilst Labour has been far less constrained as it has had no genuine challenger on the left thanks to the majoritarian electoral system in the UK. The fact that the left wing of the SPD can claim to represent a major electoral constituency increases its importance to the party leadership, leading to its representation in the party presidium and granting it a voice in policy-making. The risks have therefore been greater for the SPD in appearing to move to the right on economic issues, as was illustrated by the implosion of electoral support for the party after the launch of the SPD–Green government's Agenda 2010 reform programme. Furthermore, Agenda 2010 resulted in the splintering of the party on the left, breathing life into a new Left Party that could compete with the SPD at the national level.[19] For both Labour and the SPD, the failure to deliver to core supporters when in government has led to efforts to re-emphasise core issues such as 'public services' in response to these losses.[20] The SPD's programmatic alternatives have also been constricted by the nature of coalition government in Germany. Whilst co-operation with the Green Party (1998–2005) provided a number of particular constraints, Germany's federal structures (in stark contrast to the centralised Westminster model of the UK) added further pressures on party policy after the coalition lost control of the Bundesrat early in its first term.[21] Additional defeats in state elections resulted in a de facto Grand Coalition by the end of the SPD–Green government's second term. The formal Grand Coalition with the Christian Democrats (with the SPD as the junior partner) since 2005 has led to an even greater focus on the national context.

Just as systems of party competition and political opportunity structures define party policy in a strategic sense, the national economic situation defines how policy is actually implemented. Although it is clearly beyond the scope of this discussion to build up a detailed economic profile of the two countries, key economic data is revealing. For example, whilst the Labour Party increased public spending significantly after it came to power,[22] this is relativised by different starting points: in 1997, public spending in the UK was 42 per cent of Gross Domestic Product (GDP), compared to 48 per cent in Germany.[23] Furthermore, average debt as a percentage of GDP was recorded at 53 per cent in the UK and 60 per cent in Germany in 1997, which had diverged to 44 per cent and 68 per cent respectively in 2004.[24] This gives some indication of the extreme 'resource crunch' faced by the SPD in government, explaining why it faced increasing pressure to slim down the welfare state (in contrast to Labour, which has sought to expand it). In quantitative terms, what we saw after the two parties came to power in the late 1990s was, therefore, some convergence towards similar models even after leaders of the two parties had stopped talking the same rhetorical language. In contrast to the different structural challenges, these two parties have also faced a number of common problems such as ageing populations and the increasing cost of healthcare, which in themselves encourage convergent policy choices.

Common challenges are also provided by the international context, which has been an important theme in the Third Way debate. At the European level, the penetration of the EU into erstwhile domains of domestic policy in recent years has forced social democratic parties to respond to the challenges of an Internal Market that demands the reduction of state subsidies and a single currency that sets limits to state spending. European integration has implications for policy convergence and policy learning, as integration pressures constrain party policy (especially in government), deepen interdependence in the EU, and promote the use of similar policy instruments in the pursuit of similar policy goals. Whilst the Blair–Schröder paper in 1999 provided a generalised agenda for social democratic parties, more specific disagreements have emerged in recent years over the operation of the Internal Market (for example, over EU competition and the infamous services directive) and the future of the EU as a social model. The latter issue led to a fierce exchange of views between Blair and Schröder (partly conducted through the German press) in June 2005.[25] On the broader international level, the issue of 'globalisation' has provided a key debating point for modern social democracy. Whatever the realities of the situation, both Tony Blair and Gerhard Schröder have argued that their parties and countries must adapt to global pressures (for example in the area of labour market flexibility).[26] Schröder, for example, warned 'leftist critics' of his reform programme to 'modernise or die'.[27] Though foreign policy has certainly complicated relations between the two parties – the opposing positions on the Iraq conflict positively poisoned relations between Schröder and Blair – this does not change the fact that the two parties continue to face similar policy challenges with regard to the running of domestic economies, the functioning of public services and the viability of welfare states. In short, while faced with fundamentally different opportunity structures, the two parties have converged towards a corridor of European values within which social democracy may still have 'several different futures'.[28]

PROGRAMMATIC CONVERGENCE AND POLICY LEARNING

It is self-evident that some similarities exist in the methods of modernisation that the SPD and Labour have sought to undertake, and an analysis of their programmatic agendas sheds much light on these developments. The only serious way of comparing the parties' political profiles is by analysing their programmes and policy aims within the contexts outlined above. A broad interpretation of what constitutes a party programme (incorporating election manifestos, party programmes and statutes, lead motions at conferences, individual policy papers and major statements made by party leaders) is important in capturing the nuances of party policy.[29] Analysing election manifestos along a left–right spectrum is not enough.[30] For example, Labour implemented significant increases in spending on public services (in particular, education and health) in a quantitative sense, but also made qualitative changes to its delivery through the increased use of the private sector (for example Private

Finance Initiatives). It is not therefore sufficient to add up references to 'public services' in Labour Party manifestos to see the full picture.

Pinpointing examples of overt policy transfer is not an exact science, but there is none the less clear evidence that transfer and learning has occurred in a number of areas between the Labour Party and the SPD. The Labour Party under Tony Blair came to power in the UK with a landslide victory in 1997. A year later, Gerhard Schröder led the Social Democrats to government in Germany. After the resignation of Oskar Lafontaine, the left-wing chairman of the SPD and Finance Minister in Schröder's first government, in 1999, it appeared that the two parties were setting out on parallel paths. This seemed to be confirmed by the Blair–Schröder paper published just a couple of months later, setting out the two leaders' way forward for social democracy (just prior to elections to the European Parliament). The main themes of the paper were public expenditure and reform of the welfare state. The document argued, first, that 'public expenditure as a proportion of national income had more or less reached the limits of acceptability'.[31] It furthermore encouraged greater responsibility for citizens – to accompany their rights – vis-à-vis the state (implying that it was the responsibility of the unemployed to seek work and accept job offers).[32] The Labour position was that the benefits system should be 'structured around work', linking 'opportunity' to 'responsibility' through a system of incentives for low-paid work (e.g. tax credits, low tax rates) and penalties (e.g. cuts in benefit) for those not accepting work.[33] The position adopted by the advocates of the *Neue Mitte* was, likewise, that welfare should act as a 'trampoline' rather than a 'safety net'.[34]

Co-operation and collaboration between the two parties was shaped (initially) by good relations between the two leaders and their right-hand men, Peter Mandelson and Bodo Hombach, allowing for the formation of 'transfer networks' that acted as a stimulus for policy learning. These networks acted as a community of like-minded people, not promoting a single policy through a common strategy as in the advocacy coalition framework,[35] but sharing a set of common assumptions 'in the verity and applicability of particular forms of knowledge' and thereby providing a 'cognitive base' for interaction.[36] After the retreat of the *Neue Mitte* in 1999, bilateral co-operation was relaxed, taking place mostly in multilateral fora such as the 'progressive governance network', promoted by Mandelson, and then put on hold with the souring of relations precipitated by differences over the Iraq conflict.

While the Blair–Schröder paper caused barely a ripple of excitement in the UK, there was a fierce backlash from opponents in the SPD. Within the context of the German welfare state, and given the existence of institutional veto players in the SPD, the ideas articulated in the paper appeared relatively radical. Even though the state of German public finances ultimately meant that spending would have to be cut back, this was not something that the SPD could accept in programmatic terms at this point in time. With regard to the idea that it was the responsibility of the unemployed to accept work, the argument that any job is better than none[37] was countered with the claim that the 'necessary flexibility will not lead to a lowering of social standards'.[38] The SPD's poor performance in the 1999 European elections strengthened the hand of opponents of this course. The retreat from radical change resulted in the postponement of the *Neue Mitte* agenda for the SPD's first period in office. The Labour Party interpreted the failure to implement *Neue Mitte* policy in the SPD as a lack of spine on

Schröder's part – he was not prepared to face down internal opponents as the Labour leadership had done in the 1980s and the 1990s. This interpretation is questionable given the strength of institutional veto players within the SPD. Yet, despite the apparent decoupling of the SPD from a Third Way-type agenda, the state of German public finances ultimately forced the SPD – as a governing party – to embark upon a revision of its position. The support of the SPD–Green government for 'welfare to work' policies (known collectively as the 'Hartz reforms') and cuts in public spending, led the party to emphasise an 'active state ... that helps people to lead an independent life'.[39]

Whilst the motivations for programmatic convergence have emanated from a number of sources – demographic challenges, the constraints of the EU, perceptions about globalisation and so forth – policy learning continued to take place within the context of the European social democratic movement. Here, the transfer of policy has rarely taken place in an explicit fashion, but as the result of a subtle diffusion of policies rather like the spreading of 'ink-blots'.[40] Whilst the SPD has moved towards New Labour-type Third Way policies in recent years, the Labour Party has equally developed a greater understanding about the necessity of better funded public services. On a conceptual level, convergence between the two parties can be further illustrated by their changing usage of the key social democratic term 'social justice'. Though social justice has always been a major theme in SPD manifestos, it has been neglected by the Labour Party in recent years and has come to be seen as an antiquated notion. Social justice nonetheless became a major feature of Labour's 'social contract' in 2005, when the party argued that 'we refuse to accept false choices. The British people never wanted to choose between wealth creation and social justice ... economic dynamism and social justice must go hand in hand'.[41] The SPD, in the context of the damage inflicted on the party's support base by Agenda 2010, sent out a strikingly similar message to the Labour manifesto (only a few months earlier): 'economic prosperity and social justice are not contradictions'.[42]

In policy terms, outright convergence was limited until the SPD's second term in office (2002–2005) when it embarked upon reform of the welfare state and labour market, and attempted to make significant cuts in public spending. With regard to public spending, both Labour and the SPD have recognised the limits of demand-side economic policy. While demand-side spending has been sanctioned as social investment to accompany the labour and welfare reform mentioned above, government spending has not increased unsustainably when these parties have been in power. The SPD was faced with the task of managing the high levels of state debt built up as a result of German unity. Despite the party's relative failure in dealing with this situation between 1998 and 2005 (achieving only modest reductions in spending – from 48 to 47 per cent of GDP – and seeing an increase in debt from 62 to 68 per cent of GDP),[43] Peer Steinbrück – SPD Finance Minister in the Grand Coalition – has committed the German government to a balanced budget in the medium term. The Labour Party, following several years of budgetary restraint after coming to power (initially along the lines of Conservative spending plans), introduced significant increases in spending, but only in the context of the UK's previously low levels of public expenditure and public debt.

Through necessity in government, the SPD gradually began to accept welfare to work as a policy alternative. The SPD had already, in the late 1990s, sought to introduce the notion of 'responsibility' for 'recipients of social benefits to accept jobs that are offered to them'.[44] The 2002 programme was more explicit in its intention to provide 'both incentives and penalties for the unemployed', in combination with job creation schemes such as the 'Jump' programme to combat youth unemployment.[45] Only at the beginning of its second term in 2002, in the face of burgeoning unemployment (rising above the politically sensitive five million mark), did the SPD embark upon a series of measures to promote labour market flexibility (the Hartz reforms). Official party policy stated in 2005 that 'whoever has not found their desired job … must be prepared to accept another job offer'.[46] Given the Labour government's success in keeping levels of unemployment low, the SPD has adopted a much more New Labour approach to the unemployed, even mimicking Labour initiatives to improve the situation such as the re-designation of employment offices as employment agencies ('Job Centres'). With the haemorrhaging of core supporters in local, Land and European elections, the party nevertheless felt it necessary to reassure its supporters that it would 'preserve the welfare state' (with its main role being that of 'social levelling'), as well as an 'active state … that helps people to lead an independent life'.[47] The SPD has also made a significant movement in the direction of Third Way-style policies in the Grand Coalition, agreeing – for instance – to raise the retirement age to 67 (a measure sponsored by SPD Minister for Employment and Social Affairs, Franz Müntefering).

Although the Labour Party had already accepted the principle of welfare to work by the mid-1990s, it was faced with a different problem. Labour was keen to throw off the mantle of a tax-and-spend party (as it was successfully portrayed by the Conservatives in the 1980s), by emphasising its fiscal prudence. Yet by the end of its first term in office, the relatively low levels of public funding for education and health in the UK caused the Labour government to substantially increase investment in public services. This is borne out by the fact that public spending (as a proportion of GDP) increased from 41 per cent to 44 per cent in the UK between 1997 and 2004.[48] Labour increasingly sought to bring the private sector into public services by, for example, introducing Private Finance Initiatives for school and hospital building programmes and using the private sector to 'extend patient power and choice'.[49] Yet welfare to work remained the central component in this strategy, offering opportunity with responsibility as well as a minimum guaranteed 'take-home pay' for those willing to accept low-paid work.[50] The centrepiece of this was, a job creation scheme – the 'New Deal' – funded initially by a windfall tax on recently privatised utilities.

On a conceptual level, Labour and the SPD have both acknowledged the need to balance economic progress with social justice, but have also moved (to varying degrees) towards an emphasis on equality of opportunity. The Labour Party has tried to improve public services (from relatively low levels), while the SPD has tried to maintain key aspects of the German social model (for example worker representation in companies). Therefore, policies have converged both quantitatively (e.g. the efforts of the Labour government to 'bring UK health spending up to the EU average')[51] and qualitatively (e.g. the SPD's adoption of 'welfare to work' policies).[52] Although significant differences still remain in areas such as worker protection and labour market flexibility, even here the gap has narrowed (for example the introduction of the minimum wage in the UK, the relaxation of laws on dismissal in Germany).

CONCLUSION

This contribution has emphasised that even where political parties have ostensibly similar aims and goals, there are clear limits to the amount of convergence that we should expect to see in terms of policy outputs. In many ways, this should not come as too much of a surprise given the different institutional frameworks and political histories that inevitably exist across national borders. The conditionality of these contexts means that pinpointing active and conscious policy transfer and policy learning is not a simple process; it is rather more that parties get pulled by the gravitational fields of institutional, national and international circumstances. Even then, this pull only prompts them to prioritise certain problems and certain challenges. It does not dictate that the actors involved will automatically come to the same solutions. Viewed in this way, the SPD has been 'stretched' between divergent institutional and national contexts while the Labour Party created policy in a fundamentally different post-Thatcher United Kingdom polity.

The impact of international processes such as Europeanisation and globalisation has assisted Labour and the SPD in framing their policies to suit the challenges posed by international institutions and processes. There were none the less clear differences in terms of the desirability of bringing in Third Way ideas and the feasibility of then actually doing so in practice. Gerhard Schröder clearly believed that Blair's Labour Party could act as a source of policy inspiration when he entered government in 1998, but the institutional blockages he faced proved a considerable hindrance to actually delivering on his rhetoric. Such policies only became feasible – perhaps even unavoidable – from 2002 onwards, and even then Schröder faced challenges of a significantly larger magnitude than Blair had done in the UK. Diffusion theory tells us that organisations 'emulate' policies 'because the other state provides a timely model which may be seen as the solution to a vexing local political problem' – and, even if it took a number of years to actually come to fruition, this might well be the most applicable way of understanding why the SPD advocated Agenda 2010 in the way that it did.[53]

NOTES

1. For more on lesson-drawing, see in particular R. Rose, *Lesson-Drawing in Public Policy. A Guide to Learning Across Time and Space* (Chatham, NJ: Chatham House, 1993). See also the introduction to this collection.
2. C. Pierson, *Hard Choices: Social Democracy in the Twentieth Century* (Cambridge: Polity, 2001), p.30.
3. W. Merkel, 'The Third Ways of Social Democracy', in A. Giddens (ed.), *The Global Third Way Debate* (Cambridge: Polity, 2001); A. Giddens, *Where Now for New Labour?* (Cambridge: Polity, 2002), pp.18–19.
4. A. Etzioni, *The Third Way to a Good Society* (London: Demos, 2000), pp.13–14.
5. See for example S. Hale, W. Leggett and L. Martell (eds.), *The Third Way and Beyond* (Manchester: Manchester University Press, 2004).
6. W. Streeck and C. Trampusch, 'Economic Reform and the Political Economy of the German Welfare State', *German Politics* 14/2 (2005), pp.174–95.
7. Rose, *Lesson-Drawing in Public Policy*.
8. P.M. Haas, 'Introduction: Epistemic Communities and International Policy Coordination', *International Organization* 46/1 (1992), pp.1–35.
9. D. Dolowitz and D. Marsh, 'Who Learns What from Whom: A Review of the Policy Transfer Literature', *Political Studies* 44/2 (1996), pp.343–57; D. Dolowitz and D. Marsh, 'Learning from Abroad: The Role of Policy Transfer in Contemporary Policy-Making', *Governance* 13/1 (2000), pp.5–24.

10. D. Stone, 'Learning Lessons and Transferring Policy across Time, Space and Disciplines', *Politics* 19/1 (1999), p.51.
11. For further attempts at doing this see in particular M. Evans and J. Davies, 'Understanding Policy Transfer: A Multi-level, Multi-disciplinary Perspective', *Public Administration* 77/2 (1999), pp.361–86; Stone, 'Learning Lessons'; W. Jacoby, *The Enlargement of the European Union and NATO: Ordering from the Menu in Central Europe* (Cambridge: Cambridge University Press, 2004), Dolowitz and Marsh, 'Who Learns What from Whom'; Dolowitz and Marsh, 'Learning from Abroad'.
12. For a good example of this see D. Hough, W. Paterson and J. Sloam (eds.), *Learning from the West: Policy Transfer and Programmatic Change in the Communist Successor Parties of East-Central Europe* (London: Routledge, 2006).
13. W. Jacoby, *Imitation and Politics* (Ithaca, NY: Cornell University Press, 2000).
14. See W. Paterson and J. Sloam, 'Learning from the West: Policy Transfer and Political Parties', *Journal of Communist Studies and Transition Politics* 21/1 (2005), pp.33–47.
15. Ibid., pp.33–47.
16. See W. Paterson, 'Political Parties and the Making of Foreign Policy', *Review of International Studies*, 1981, pp.227–35; J. Sloam, *The European Policy of the German Social Democrats: Interpreting a Changing World* (Basingstoke: Palgrave, 2004).
17. For an analysis of SPD strategy in the 1998 federal elections see E. Noelle-Neumann (ed.), *Kampa. Meinungsklima und Medienwirkung im Bundestagswahlkampf 1998* (Freiburg: Alber, 1999).
18. A. Panebianco, *Political Parties: Organisation and Power* (Cambridge: Cambridge University Press, 1988).
19. See D. Hough, M. Koβ and J. Olsen, *The Road to Normality? The Left Party in Contemporary Germany* (Basingstoke: Palgrave, 2007).
20. See Labour Party, *Ambitions for Britain* (London: Labour Party, 2001), available at http://www.psr.keele.ac.uk/area/uk/e01/man/lab/lab01.htm (accessed 4 April 2006); SPD, *Erneuerung und Zusammenhalt – Wir in Deutschland* (Berlin: SPD, 2002), available at SPD-Vorstand, http://www.spd.de/servlet/PB/show/1019292/Regierungsprogramm percent20der percent20SPD.rtf (accessed 4 April 2006).
21. A. Lijphart: *Democracies: Patterns of Majoritarian and Consensus Government in Twenty-one Countries* (New Haven, CT: Yale University Press, 1984).
22. The Labour Party nevertheless left its major increases in public spending until its second term (beginning in 2001), after UK public debt had been reduced from 53 per cent to 41 per cent of GDP – OECD, *Economic Outlook No. 78* (2005), Annex Table 32, available at http://www.oecd.org/dataoecd/5/51/2483816.xls (accessed 4 April 2006).
23. Ibid., Annex Table 25.
24. Ibid., Annex Table 32.
25. The debate between Blair and Schröder was partly conducted on the pages of *Bild* magazine in June 2006 (just prior to the UK's EU presidency).
26. For a thorough discussion of this point see M. Watson and C. Hay, 'The Discourse of Globalisation and the Logic of No Alternative: Rendering the Contingent Necessary in the Political Economy of New Labour', *Policy and Politics* 31/3 (2003), pp.289–305.
27. G. Schröder, 'Modernise or Die', *The Guardian*, 8 July 2003, available at http://www.guardian.co.uk/print/0,3858,4707676-107025,00.html (accessed 4 April 2006).
28. W. Paterson and A. Thomas, *The Future of Social Democracy* (Oxford: Clarendon, 1986), p.16.
29. Paterson and Sloam, 'Learning from the West', pp.33–47.
30. For a more detailed criticism of the manifestos approach Paterson and Sloam, 'Learning from the West'.
31. T. Blair and G. Schröder, 'Europe: The Third Way/die Neue Mitte', in B. Hombach (ed.), *The Politics of the New Centre* (Oxford: Blackwell, 2000), p.164.
32. Ibid.
33. Labour Party, *Ambitions for Britain*; T. Blair, *The Third Way: New Politics for the New Century* (London: Fabian Pamphlet 588, 1998).
34. Hombach (ed.), *The Politics of the New Centre*
35. P. Sabatier and H. Jenkins-Smith (eds.), *Policy Change and Learning: An Advocacy Coalition Approach* (Boulder, CO: Westview, 1993), pp.16–20.
36. P. Haas (ed.), *Knowledge, Power, and International Policy Coordination* (Columbia: University of South Carolina, 1999), p.3.
37. Hans-Martin Bury (Berlin: 'Vorwärts', November 1999).
38. SPD, *Wegmarken für ein neues Grundsatzprogramm – Sozialdemokratische Vorstellungen zur nachhaltigen Gestaltung der globalen Epoche* (Berlin: SPD, Interim Report of the Programme Commission, 2001), p.20.

39. SPD, *Vertrauen in Deutschland* (Berlin: SPD, 2005), available at http://www.spd.de/040705_Wahlmanifest.pdf, p.9 (accessed 4 April 2006).
40. J. Walker, 'The Diffusion of Innovation among the American States', *American Political Science Review* 63 (1969), pp.880–99. Interaction in these transfer networks is similar to the concept of 'normative isomorphism', where transorganisational networks provide arenas through which 'new models diffuse rapidly'. See P. Dimaggio and W. Powell, 'The Iron Cage Revisited: Institutional Isomorphism and Collective Rationality in Organizational Fields', *American Sociological Review* 48/1 (1998), pp.147–60, here pp.150–52.
41. Labour Party, *Britain Forward Not Back* (2005), available at http://www.labour.org.uk/ fileadmin/ manifesto_13042005_a3/pdf/manifesto.pdf (accessed 4 April, 2006), pp.9, 15.
42. SPD, *Vertrauen in Deutschland*, p.8.
43. OECD, *Economic Outlook No. 78*, Annex Tables 25 and 32.
44. SPD, *Arbeit, Innovation und Gerechtigkeit* (Bonn: SPD, 1998).
45. SPD, *Erneuerung und Zusammenhalt – Wir in Deutschland*.
46. SPD, *Vertrauen in Deutschland*, p.29.
47. Ibid., p.9.
48. OECD, *Economic Outlook No. 78*, Annex Table 25.
49. Labour Party, *Britain Forward Not Back*, p.60.
50. Labour Party, *Ambitions for Britain*, pp.26–7.
51. Ibid.
52. Ibid.
53. R. Eyestone, 'Confusion, Diffusion, and Innovation', *American Political Science Review* 71/2 (1977), pp.441–7, here p.441.

Germany, Britain and the European Union: Convergence through Policy Transfer?

SIMON BULMER

INTRODUCTION

Germany and Britain are two medium-sized powers in global politics and the global political economy. They have common membership of a number of international organisations, most notably the European Union. Should we therefore expect policy convergence or policy exchange between the two states? This contribution aims to offer some answers to that question. It does so in three parts. First, it explores what the real-world pressures are that may lead to policy convergence. What are the underlying forces at work? Why is it that policy convergence may take place? Secondly, what analytical or theoretical tools can help shed light on the pressures for convergence? Three forces for convergence are explored: globalisation, Europeanisation and the preferred framework deployed in what follows, namely policy transfer. Thirdly, in developing an institutionalist exposition of policy transfer it explores the obstacles and opportunities for transfer between Germany and Britain within a European and global context.

It is argued that the EU is the most systematic mechanism for policy convergence between the two states. There are some notable instances of especially German but also British policies being adopted at EU level and thereafter being transferred down to the 'other' state. However, while the EU is a force for convergence, the general pattern of policy transfer between the two states via the Brussels detour is one of synthesis. That is to say, with the preferences of 27 member states, as well as those of the European Commission and Parliament, to be taken into account in policy-making, German and British views need to be accommodated in overall agreement: hence the synthetic character of the policy transfer. The argument and policy transfer framework are not subject to detailed empirical investigation in this study, which aims to inform the subsequent policy cases examined in this collection.

EXPLAINING POLICY CONVERGENCE

Christoph Knill has offered a valuable definition of convergence:

> Policy convergence can be defined as any increase in the similarity between one or more characteristics of a certain policy (e.g. policy objectives, policy instruments, policy settings), across a given set of political jurisdictions (supranational institutions, states, regions, local authorities) over a given period of time. Policy convergence thus describes the end result of a process of policy change over time towards some common point, regardless of the causal process.[1]

Analytically it can be explained in different ways, with emphasis being placed on the processes behind convergence or upon the outcomes.[2] Empirically, three underlying forces can explain convergence between the policies of Britain and Germany: globalisation, Europeanisation, and the facilitating role of other international arenas including bilateral relations. However, it is also important to recognise that convergence might not be the product of any of these forces at all. It could be down to pure coincidence that two states deploy the same policy devices, although such an explanation would lack credibility if convergence went beyond isolated instances. The key analytical point is that it is important to identify clear causality for convergence. If the root cause of similarity or convergence cannot be determined, then it might be attributable to coincidence. Most typically, however, it is likely to be attributable to the underlying forces identified earlier, and to which attention is now turned. One important point is worth making before doing so: that these potential explanations may be less easily disentangled in practical than they can be in analytical terms.

Globalisation

Globalisation presents a range of pressures for policy change that may result in policy convergence. Technological change has become a strong driver of globalisation, as new advances have presented challenges for sectors traditionally based in national markets. New technologies have required increasingly large capital investments. The civil aerospace industry is an obvious example of this dynamic, with the market for airliners with 100+ seating capacity now confined to two manufacturers: Boeing and Airbus. The latter absorbed the main airliner producers in France, Germany, Britain and Spain. Similar technology policy challenges are presented for the four governments each time Airbus seeks launch aid in order to develop a new airliner. It follows that there is some convergence of British and German policy on aviation technology. The case of Airbus highlights another component of globalisation, namely the need for companies to have access to international capital markets and/or engage in cross-border concentrations or joint ventures in order to recoup their investment. Airbus was owned by two companies: the European Aeronautic Defence and Space Company (EADS) and British Aerospace (the latter sold its stake in autumn 2006) EADS was established in 2001 through the merger of Aérospatiale-Matra of France, Construcciones Aeronáuticas SA (CASA) of Spain and Daimler-Chrysler Aerospace

AG (DASA) and its shares are traded on several stock exchanges.[3] This corporate consolidation has presented policy challenges for Airbus partners, including on company law and industrial relations and these impact on other areas of British and German public policy as well as that of the EU.

In addition to these technology-related dynamics, globalisation also promotes the development of international policy trends. These trends may be facilitated by companies in the private sector, think-tanks, expert groups and international agencies. We may illustrate these dynamics through reference to air transport liberalisation. Originally set in motion by the domestic de-regulation of air transport in the United States in 1978, the ideas resonated in the UK and the Netherlands.[4] Companies may identify new market opportunities arising from a change of public policy, such as when British Airways and British Midland advocated liberalisation of air travel within the European Union. Think-tanks and epistemic communities serve as arenas within which the international dissemination of policy ideas may occur.[5]

Developments of this kind arising from globalisation may take effect in different ways. One variant is herding: the notion that states do not simply orient their policy response to objective indicators but, like portfolio managers on the stock markets, discount that information in favour of attentiveness to the signals of their peers.[6] Regulatory competition implies an approach whereby states focus on providing an optimal business environment for domestic industry/entrepreneurs or to attract inward investment.[7] The related 'competition state' analysis sees states losing some of their traditional powers, notably the facility for Keynesian demand management in favour of supply-side economic policies, in the face of the process of globalisation. Whether the competition-state model leads to national convergence around a neo-liberal, lean-welfare model of capitalism, as argued by Philip Cerny, is open to challenge.[8] Not only that, but there is an important debate as to whether regulatory competition does lead to a convergence downwards in terms of regulatory standards (the so-called Delaware effect) or upwards, towards higher standards (the California effect).[9]

Globalisation has been a prominent concern for public policy analysts but it may sometimes appear to be a cause looking for an effect. The more thorough-going analyses have sought to identify the mechanisms triggering domestic policy change. They have highlighted such factors as independent problem-solving, international harmonisation, regulatory competition and transnational communication.[10] However, as is well known from the 'varieties of capitalism' literature, assumptions of convergence are highly contested.[11] National cultural traditions and norms are not easily swept away in the face of globalisation. The national institutional structures in which public policy is embedded are resistant to change and represent formidable obstacles to the dynamics of globalisation. National governments remain key actors in most international negotiations and they set the rules for domestic economic governance. Globalisation is clearly of considerable background importance to policy convergence between the two states. What of the EU's role?

Europeanisation

Membership of the EU is another potential explanation for policy convergence. EU membership brings with it obligations to comply with policy agreements reached at supranational level, resulting in what is referred to as Europeanisation. The EU does not have a monopoly over Europeanisation, since other agencies such as the Council of Europe may have comparable impacts. However, it is the policy spread, institutional density and legal character of the EU which make it central to Europeanisation. Over the period since the early 1950s the obligations associated with supranational integration in the contemporary EU have developed across almost the full range of socio-economic policies: from coal and steel, through agriculture, the single market to – at least for member states of the euro-zone – monetary integration. As is well known, the EU's policy portfolio has extended beyond purely economic policy to include social and environmental matters. Foreign policy cooperation has been developed to include security and defence policy. Finally, home affairs cooperation has developed across a range of sub-fields: from asylum and immigration policy through counter-terrorism and combating organised crime to cooperation on criminal law. Apart from in the event of an opt-out provision, such as the UK's on joining the euro-zone or on joining the passport-free zone colloquially known as 'Schengenland', all these policy areas bring some kind of obligation. However, the nature of the obligation varies from a political commitment to consult or exchange ideas and practices at one end of the spectrum to legal requirements at the other.

Europeanisation brings with it similar dynamics to those identified above with globalisation but amongst a geographically close set of countries with similar policy concerns. In fact, there is something of a tension evident in political discourses within the EU as to whether Europeanisation is an effort to mitigate the effects of globalisation or to embrace it.[12] As an intellectual discourse Europeanisation has become pervasive in the study of the EU.[13] As with globalisation, there is a strong emphasis upon *policy* impact.[14] However, it should be pointed out that the close association of Europeanisation with the EU, which is a political system in its own right, means that there are also studies of its impact upon domestic political systems and political forces. Whilst not the focus of attention in this discussion, it should be noted that these other two forms have an indirect impact on the Europeanisation of policy. Member state political systems are more closely intertwined within the EU, notably through the frequent bilateral diplomacy that flanks the more obvious multilateral variant. In addition, collaboration between party families, most obviously in the European Parliament, and between national interest groups in their transnational counterparts, also offer opportunities for policy learning by governments and non-governmental actors alike.

The impact of the EU on domestic policy is significant because of its policy reach and the mechanisms by which it penetrates the national policy process. However, Europeanisation is also an analytical framework to which attention is now turned. The Europeanisation of policy 'entails two steps: adoption at EU level and then incorporation at domestic level'.[15] The first step must not be neglected, for member governments are able to shape EU policy in the first place but there is an abundant *policy-making* literature to account for this preliminary step.[16] The two steps are, of course, inter-related. As Tanja Börzel has observed, the Europeanisation experience of a member state may well be influenced by its role in policy-making, thus linking the uploading and downloading phases of Europeanisation.[17] Thus if a member state is successful in shaping EU policy according to its own domestic model, it should experience relatively painless adaptation at the downloading stage.

If domestic incorporation is to create convergence – which need not necessarily be the outcome[18] – then what are the mechanisms that promote it? The first major study of Europeanisation advanced the argument that adaptational pressure arising from the 'goodness of fit' of EU policy with domestic policy constituted the dynamic and mechanism of adjustment.[19] Specifically, the adjustment process was deemed most likely to take place in the case of moderate goodness of fit.[20] However, a lively debate emerged as to whether goodness of fit was, in fact, a pre-requisite of domestic adjustment.[21] Other analysts have advocated a more nuanced approach, arguing that different patterns of governance within the EU are associated with different mechanisms of change.[22]

Bulmer and Radaelli have identified three ideal-typical modes of governance in the EU.[23] First, where the EU has strong powers and applies them through positive integration, namely through creating a detailed policy regime such as in European Monetary Union, goodness of fit provides a good 'default' account of the pressures for domestic adaptation.[24] In other words, the positive integration typically associated with market-correcting measures brings with it a strong policy template. However, secondly, in many areas of strong supranational powers, such as the market-making rules relating to the internal market, there is a minimalist policy template and considerable discretion left to economic actors in the member states. Under these circumstances regulatory competition offers a better default explanation of adaptational pressures than goodness of fit. Thirdly, there are the many areas of EU policy where supranational powers are limited or even non-existent. These include traditional intergovernmental coordination, such as in foreign and security policy as well as newer approaches to policy exchange through benchmarking and peer review, generally termed the Open Method of Coordination (OMC). In these cases Europeanisation takes place through policy coordination and the default explanation for domestic adaptation rests with policy learning. This framework is summarised in Table 1.

There are obvious implications of this account of Europeanisation for convergence between Germany and the UK. Both states will seek to influence European policy during its negotiation in the 'uploading' phase of Europeanisation. It should be emphasised that 'policy' encompasses not just specific rules but also ideas and values. Both states will be subject to operationalising EU policy in the 'downloading' phase, once it has been agreed. In view of the fact that the EU's authority ranges between coercion and mild encouragement, the pressures for convergence vary from policy to policy. They also vary according to the policy instrument that is chosen. Hence Regulations require no separate domestic legislation, whereas Directives necessitate a domestic transposition stage of legislation. Thus Regulations should lead to convergence, whereas Directives may promote convergence of policy principles or of ideas but not necessarily of policy execution. That is because Directives are utilised specifically where the EU is mindful of different national routes to achieving a common policy goal. Indeed, depending on domestic constitutional provisions Germany's federal system and, since 1999, the UK's system of asymmetric devolution permit different modes of transposition *within* the member state where the EU legislation allows. Finally, it should be noted that domestic discretion may be abused, thus undermining the objectives of an EU Directive and limiting the likelihood of policy convergence.

My argument is that the sheer breadth of EU policy and its tangibility to the member states, whether in terms of political commitments or legal instruments,

TABLE 1
EUROPEANISATION AND DOMESTIC POLICY CHANGE

Mode of governance	Type of policy	Analytical core	Main mechanism	Policy examples	Default explanation
Negotiation	Any of those below	Formation of EU policy	Vertical (uploading)	Any	None specified
Hierarchy	Positive integration	Market-correcting rules; EU policy templates	Vertical (downloading)	EMU[a], Common Agricultural Policy, environmental policy	Goodness of fit
Hierarchy	Negative integration	Market-making rules; absence of policy templates	Horizontal	Internal market, utilities regulation, corporate governance	Regulatory competition
Facilitated coordination	Coordination	Soft law, OMC, policy exchange	Horizontal	OMC, CFSP[b]	Learning

Source: adapted from Tables 14.1 and 14.2 of S. Bulmer and C. Radaelli, 'The Europeanization of National Policy', in S. Bulmer and C. Lequesne (eds.), *The Member States of the European Union* (Oxford: Oxford University Press, 2005), pp.346, 354. By permission of Oxford University Press.
Notes: a. Economic and Monetary Union (EMU).
b. Common Foreign and Security Policy (CFSP).

means that it is a major force for convergence between the UK and Germany. Europeanisation as an analytical framework also has strengths, but it is not utilised further in this study.

Other International Mediation

As we have seen, the EU can serve as an important source of policy convergence. However, this role can also be played by other international organisations. The International Monetary Fund and/or the World Bank, for instance, impose conditionality upon developing countries that may encourage policy convergence. Whilst these circumstances may offer little purchase on German–British convergence, there are other international organisations that may do so. The Organisation for Economic Cooperation and Development (OECD), for example, serves as an arena for exchanges of economic policy as well as on public sector and governance issues, such as public management techniques. North Atlantic Treaty Organisation (NATO) has been a long-standing arena for identifying collective Atlantic security and defence and the Group of Eight industrialised nations (G8) economic summits serve as another arena within which economic policy ideas and practices are discussed, for instance on alleviating global poverty. In addition and partly facilitated by common membership of the EU, bilateral relations may play a role in aiding policy convergence. For a short period the Labour government under Tony Blair and its German counterpart under Gerhard Schröder identified common ground around the 'Third Way/die neue Mitte'.[25] In the event this common centre-left policy platform was short-lived. However, it illustrated the way in which ideological connections could facilitate an interchange of policy ideas such as to promote policy convergence. In sum, these international and

Synthesis and Illustration

The three explanations for policy convergence offered above have been presented as distinct from each other. In reality they are often intertwined. We can illustrate this interconnectedness of explanations with the example of European passenger air transport liberalisation: a process which was of significance to the commercial airline industry of the UK and Germany. In both states the airline industry has been transformed over the last decade or so. British Airways and Lufthansa, the national 'flagcarriers', now operate in an extremely competitive environment. Low-fare airlines such as easyJet and Ryanair provide fierce competition, having developed bases in the UK (and later in Germany). Air Berlin and German Wings have emerged as major competitors in the German market. The direct cause of both these developments was regulatory change in the European Union. However, in reality other indirect causes contributed to the changes, as will be seen.

The idea of liberalisation originated with domestic de-regulation of airlines in the United States under the Carter administration in 1978. In the 1980s the two European states most supportive of liberalisation in the European context were the UK and the Netherlands. There had been a history of a multi-airline policy in the UK and the Thatcher government took this further with privatisation of British Airways in 1987. Authorities in the Netherlands had positioned Schipol airport as a major competitor with London Heathrow for transatlantic traffic, with support from the quasi-privatised Dutch flag-carrier, KLM. For a variety of reasons, other European states regarded air transport as a public service that was excluded from competitive pressures, while state ownership of flag-carriers was the norm. The practice of revenue sharing on international routes, such as between Germany and the UK, meant that there was no incentive for, say, Lufthansa to improve service quality because all revenues were split 50/50 with its UK counterpart. The UK and Dutch governments could not press their case in the European Community because it lacked clear competence in the policy area. Hence these states tried to change thinking in the European Civil Aviation Conference (ECAC), which was then the relevant arena. In addition, the UK government sought bilateral initiatives, such as liberalisation of air transport between the UK and the Netherlands. Eventually, following court cases, the European Court of Justice declared the existing bilateral basis of intra-EC air transport to be contrary to competition rules.[26] This development transformed the EU into the key policy-making arena, since new regulatory arrangements had to fill the void created by the judgment. At this point British and Dutch thinking, as well as a report on liberalisation that had been produced under the auspices of ECAC, provided an important foundation of ideas and practice for multilateral liberalisation in the EU.

This illustration shows that globalisation had a background influence through the spread of ideas from the USA. However, there was no convergence on an American domestic model of liberalisation because the challenges posed by dismantling the existing bilateral regulation of air transport in Europe were quite distinct, notably because of the sovereignty issues entailed. Before the EC/EU became involved, the two governments pursued separate strategies, although they came together in ECAC, culminating in the 1982 Competition in Air Services (Compas) Report.[27] The Anglo-Dutch bilateral agreements on liberalisation in 1984 and 1985 were important in seeking to demonstrate to other member states what a multilateral Europe-wide agreement could offer.[28] However, Europeanisation is arguably the most suitable framework for understanding the liberalisation process. It was in the EC/EU that liberalisation gathered momentum with three packages of legislation being agreed in 1987, 1990 and 1992, leading to full liberalisation in 1997. Contrary to some policy areas, such as on the environment, the UK played the role of leader on air transport liberalisation, whereas Germany played a cautious role. Apart from its general view of air transport as a public service, there were special circumstances relating to German aviation, notably the pre-unification ban on Lufthansa and other West German airlines from flying to/from West Berlin. For Germany, therefore, intra-EU and domestic liberalisation was a clear product of the new EU regulatory regime, whereas for the UK domestic liberalisation dated from the early 1980s.

The above exposition of the air transport case shows how globalisation, bilateralism, Europeanisation and the role of international agencies and bilateralism (here ECAC and the British/Dutch governments) were closely inter-twined.[29] The threefold classification of drivers of policy convergence may not be so discrete in empirical accounts as is the case analytically. The air transport case is by no means exceptional in this respect. Comparable circumstances also applied in other utilities sectors, although the exact balance between the dynamics differed.[30] The original '1992' single market programme was driven in part because of the threat of the EC falling behind in industrial competitiveness with Japan and the USA.[31]

In the next section we explore in greater detail the concept of policy transfer as a means of explaining the scope for policy convergence between Germany and the UK. Policy transfer, it is argued, offers a more neutral framework for tracing the process whereby the exchange of policy ideas and practice between different jurisdictions may take place. In other words, it does not necessarily privilege the EU or globalisation as the dynamic behind convergence. Moreover, it can encompass bilateral policy exchange between two EU member states but under circumstances where EU membership *per se* may not be a decisive factor in the policy transfer. In short, policy transfer privileges the process of tracing the mechanisms of transfer and leaves the source of adaptational pressure to empirical investigation.

CONVERGENCE THROUGH POLICY TRANSFER?

In the words of Dolowitz and Marsh, policy transfer is 'a process by which ideas, policy, administrative arrangements or institutions in one political setting influence policy development in another political setting'.[32] Policy transfer may be entirely voluntary in nature, but it may be coercive under certain circumstances, such as the conditionality of World Bank donor aid. As a separate observation,[33] policy transfer may be conducted on a 'rational' basis, akin to Richard Rose's prospectus for policy-makers on how to conduct lesson-drawing.[34] In reality, however, a range of factors may result in policy transfer being conducted under conditions of bounded rationality. Thus policy transfer or learning is much more likely to take place 'within an established structure of core beliefs, behaviours, and structures'.[35] These constraints serve to restrict the scope for policy transfer in practice.

Reviewing their own model in 2000, Dolowitz and Marsh identified six key questions associated with empirical research on policy transfer:[36]

- why do actors engage in policy transfer;
- who are the key actors;
- what is transferred;
- what are the sources of inspiration in the transfer process;
- what is the character of the transfer; and
- what factors constrain or facilitate policy transfer?

Finally, Dolowitz and Marsh pointed to the possibility that policy transfer may fail and also to the circumstances surrounding such situations. Answers to the above questions are, on the one hand, matters for empirical research. On the other hand, the purpose of this piece is to suggest some answers based upon the known circumstances of British-German relations and the two states' common membership of the EU and other international organisations. In this section we consider some of the questions posed by Dolowitz and Marsh in the specific context of Britain, Germany and their common membership of the EU.

Why would German and British Political Actors Engage in Policy Transfer?

As medium-sized states in a globalised economy there are many common economic challenges faced by the two countries, as discussed earlier. The range of common challenges is very wide and is reflected by the contributions to this volume, encompassing issues such as immigration and health policy. However, the two states have common membership of several international organisations, notably the EU. Richard Rose has made a useful distinction between parallel and interdependent policy programmes as the context for lesson-drawing.[37] In the former case different states may be grappling with the same policy problems, say Britain and the USA, thus already prompting some interest in lesson-drawing. However, in situations of interdependence, that is where states have close trading relations or are members of the same international organization, 'national governments must pay attention to what is done elsewhere or risk failure'.[38] This is the situation faced by Britain and Germany as similar-sized members of an institutionally dense organization such as the EU. For example, each state needs to keep a watchful eye on its counterpart's economic policies in order to ensure that its competitive position is not affected adversely.

It is important to indicate that two different policy transfer scenarios may arise, and they reflect respectively Rose's distinction between parallelism and interdependence. The first is one where either British or German actors are seeking a new policy or institutional solution and, recognising the similarities of political and economic development, turn to the other state to see how it has addressed the same problem. For example, before British devolution the Scottish Office paid close attention to the Bavarian state government as one of several exemplars of sub-national devolved authority.[39] Since devolution the Scottish Executive has signed two bilateral agreements with German Länder, namely Bavaria and North Rhine-Westphalia. These agreements aim to develop political alliances and policy initiatives.[40] The second scenario is where policy transfer between the two states is mediated by the international organisation to which both states belong, most obviously the EU.[41] For instance, Germany was a major source of inspiration for the early stages of European environmental legislation. At this time the UK government was an environmental 'laggard' and slow to adapt to the new policy. However, as it came to take on its legal obligations, the UK government was in effect downloading from the EU policies which had a strong German imprimatur.[42] Thus the policy transfer from Germany to the UK was indirect, because it was taking place via Brussels, but also limited in degree because EU policy is inevitably the product of multinational negotiation and not simply the adoption of German legislation. It is worth emphasising that these two examples reflect variation in the extent to which policy transfer is voluntary. In the case of parallelism the process is voluntary. In the case of interdependence there may well be international pressure or, in the case of the EU, legal obligations arising from membership. The greatest degree of coercion is likely to arise where one or other member state is overruled in the Council of Ministers under qualified majority voting but is bound none the less to put policy into practice.

Who are the Key British and German Actors that Might be Engaged in Policy Transfer?
Several different types of actor may become involved.[43] *Politicians and civil servants* are major potential agents of transfer. National ministers and senior officials of the two states have quite frequent meetings as a result of bilateral relations, albeit not at such regular intervals as in the Franco-German partnership. If a minister or government head strikes up an important bilateral *political* relationship, this may enhance the chances of policy transfer, as was thought possible in the early period when both Blair and Schröder headed the two governments. The potential for such policy transfer may be heightened by collaboration in a transnational political party: in this case, the Party of European Socialists (PES).[44] For example, PES leaders (or their representatives) meet several times a year, typically ahead of an EU summit (the European Council). However, a common ideological context is not necessary for policy transfer or joint initiatives. A range of economic policy initiatives made within the EU under Tony Blair's governments were the result of his relations with centre-right counterparts: José-Maria Aznar in Spain, and Silvio Berlusconi in Italy. Similarly, the Anglo-French St. Malo agreement, which laid the foundation for the European Security and Defence Policy (ESDP), was an initiative of Blair with the Gaullist President, Jacques Chirac. The examples highlighted here are at government head level but they may be at any level of government, including the subnational one. UK devolution, as noted above, has opened new opportunities for policy transfer as new British authorities seek to draw on the long-established experience of German counterparts.

Institutions may also be agents of policy transfer. In most cases politicians and/or civil servants lie behind governmental developments. However, there are cases where the potential for policy transfer is directly attributable to institutional dynamics. Three examples will suffice here. First, as is already evident, *supranational institutions* are particularly important potential agents of policy transfer. There are a number of international bodies that may function in this way but, owing to its significant powers, the EU is the most developed of these. As Dolowitz and Marsh point out, other organisations such as the International Monetary Fund, the United Nations and its agencies, the Group of Seven/Eight (G7/G8) and the OECD 'are increasingly playing a role in the spread of ideas, programs and institutions around the globe'.[45] As a result of its institutional density, the EU may also promote transfer indirectly. One example is the cooperation between EU member state parliaments in the Conference of European Affairs Committees (COSAC). This body offers the opportunity for one parliament to learn from one of its counterparts how to improve practice in ensuring national parliamentary control over European legislation. Another example relates to the development of forums which bring together EU regulators, such as the Florence Forum for electricity regulators or the European Regulators Group in telecommunications.[46] In both these cases inter-institutional arenas have been set up with the specific task of exchanging information and good practice. Although established under the EU's auspices the forums are not formal institutions of the EU. On a more *ad hoc* basis bilateral German–British arrangements might develop, especially where one of the two states is at the institutional design stage and wishes to review existing practice in order to inform its own choices. In a similar vein, *consultants* might review practice in the other state as part of their advisory work for government or other institutions.

Finally, beyond government itself, *non-governmental organisations* (NGOs), think-tanks and other policy-related forums may offer a platform for policy transfer.[47] As with governmental counterparts British and German interest groups normally meet within EU-level organisations. *Think-tanks* may also offer opportunities for transfer. For instance ideas on European constitutionalism are circulated amongst such as bodies as Chatham House and the Federal Trust in London with counterparts such as the Institut für Europäische Politik or the Bertelsmann Foundation in Germany. Other more diffuse opportunities for policy transfer are offered by bilateral arenas, notably the long-standing annual Königswinter Conference or the more recently established German–British Forum. A final potential agent of policy transfer is *transnational business*. Strong private sector links exist between the two states, such as the strong representation of the German financial sector in the City of London. These links offer the possibility not only for exchange of private sector practices but also of lobbying for public policy change at all levels of governance, including of the EU itself. In each of the above cases the policy exchange needs to be advocated with government in order to have influence.

With all these potential sources of policy transfer, overlaid by the EU itself, one might expect an ineluctable convergence between the two states to be underway. However, things are not that simple. There are all manner of obstacles – historical, political and cultural – to policy transfer taking place. We will consider these in due course. At this stage, the discussion is only concerned with the *potential* for policy transfer.

The Sources, Subject and Character of Policy Transfer

These aspects of policy transfer are best dealt with either in the specific context of case studies or, briefly, in abstract terms. The latter approach is adopted here. The *sources* of inspiration for policy transfer are likely to be different levels of governance within the two states as well as independent agencies within them. Once again the EU's role as a potential intermediating agency, or outright source itself, is underlined. Eight different *subjects* of potential policy transfer are identified by Dolowitz and Marsh: 'policy goals, policy content, policy instruments, policy programs, institutions, ideologies, ideas and attitudes and negative lessons'.[48] As regards the character of policy transfer, different analysts have deployed different terminology. At one end of the spectrum policy transfer may resemble copying or emulation. That is to say, there is an attempt to adopt more or less wholesale a policy framework from another political system, retaining a large degree of fidelity. At the other end of the spectrum is a situation where no policy transfer takes place. In the middle ground terms such as synthesis or influence are deployed. The former is particularly relevant to transfer that takes place via the EU, since its policies typically draw upon several member states' practice. Synthesis is also an appropriate term where a 'foreign' policy model requires fundamental translation in order to make the journey from one political system to another. For example, in work on the telecommunications sector, Peter Humphreys found that the German authorities, with their different traditions – especially their reliance on administrative law – had problems in translating the UK model of independent regulatory agencies into their own circumstances.[49] Inspiration or influence are both terms which indicate a limited level of policy transfer.

WHAT FACTORS CONSTRAIN OR FACILITATE POLICY TRANSFER? AN INSTITUTIONALIST PERSPECTIVE

Policy transfer as a practice has many attractions. Through reference to practice in comparable political systems policy-makers may be able to pre-empt 'policy disasters' at home or draw lessons from experience abroad with a view to offering a better solution at home. However, better potential knowledge of comparable political systems and their practices is no guarantee for the avoidance of policy disasters, as the British examples of the 'poll tax' and rail privatisation demonstrate. Significantly, these were policies pursued during an era of 'conviction politics' in the UK, when stringent ideological tests were applied to potential policy solutions. Thus, policy is not determined solely by a rational process of searching amongst the available repertoire of solutions in similar political systems. Despite the increased scope for gaining information on such solutions as a result of greatly improved communications, there are various other calculations that impact on policy choice. A central one is that policy-makers may feel that they can learn from experience in their own political arena without having to go to an alien context for the purposes of policy transfer. Indeed, an even stronger endogenous account of policy choice was offered by Richard Rose when he argued that politicians' choices are pre-determined by their policy inheritance.[50]

In reviewing the constraints on, or opportunities for, policy transfer a 'shopping list' approach is eschewed in favour of an institutionalist perspective. Institutionalism is an encompassing framework.[51] At one end of the spectrum it encompasses calculus-based understandings of institutional incentives and how they may impact upon political action: in this case the propensity to undertake policy transfer. At the other end of the spectrum emphasis is placed upon more sociological accounts that emphasise how norms and values superimpose a 'logic of appropriateness' upon calculus-based understandings of behaviour within institutions. This account is at the latter end of the spectrum and is also sensitive to the importance of time (historical institutionalism).

The importance of policy inheritance is a useful starting point for considering the constraints on, and opportunities for, policy transfer. Historical institutionalists classically point out that policies and institutions are notoriously 'sticky'. Path-dependency of policies may develop; major obstacles to institutional reform may accumulate.[52] The standard operating procedures that characterise the governmental process may act to screen out certain solutions, including policy transfer.[53] Similarly, the beliefs and ideology attached to systems of government may screen out certain policy solutions that do not, on the face of it, fit domestic circumstances. As well as the more ideational aspects of political culture, such as the predilection for Anglo-Saxon economic policy ideas in UK politics, this cultural dimension may include Germany's preference for administrative-legal solutions in public policy. Different understandings of the role of the state are also relevant; Germany's statism contrasts with the British understanding of the state being at arm's length from civil society. Nevertheless, care needs to be taken not to present these circumstances as deterministic in nature, for change does occur. It stems not only from major critical junctures such as the end of the Cold War and its impact on foreign policy, or the 11 September 2001 attacks and their impact on internal security policy. Change also occurs in the more routine policies, as pressure builds up over time, eventually precipitating a new policy trajectory.

Seen in comparative context, political systems have different veto points and opportunity structures that may be exploited to bring about change. On many of the structural characteristics of political systems, such as those identified by Lijphart,[54] Germany and the UK find themselves on opposite sides of the divide, so to say:

- federalism v. centralism (although the UK has moved closer to federalism since 1999);
- majoritarian v. coalition government; and
- adversarial v. consensus/consociational governance.

The presidential v. parliamentary division is the main cleavage where the two systems display similarity. Schmidt and Radaelli have highlighted how different national institutional settings may affect the form taken by the important discursive dimension of facilitating policy change.[55] Finally, Olsen and Peters, indicate that the comparative openness of government to the recruitment of outsiders helped account for different national patterns of public management reform.[56] The significance of these structural differences is that the mechanisms of policy transfer are likely to differ significantly between the two states.

The EU has its own institutional and policy legacies that are superimposed on those of the member states. However, it is important to recognise that the interaction between tiers of governance in a multi-level system may not have the effect of reinforcing inertia. It may open up possibilities for one level of government to bring about change. A much cited example is the so-called *vincolo externo* whereby Italian economic policy-makers could invoke commitments on monetary union, entered into in the Maastricht Treaty, as a way of forcing through domestic reforms that had previously proved impossible.[57] Equally, the EU is one of the most dynamic political systems, expanding in terms of policy range, institutional development and geographical scope, especially over the period from the mid-1980s. The transfer upwards of policy responsibilities has been one way of breaking out of domestic policy inertia, especially where there has been a risk of policy failure at home due to the increased cross-border nature of the issues. Economic competitiveness (translating into the EU's single market programme and the so-called Lisbon Agenda on economic reform amongst various initiatives), pollution control and internal security are key examples. Policies that have gained credibility at member state level may then be exported to the EU and enable other states to break out of domestic inertia. Thus, the Bundesbank model of central banking formed a central plank of monetary union, while the privatisation of utility sectors in Britain was a prominent experience influencing the later negotiations on liberalisation at EU level.[58] These illustrations indicate that while the weight of history can indeed be an obstacle to policy transfer, the multi-level governance of the EU may be a vehicle for breaking free of policy legacies when they become counter-productive in a changing global environment.

CONSTRAINTS AND OPPORTUNITIES IN THE BRITISH-GERMAN-EU CONTEXT: CONCLUSION

In light of the above considerations, what are the prospects for policy transfer occurring between Britain and Germany? First, we need to summarise the different potential pathways implicit in what has gone before. There are three different routes by which policy transfer may occur.[59] The most straightforward form of policy transfer is bilateral. One government (at national/subnational level) engages in policy transfer with the other. A modified variant of this is where this bilateral exchange is mediated in a very limited way by the EU under conditions of policy coordination, such as in the Open Method of Coordination. This transfer might take place under a political commitment, such as the Lisbon Agenda's commitment to making the EU the world's most competitive economic arena by 2010. The EU facilitates transfer but it does so by offering arenas for learning rather than by putting in place legal obligations. The third possibility relates to where the EU has hierarchical powers. In other words European law can impose compliance at member state level. In this case there are separate uploading and downloading phases of policy transfer. In the uploading phase policy transfer to the EU is subject to institutional constraints inherent to the EU. It is difficult for one state to make a decisive impact on policy, especially in an EU of 25 states. However, if one state is successful the EU may have significant powers to secure compliance. Hence, although EU agreement is unlikely to reflect one state's policy, the downloading policy transfer effect is likely to be greater than in pure bilateral exchange between the two states, Hence the sheer penetration of policy in the two states by the EU may make this indirectly-routed policy transfer of considerable significance. As has been mentioned already, there are instances where each state has been particularly influential in the ideas, specific policy model or institutional arrangements: for instance, Germany on early environmental policy and monetary union; the UK on the ideas behind market liberalisation since the 1980s, including of the utilities sectors (electricity, air transport and telecommunications). When, from 1988 onwards, the UK government finally adapted to its obligations to comply with European environmental legislation, it was in effect downloading policies that had been strongly influenced by Germany.[60] Were the UK to join the single currency – an unlikely prospect at the time of writing – a similar form of indirect policy transfer would take place. In the case of air transport, EU legislation has obliged Germany to follow a competitive model inspired by the UK.

In comparing the two states some broad conclusions can also be drawn, although these are general and need empirical investigation. The UK political system has a number of characteristics that make it open to policy transfer as an importer. Its majoritarian system, its relatively centralised polity, where the devolved authorities lack the formal veto powers that the Bundesrat has over much German federal legislation, its openness to outsiders such as government consultants are potential facilitators of policy transfer. The English language should not be under-estimated as a vehicle for policy transfer amongst epistemic communities. For Germany, by contrast, there are

FIGURE 1
GERMANY, THE UK AND THE EU: A POLICY TRANSFER FLOW-CHART

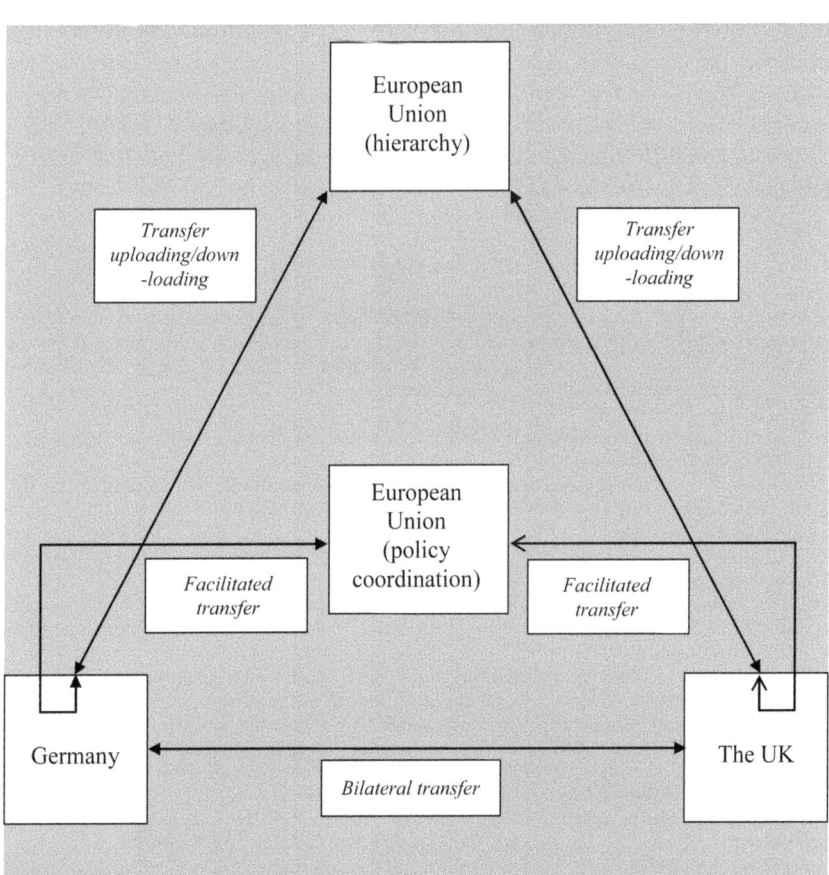

some institutional features which suggest a reduced susceptibility to policy transfer by import. These include the predominance of coalition government, the potential for gridlock between the two chambers of parliament in the federal system and a relatively closed administrative structure.[61] These features make herding less likely, although they may encourage a more considered approach to policy. The consensual political system may also make it easier and less conflictual to secure policy change once it is recognised by key actors as being necessary.

These observations must be augmented by others relating to the susceptibility to transfer *with each other*: a key issue in this volume. The UK has biases towards Anglo-Saxon policy solutions: ideological, linguistic, the 'special relationship' with the USA and so on. Its welfare state tradition differs from Germany and its model of capitalism does too. The legal and regulatory traditions of the two systems are both quite distinct. And it is these differences which make the role of the EU all the more remarkable. For, with the notable exceptions of the single currency and passport controls both states are inextricably linked in a complex process of policy transfer through the EU. Part of EU policy activity is concerned with Europe-specific matters but another part of its activity relates to finding EU-specific solutions to problems on the global agenda. The direct adoption of each other's policy solutions may be rare but indirect influence and synthesis *via the EU* is an ongoing process. The extent of inter-connectedness is high. And the accumulated size of the joint policy inheritance – the EU's *acquis communautaire* – has become very large. It is the common membership of the EU, I conclude, that is *in principle* the most important driver of policy convergence between Britain and Germany. It is also a significant potential vehicle for policy transfer between the two states.

NOTES

I thank Stephen Padgett, Peter Humphreys and David Dolowitz, with whom I collaborated in researching policy transfer within the EU as part of an ESRC-funded project on regulating the utilities sectors (award no L216252001-A). I am also grateful to Claudio Radaelli and colleagues within the European Politics Research Unit, University of Manchester, for discussions on Europeanisation. The usual disclaimer applies.

1. C. Knill, 'Introduction: Cross-national Policy Convergence: Concepts, Approaches and Explanatory Factors', *Journal of European Public Policy* 12/5 (2005), p.768.
2. See Edward Turner and Simon Green's discussion in this volume; also Knill, 'Introduction', pp.764–74.
3. For further information on the history of Airbus, see http://events.airbus.com/about/history.asp (accessed 21 July 2006).
4. See S. Bulmer, D. Dolowitz, P. Humphreys and S. Padgett, *Policy Transfer in European Union Governance: Regulating the Utilities* (Abingdon: Routledge, 2007), Chapter 3.
5. See for instance the platform provided by the Adam Smith Institute in the case of air transport liberalisation in the EU: S. Barrett, *Flying High: Airline Prices and European Regulation* (London: Avebury/ Adam Smith Institute, 1987).
6. See D. Levi-Faur, 'Herding towards a New Convention: On Herds, Shepherds and Lost Sheep in the Liberalization of the Telecommunications and Electricity Industries', *Nuffield College Working Papers in Politics*, Oxford: 2002-W6, 7 Feb. 2002, available at http://www.nuff.ox.ac.uk/Politics/ papers (accessed 9 Aug. 2006). The herding literature originated in economics. See in particular S. Bikhchandani, D. Hirshleifer and I. Welch, 'Learning from the Behavior of Others: Conformity, Fads, and Informational Cascades', *Journal of Economic Perspectives* 12/3 (1998), pp.151–70.
7. See K. Gatsios and P. Holmes, 'Regulatory Competition', in P. Newman (ed.), *The New Palgrave Dictionary of Economics and the Law*, Vol.3 (Basingstoke: Palgrave, 1998), pp.271–5.
8. For Cerny's argument, see P. Cerny, 'Paradoxes of the Competition State: The Dynamics of Political Globalisation', *Government and Opposition* 32/1 (1997), pp.251–74. For a review of other literature

on the competition state, see G. Strange, 'Symposium: Globalisation and Social Democracy – Beyond "Third Wave" Globalisation Analysis: A Critical Review of Structural Dependency Theory in International Political Economy', *European Political Science* 2/2 (2003), pp. 42–6.
9. See D. Vogel, *Trading Up: Consumer and Environmental Regulation in a Global Economy* (Cambridge, MA: Harvard University Press, 1995).
10. See the review by Knill, 'Introduction', pp.769–72.
11. See P. Hall and D. Soskice (eds.), *Varieties of Capitalism: The Institutional Foundations of Comparative Advantage* (Oxford: Oxford University Press, 2001).
12. See C. Hay and B. Rosamond, 'Globalisation, European Integration and the Discursive Construction of Economic Imperatives', *Journal of European Public Policy* 9/2 (2002), pp.147–67.
13. For major book-length studies on the subject, see M.G. Cowles, J. Caporaso and T. Risse (eds.), *Transforming Europe: Europeanization and Domestic Change* (Ithaca, NY: Cornell University Press, 2001); K. Featherstone and C. Radaelli (eds.), *The Politics of Europeanisation* (Oxford: Oxford University Press, 2003); and P. Graziano and M. Vink (eds.), *Europeanization: A Handbook for a New Research Agenda* (Basingstoke: Palgrave, 2007).
14. For concise reviews, see S. Bulmer and C. Radaelli, 'The Europeanization of National Policy', in S. Bulmer and C. Lequesne (eds.), *The Member States of the European Union* (Oxford: Oxford University Press, 2005), pp.338–59; A. Lenschow, 'Europeanisation of Public Policy', in J. Richardson (ed.), *European Union: Power and Policy-making* (Abingdon: Routledge, 2006), pp.55–71.
15. Bulmer and Radaelli, 'Europeanisation', p.341.
16. See M. Pollack, 'Theorizing EU Policy-making', in H. Wallace, W. Wallace and M. Pollack (eds.), *Policy-making in the European Union*, 5th edition (Oxford: Oxford University Press, 2005), pp.13–48.
17. See T. Börzel, 'Pace-Setting, Foot-Dragging and Fence-Sitting: Member State Responses to Europeanization', *Journal of Common Market Studies* 40/2 (2002), pp.193–214.
18. Claudio Radaelli identifies, for example, four possible outcomes in terms of domestic policy change: retrenchment, inertia, absorption and transformation: see C. Radaelli, 'The Europeanization of Public Policy', in Featherstone and Radaelli (eds.), *The Politics of Europeanisation*, pp.37–40. This classification system is separate from the question of convergence but neither inertia nor retrenchment is consistent with convergence. In the unusual event of retrenchment, policy divergence might take place. See for example the outcome of the Europeanisation of transport policy in Italy: A. Héritier, D. Kerwer, C. Knill, D. Lehmkuhl, M. Teutsch and A.-C. Douillet, *Differential Europe. The European Union Impact on National Policymaking* (Lanham, MD: Rowman and Littlefield, 2001).
19. T. Risse, M.G. Cowles and J. Caporaso, 'Europeanization and Domestic Change: Introduction', in Cowles *et al.* (eds.), *Transforming Europe*, pp.1–20.
20. In the event of very poor fit, it would be unlikely that adjustment would be possible. By contrast, in the case of a strong degree of fit, little adjustment would be needed.
21. For reviews of this debate, see Radaelli, 'The Europeanization of Public Policy', pp.44–6.
22. See C. Knill and D. Lehmkuhl, 'The National Impact of European Union Regulatory Policy: Three Europeanization Mechanisms', *European Journal of Political Research* 41/2 (2002), pp.255–80; Bulmer and Radaelli, 'Europeanisation'.
23. For fuller exposition of this explanatory framework, see Bulmer and Radaelli, 'Europeanisation'.
24. In each case the suggested 'default' mechanism of Europeanisation requires empirical testing, of course.
25. See L. Funk (ed.), *The Economics and Politics of the Third Way* (Hamburg: Lit-Verlag, 1999). See also the contribution by Hough and Sloam in this volume.
26. In the *Nouvelles Frontières* judgment of the ECJ (joined cases 209-213/84, *Ministère Public v. Asjes and others* [1986] ECR 1425).
27. European Civil Aviation Conference (ECAC), 'Report on Competition in Intra-European Air Services', ECAC Doc. No. 25 (Paris: ECAC, 1982).
28. See H. Stevens, 'Liberalisation of Air Transport in Europe: A Case Study in European Integration', working paper (London: LSE, European Institute, 1997), pp.13–15.
29. As a further twist to the mixture of sources it is possible to present ECAC as both an international agency or as a vehicle for Europeanisation.
30. See Bulmer *et al.*, *Policy Transfer*.
31. See, for example, W. Sandholtz and J. Zysman, '1992: Recasting the European Bargain', *World Politics* 42/1 (1989), pp.95–128.
32. D. Dolowitz and D. Marsh, 'Who Learns What and from Whom? A Review of the Policy Transfer Literature', *Political Studies* 44/2 (1996), p.344.
33. Dolowitz and Marsh conflate judgements about whether policy transfer is rational or otherwise with their evaluation on whether it is voluntary or coercive. These are considered to be two separate issues here.
34. R. Rose, *Learning from Comparative Public Policy: A Practical Guide* (Abingdon: Routledge, 2005).

35. J.P. Olsen and B.G. Peters, 'Learning from Experience?', in J.P. Olsen and B.G. Peters (eds.), *Lessons from Experience. Experiential Learning in Administrative Reforms in Eight Democracies* (Oslo: Scandinavian University Press, 1996), p.9.
36. D. Dolowitz and D. Marsh, 'Learning from Abroad: The Role of Policy Transfer in Contemporary Policy-making', *Governance* 13/1 (2000), p.8.
37. Rose, *Learning from Comparative Public Policy*, pp.18–22.
38. Ibid., p.20.
39. See the Scottish Office's press release 'Scotland can help shape a new Europe – Donald Dewar', in which the then Secretary of State reports on the visit of his colleague Henry McLeish to Bavaria, Scottish Office News Release 1900/97, 1 Dec. 1997, available at http://www.scotland.gov.uk/news/releas97/pr1900.htm (accessed 12 Sept. 2006).
40. The agreement with North Rhine-Westphalia covers EU policy, science and technology and the stimulation of entrepreneurship; that with Bavaria covers land use planning and design of development; justice; education; tourism; environment and administration. Specifically, part of the Bavarian agreement includes a commitment to information exchange on good practice in planning, including planning for new developments and housing quality. See Scottish Parliament European and External Relations Committee Report, SP Paper 297, available at http://www.scottish.parliament.uk/business/committees/europe/reports-05/eur05-01-02.htm#_ftnref23 (accessed 11 Sept. 2006).
41. On EU-mediated policy transfer generally, see S. Bulmer and S. Padgett, 'Policy Transfer in the European Union: An Institutionalist Perspective', *British Journal of Political Science* 35/1 (2005), pp.103–26, and C. Radaelli, 'Policy Transfer in the European Union: Institutional Isomorphism as a Source of Legitimacy', *Governance* 13/1 (2000), pp.25–43. Also see Bulmer *et al.*, *Policy Transfer*.
42. In the early years of environmental policy specific initiatives bore a strong German imprint, for example the large combustion directive and the packaging directive, see A. Weale, 'Environmental Rules and Rule-making in the European Union', *Journal of European Public Policy* 3/4 (1996), p.603. There was also a strong influence from German regulatory philosophy: see A. Sbragia, 'Environmental Policy: Economic Constraints and External Pressures', in H. Wallace and W. Wallace (eds.), *Policy-making in the European Union*, 4th edition (Oxford: Oxford University Press, 2000), p.306. However, as both authors note, in more recent times the UK has been influential in other areas of environmental legislation, causing some discomfiture in Germany.
43. See Dolowitz and Marsh, 'Learning from Abroad', pp.8–12 for general discussion.
44. For details of the cooperation that takes place within the Party of European Socialists, see S. Hix and U. Lesse, *Shaping a Vision: A History of the Party of European Socialists, 1957–2002* (Brussels: PES, 2002), available at http://www.pes.org/downloads/History_PES_EN.pdf (accessed 12 Sept. 2006).
45. See Dolowitz and Marsh, 'Learning from Abroad', p.11.
46. See Bulmer *et al.*, *Policy Transfer*, Chapter 4 for discussion of policy transfer in these bodies, albeit on an EU-wide basis.
47. On the role of think-tanks in policy transfer, see D. Stone, 'Non-Governmental Policy Transfer: The Role of Independent Policy Institutes', *Governance* 13/1 (2000), pp.45–62.
48. Dolowitz and Marsh, 'Learning from Abroad', p.12.
49. See Bulmer *et al.*, *Policy Transfer*, p.122.
50. R. Rose, 'Inheritance before Choice in Public Policy', *Journal of Theoretical Politics* 2/3 (1990), pp.263–91. See also R. Rose and P. Davies, *Inheritance in Public Policy: Change without choice in Britain* (New Haven, CT: Yale University Press, 1994).
51. For a classic review, see P. Hall and C. Turner, 'Political Science and the Three New Institutionalisms', *Political Studies* 44/5 (1996), pp.936–57.
52. See P. Pierson, *Politics in Time: History, Institutions and Social Analysis* (Princeton, NJ: Princeton University Press, 2004). Also see K. Thelen, *How Institutions Evolve: The Political Economy of Skills in Germany, Britain, the United States, and Japan* (Cambridge: Cambridge University Press, 2004).
53. On the role of standard operating procedures and the institutional 'logic of appropriateness', see J. March and J. Olsen, *Rediscovering Politics: The Organizational Basis of Politics* (New York: The Free Press, 1989).
54. A. Lijphart, *Democracies: Patterns of Majoritarian and Consensus Government in Twenty-One Democracies* (New Haven, CT: Yale University Press, 1984); A. Lijphart (ed.), *Parliamentary Versus Presidential Government* (Oxford: Oxford University Press, 1992). More specifically on the impact of political systems on policy choice, see R.K. Weaver and B.A. Rockman (eds.), *Do Institutions Matter? Governance Capabilities in the United States and Abroad* (Washington, DC: The Brookings Institution, 1993).
55. See. V. Schmidt and C. Radaelli, 'Policy Change and Discourse in Europe: Conceptual and Methodological Issues', *West European Politics* 27/2 (2004), pp.183–210.

56. J. Olsen and B. Peters, 'Learning from Experience?', in Olsen and Peters (eds.), *Lessons from Experience*, pp.26–8.
57. K. Dyson and K. Featherstone, *The Road to Maastricht: Negotiating Economic and Monetary Union* (Oxford: Oxford University Press, 1999), pp.485–507.
58. On EMU, see ibid., pp.370–451. On three utilities sectors, see Bulmer *et al.*, *Policy Transfer*, Chapter 3.
59. I omit from this account the possibility that policy transfer involves another, non-EU European or international institution.
60. See A. Jordan on this downloading in *The Europeanization of British Environmental Policy* (Basingstoke: Palgrave, 2002).
61. It should be noted that the top levels of officials turn over with a change of government because they are designated political appointments.

Balancing Territorial Politics and Social Citizenship in Germany and Britain: Constraints in Public Opinion

CHARLIE JEFFERY

INTRODUCTION

One of the classic aspirations of welfare states is that their policies should have a uniform state-wide reach. The aim is to ensure equity of provision for all citizens irrespective of where they live within the state. One of the classic aspirations of federal, devolved or other forms of decentralised government is diversity of policy provision. The aim is to reflect the distinctive preferences of different, territorially demarcated communities within the state.

There is an obvious tension here between aims of equity and diversity. This contribution explores that tension in the cases of Germany and Britain. Both Germany and Britain have evolved strong normative commitments to delivering the social policies of the welfare state on a uniform, state-wide basis. In both countries equity aims have been seen as more important than diversity aims. But in both countries there are now significant challenges to that prioritisation. Britain's devolution reforms have responded to demands for self-government outside England and opened up new possibilities for territorial policy variation between the different parts of Britain. And in Germany the territorial cleavages that resulted from national unification in 1990 have prompted a new territorialism which has unpicked some of the inherited consensus on uniform policy provision.[1] To use the language of this collection, Britain and Germany appear to be facing similar challenges to their established patterns of welfare statehood and to be responding in similar, or convergent, ways.

Research on these challenges is now accumulating, with a strong focus in Britain on the extent of territorial policy variation seen so far since devolution and the institutional relationships between the British central and devolved governments which facilitate or constrain that variation.[2] In the German case the focus has been on the agendas of 'competitive' federalism promoted by some of the Länder, the constitutional relationships between the institutions of central government and those of the Länder, in particular in the light of the federalism reform discussions of the last few years, the federalism reform of 2006, and the mechanisms of fiscal equalisation.[3] Amid this strong institutional focus relatively little attention has been given in Britain[4] or Germany[5] to the views of the general public on the balance of equity and diversity aims, and whether or how those views act as a constraint on the operation of political institutions. This contribution is an attempt to begin filling the gap.

After setting out dominant understandings of equity in the welfare state, it explores evidence from UK and German public attitude surveys on the relative weighting citizens give to equity and diversity goals, and the trade-offs and interactions that exist between them. Those interactions are then reviewed through a discussion of citizenship in the modern state as comprised of distinctive, but inter-related clusters not just of classic civil and political rights, but also of social rights. That conception of a supplementary, social citizenship was articulated by the English sociologist T.H. Marshall amid the ambitious expansion of British welfare state programmes after the Second World War.[6] It has been enduringly influential in Britain, but also in Germany and beyond as an explanation and justification for the uniform, state-wide reach of postwar welfare policies.[7] But it has also been understood in too static a way, which arguably underplays the potential for social citizenship to become detached from the statewide setting, and to become territorially differentiated. There is growing evidence across a number of decentralised states for this trend towards a territorialisation of social citizenship.[8] The discussion concludes by proposing explanations for this apparent convergence in trajectories of welfare policy change in a discussion of scenarios in which a territorialisation of social citizenship appears possible, even likely, in both Germany and the UK.

SOCIAL CITIZENSHIP IN GERMANY AND BRITAIN

Both Britain and Germany have had strong normative commitments that social rights should be enjoyed on a state-wide basis, and should not be subject to significant territorial variation. Both have seen those commitments challenged over the last ten years or so.

In the German case the commitment to state-wide social rights is unusual given that federal systems of government are generally understood as barriers to welfare state development.[9] Germany stands out from that wider pattern. It does so in part because its founding welfare institutions – the Bismarckian social insurance reforms of the late nineteenth century – pre-dated the contemporary federal system, in part because of the challenges of national integration faced then and later.[10]

The purpose of the Bismarckian welfare institutions was one of national integration, of establishing loyalties to a nascent German nation state under Prussian leadership that transcended both the particularisms of the other German states and the emerging social conflicts produced by industrialisation. That nationalising ambition was revived and extended after World War Two in the form of a commitment to maintaining 'uniform living conditions' across the West German state. That emphasis on state-wide uniformity was a profound aspiration for a West German state focused on rebuilding a sense of moral order after the Third Reich, but also struggling to accommodate the 12 million or so refugees expelled from Poland, Czechoslovakia and elsewhere in Eastern Europe, or fleeing from East Germany. In those circumstances 'regional diversity seemed to be something obsolete, which had to be overcome'.[11] And it was largely overcome with the evolution, by the 1970s, of a comprehensive, national welfare state, whose policies were delivered with a high degree of territorial uniformity by a densely interwoven set of institutional and fiscal relationships between central and Länder institutions.

The nationalising ambition of the German welfare state was renewed yet again as a mechanism of national integration after 1990. Prior to the formal unification of the two German states the terms of an 'economic, monetary *and social* union' were agreed, expressing a remarkable commitment to west–east solidarity. But that solidarity came at a high price. Maintaining uniform living conditions in the context of united Germany levies higher costs on the west in terms of higher taxation generally, and of higher equalisation transfers within the federal system more specifically. Debate about the costs and benefits of social equity has, as a result, become more vivid and polarised, opening up challenges not only to the level of social rights but also to their state-wide scope. Some of the economically stronger Länder in southern Germany have pressed with growing persuasive effect for the relaxation of the commitment to state-wide uniformity, arguing for greater legislative and fiscal autonomy for the Länder (or, to put it differently, for fewer obligations of solidarity between the Länder).[12] Bavaria has been at the forefront of these demands, but has also been flanked by Baden-Württemberg and, at times, Hesse. The agreement in mid-2006 on a reform to the distribution of competences in the federal system represents a step in this southern direction. At the same time, some of the economically weaker Länder, especially those in the east, have argued for, and won, special treatment outside of the standard redistributive mechanisms, and financed by asymmetrical deals with the federal government, to alleviate continuing problems of economic adaptation.[13]

The outcome is that, under challenge from both a rich south and a poor east, the inherited commitment to a uniformity of living conditions is one that no longer binds so tightly as a common, national project. The German Länder increasingly pursue – in line with the forecast first made close to a decade ago – a 'Sinatra doctrine', each wanting to 'do it my way', increasingly subverting state-wide solidarity, increasingly defining the interests of their citizens within a narrower territorial setting.[14]

The question this contribution addresses is whether, or in what circumstances, citizens might want to have their interests defined differentially in narrower territorial settings with, as a consequence, higher or lower levels of social rights, rather than in a state-wide setting in which social rights of citizenship are not territorially differentiated. The same question can be posed of Britain. Contrary to textbook myth, Britain has never been a unitary state. Rather it is a union state in which different parts of Britain joined with its English core under quite different conditions over a period of centuries.[15] Those different conditions of union were permissive of notable territorial policy variations which persisted until, and then were taken forward by, devolution. The notion of a common citizenship across Britain has, in other words, always been 'attenuated by the existence of separate institutions with separate histories'.[16]

However, the post-war welfare state – the inspiration for Marshall's conception of a social citizenship – encompassed aspirations and, in part, a policy practice which were powerfully integrative.[17] The most obvious example is the imagery attached to the *National* Health Service and its mantra of healthcare 'free at the point of need' everywhere in Britain, but also that of *national*isation of industry. Nationalisation also had territorially integrative substance, with much of the industry taken into public ownership based outside the affluent south-east. Together with a regional policy designed to even out regional economic disparities (even if it rarely succeeding in doing so) there was a commitment to keeping differences in living conditions across Britain, despite the accumulated territorial differences of the union state, within a narrow range.

The commitment to this UK variant of a state-wide social citizenship has been most closely associated with the Labour Party. It is something of an irony that history twice dealt Labour the hand of promoting devolution: in the 1970s to weaken the appeal of the Scottish nationalists; and in the 1990s as compensation to an anti-Conservative Scotland for the Thatcher years. Labour has always found devolution problematic for questions of social citizenship. The classic Labour view has been that disadvantage was never in essence territorial, but always and everywhere a product of entrenched class relationships which the labour movement could only change by using the levers of the state's power across its whole territory. Devolution challenged that state-wide reach. For key figures like Aneurin Bevan in the 1940s, Neil Kinnock in the 1970s and Gordon Brown from the early 1980s onwards devolution and 'a British socialist advance' have been, as Brown put it in his 1981 doctoral thesis, 'conflicting aspirations': 'no one was able to show how capturing power in Britain – and legislating for minimum levels of welfare, for example, could be combined with a policy of devolution for Scotland'.[18] That dilemma remains, and has been addressed most systematically since devolution by Gordon Brown in a series of speeches about the binding effect of shared values that extend across the boundaries of Britain's nations. In those speeches Brown has argued that while Britain has been 'increasingly strengthened, not divided by the reality of our diversity' since devolution there are also lines in the sand that cannot be crossed:

> Today when people talk about the National Health Service whether in Scotland, Wales or England people think of the British National Health Service ... And its most powerful driving idea is that every citizen of Britain has an equal right to treatment regardless of wealth, position or race and, indeed, can secure treatment in any part of Britain ... When we pool and share our resources and when the stronger help the weak it makes us all stronger ... I believe that the common bonds and mutual interests linking our destinies together is as real for other public services: the ideal that every child in Britain should have an equal opportunity in education. And the equally strong belief, widely felt throughout the country, that everyone in Britain who can work has the right and responsibility to do so. When Scots, English or Welsh talk of the right to work, they do not normally distinguish between the rights of the Scottish, Welsh or English miner, computer technician, nurse or teacher.[19]

Devolution in other words can only go so far: it must not threaten the vision of state-wide policy provision which was championed after the Second World War and which encapsulates Marshall's notion of a social citizenship. Of course, in practice, it does threaten that vision. In part because of the long-term territorial differentiation wired into the union state, in part reflecting policy decisions made since devolution, the realities of health care provision, educational opportunity and labour markets increasingly do not match Gordon Brown's state-wide aspirations, but instead vary significantly by territory. In Scotland, for example, health care is delivered differently than in England, there are no up-front tuition fees for university students, and teachers are paid more. In some views the likelihood is that the institutional arrangements for devolution are likely to amplify such variations over time,[20] opening up the prospect of a territorialisation of the social content of citizenship and the erosion of a Britain-wide welfare statehood.[21]

Whether this is what citizens want either in Britain, or indeed in Germany, is unclear. It may be that citizens, irrespective of what their governments think or do, are continued adherents of uniform, state-wide social rights. In that case public attitudes may act as a de facto constraint on the leeway of governments to pursue and implement territorial variations in social rights. It may be that citizens are unconcerned about, or more actively favour, greater territorial variation. In that case public attitudes may facilitate the erosion of uniformity and the emergence of new, territorialised notions of social citizenship. The next section explores these competing propositions by drawing on findings from public attitudes research in Germany and Britain.

PUBLIC ATTITUDES, TERRITORIAL POLITICS AND SOCIAL CITIZENSHIP

Comparing public attitudes across two states is clearly not straightforward, in part because it is rare for public attitudes research to pose the same questions in the same ways at the same time in different places. The data presented below were generated by different sampling methods and rest on different sample sizes (though all the surveys consulted were done by reputable survey teams). In the absence of a systematic and coordinated programme of international comparative survey work the conclusions that can be drawn necessarily have to be broad-brush. But the aim here is not precise, statistical comparison, but rather to illustrate the possibility that state-wide equity is not always the only thing on people's minds when they think about the level of government at which social rights are delivered.

Moreover, public attitudes research is only carried out in a particular country on questions deemed there to be sufficiently interesting and important to be worth funding. Perhaps surprisingly, given the high profile of debates about a more 'competitive' federalism with greater territorial autonomy, public attitudes on questions of equity vs. diversity have not been probed systematically in Germany. There are very few surveys which have set out to explore public views on the purposes and operation of the federal system, and the most comprehensive available dates from 1995.[22] The situation in Britain is very different, with a substantial investment of public funding since 1997 in academic surveys on public attitudes about devolution, plus significant commercial polling around devolution themes. For these reasons the following sections start with a discussion of the fuller British data, using these then to open up perspectives on the scantier German data.[23]

Do Citizens Want Devolution/Federalism?

A logical starting point is to ask whether or not people actually want a political system that combines state-wide and territorial (devolved/Länder) government. Opposition to territorial government would, intuitively, seem to indicate opposition to significant territorial policy variation. Devolution is, in fact, strongly supported in Scotland and Wales. It is the most popular constitutional preference in Scotland, supported consistently by a clear majority. In Wales the devolution variant of 'Parliament' (i.e. the more powerful model of devolution that exists in Scotland) is the most popular constitutional option. Taken together with the 'Assembly' variant (i.e. the less powerful model of devolution that applies currently in Wales) there is around 65 per cent support for devolution.[24] The greater popularity of the 'Parliament' model in Wales suggests an appetite for further-reaching devolution. That appetite is even more voracious in Scotland: around two-thirds of Scots agreed that the Scottish Parliament should have 'more powers' in surveys carried out in 2001 and 2003.[25] In similar vein large majorities of the Scots and the Welsh feel that while the British government at Westminster *does* have 'most influence' over the way their part of Britain is run, it *ought not* (Table 1); rather, the devolved institutions ought to have 'most influence'.

Significantly the part of Britain that does not have devolution – England – does not want it. The English are generally happy with centralised government from London, agree that it both does and ought have most influence on the way England is run, and are unpersuaded by the devolution options of an England-wide parliament or elected regional government (the latter confirmed in the 78:22 rejection of regional devolution in north-east England in November 2004). The current situation of 'asymmetrical' devolution implemented outside of England only is in other words consistent with public opinion everywhere (although, as discussed below, there is some evidence for there being concern in England that the Scots may have an unduly favourable deal from the current devolution arrangements).

Germany has a symmetrical federal system, with all 16 Länder having the same powers. In the early years of the West German state the existence of the Länder tier of government was distinctly unpopular. In 1953 60 per cent of West Germans thought it would be 'good' or 'very good' if the institutions of the Länder were dissolved (Table 2). From that peak of distaste the pattern of opinion gradually reversed so that by 1974 a majority was against the dissolution of the Länder institutions, and by 1992 around three-quarters in both west and (the newly joined) east Germany rejected the prospect of dissolution.

That picture of general acceptance of Länder government is confirmed in questions asked in surveys in the mid-1990s on whether the Länder had too much or too little influence on German politics. Hardly anyone felt they had too much influence. The majority of east Germans felt they had too little influence, reflecting a concern

TABLE 1
VIEWS ON THE INFLUENCE OF WESTMINSTER (%)

	Scotland		Wales		England	
	2001	2003	2001	2003	2001	2003
Does have most influence	66	64	61	54	75	71
Ought to have most influence	14	21	25	29	54	50

Source: J. Curtice, 'Restoring Confidence and Legitimacy? Devolution and Public Opinion', in A. Trench (ed.), *Has Devolution Made a Difference. The State of the Nations 2004* (Exeter: Imprint Academic, 2004), p.220.

TABLE 2
VIEWS ON THE DISSOLUTION OF LÄNDER INSTITUTIONS AND THE CONCENTRATION OF GOVERNMENT AT THE FEDERAL LEVEL (%)

	West							East
	1952	1953	1960	1974	1978	1985	1992	1992
Not good/quite bad	21	17	41	55	63	70	72	74
Indifferent	5	4	6	9	8	6	6	5
Very good/good	49	60	25	17	9	7	6	7
Don't know	25	19	28	19	20	17	16	14

Source: N. Grube, 'Föderalismus in der öffentlichen Meinung der Bundesrepublik Deutschland', *Jahrbuch des Föderalismus 2001* (Baden-Baden: Nomos, 2001), pp.102-3.

discussed more fully below that the political system appears weighted against the east. Views among west Germans were evenly split, with 38 per cent judging that the Länder had too little influence and another 38 per cent that the level of influence was 'just right'.[26] Unfortunately the German data do not generally provide reliable figures disaggregated by Land. One 2003 survey did ask whether Bavarians felt they should have more autonomy within Germany or even separate statehood; 24 per cent of Bavarians supported more autonomy and 17 per cent independence.[27] Even in Bavaria, the traditional source of proposals for greater Länder autonomy, the greater weight of public opinion is tilted towards the status quo of the federal system.

What do Citizens Want from Devolution/Federalism?

If citizens in both countries are at the very least content with the status quo or in some places – Scotland, Wales and east Germany – would like to strengthen territorial government further, then why?

In both Britain and Germany the most powerful explanation has to do with voice. People like territorial government because they trust it more than central government to express their views. In Britain this has in part to do with identity. The Scots and the Welsh are much less likely than the English to identify themselves as British and much more likely to claim a Scottish or Welsh identity. This prioritisation of Scottish/Welshness over Britishness is not an effect of devolution, but rather a long-term trend extending back at least to the 1970s.[28] It would appear to support a call for more 'proximate' government, better placed to give expression to distinctive identities than remote UK institutions in Westminster. That impression is confirmed by survey data on which level of government is trusted to act in the best interests of citizens in different parts of Britain. For example, in surveys carried out in 2001 and 2003, over three-quarters of Scots trusted the Westminster government to work in Scotland's interests 'only some of the time' or 'almost never', while over 60 per cent trusted the Scottish Parliament to do so 'most of the time' or just about always'.[29] In Wales, as well, devolved government is much more trusted than the British government to work in the interests of the Welsh; the English trust much more fully in Westminster than any of the potential devolution option available to them.

This endorsement of the proximity and trustworthiness of devolved government is not that surprising. James Mitchell has noted how the devolution reforms in Scotland

and Wales had above all to do with reclaiming *ownership* of politics.[30] They were about reconnecting the Scots and Welsh with a political system felt during the years of Conservative UK government from 1979 to 1997 to have become closed, even hostile to Scottish and Welsh concerns. Devolution in that sense was about providing some level of protection against majoritisation by the more numerous English. What it was not about was a distinctive policy agenda. The campaigns for devolution in Scotland and Wales did not mobilise around distinctive policy programmes. The Scottish Constitutional Convention, which animated the devolution debate in Scotland, built a vision of devolution that was much more about symbolic politics, grounded in a claim of popular sovereignty on a Scottish territorial scale (the 'claim of right')[31] and suffused with a rhetoric of civic inclusion, participation and consultation. Wales had a paler version of the same debate, focused on inclusiveness and accountability, the latter focused in particular on making the 'quango state' in Wales accountable to a Welsh political process.

Against this background it is striking, though perhaps logical, how the Scots and the Welsh judge devolution to have made a difference since its introduction in 1999. Table 3 tracks judgements of the impact of devolution on 'voice' within Britain and on one of the policy fields, education, which falls under devolved competence in Scotland and Wales. Half or so of the population in Scotland and Wales think their voice has become louder since devolution. Only around a quarter think a positive difference has been made in education policy while half or more think that devolution has made no difference at all to education. The latter judgement may reflect perceptions of the ineffectiveness of devolved government or of the continued influence of the British government as a decision-making body for Scotland and Wales. But it may also reflect the absence of demand for divergence of policy standards. Survey data show that there are remarkably few territorial differences between the Scots, Welsh and English on questions on basic values about the role of the state or on more specific policy preferences.[32] All want the state to do much the same things on their behalves. And when asked about their attitude to the possibility of divergences of policy from one part of Britain to another, most people in Scotland, Wales and England prefer uniform provision (Table 4). Irrespective of strong territorial identities, and irrespective of the

TABLE 3
IMPACTS OF DEVOLUTION IN SCOTLAND AND WALES

	Scotland		Wales	
	2001	2003	2001	2003
Impact on Voice				
Stronger	52	49	49	52
No difference	40	41	45	42
Weaker	6	7	3	4
Impact on Education				
Better	27	23	22	27
No difference	59	59	64	53
Worse	5	7	3	6

Source: J. Curtice, 'Restoring Confidence and Legitimacy? Devolution and Public Opinion', in A. Trench (ed.), *Has Devolution Made a Difference? The State of the Nations 2004* (Exeter: Imprint Academic, 2004), pp.223–4.

TABLE 4
ATTITUDES TOWARDS TERRITORIAL POLICY VARIATION IN BRITAIN 2003 (%)

	Should be the same in every part of Britain	Should be allowed to vary
England		
Standards for services such as health, schools, roads and police	66	33
Scotland		
Standards for services such as health, schools, roads and police	59	40
Level of unemployment benefit	56	42
University tuition fees	56	40
Wales		
Standards for services such as health, schools, roads and police	55	44
Level of unemployment benefit	57	41
University tuition fees	58	40
Cost of NHS Prescriptions	63	37

Sources: Data collated by John Curtice from British and Scottish Social Attitudes survey 2003; Wales Life and Times survey 2003.

demand for the additional voice provided by devolved government, there is little appetite across Britain for territorial policy variation. The public appears to continue to favour a state-wide conception of citizenship *despite* devolution.

There are quite striking echoes of these findings in Germany. Only Bavarians claim a strong regional identification with their Land, with 41 per cent in 1995 identifying themselves 'more as Bavarians' as against 50 per cent seeing themselves 'more as Germans'. The next highest Land identity score was 21 per cent in Saxony/Thuringia. Significantly, though, east Germans were about as likely to identify themselves as 'east German' as 'German' (with around 40 per cent in each category). A 'west German' identity was claimed by only ten per cent or less of west Germans; Bavaria excepted, around 70 per cent of west Germans identified themselves as 'German'.[33]

These indices of territorialised identity at Land level in Bavaria and across east Germany as a whole suggest a similar basis for support for 'proximate' government as in Scotland and Wales. That proposition is broadly borne out by the available data, but with important nuances. Table 5 records citizen views on which level of

TABLE 5
WHICH IS MORE CONCERNED WITH THE WORRIES AND DESIRES OF THE PEOPLE, FEDERAL OR LÄNDER GOVERNMENTS?

	Germany		West		East	
	1995	2004	1995	2004	1995	2004
Federal government	10	6	11	6	6	4
Länder governments	52	34	52	36	50	29
Neither	25	42	24	40	31	50
Don't know	13	18	13	18	13	17

Source: N. Grube, 'Unverzichtbares Korrektiv oder ineffective Reformbremse? Wahrnehmungen föderaler Strukturen und Institutionen in Deutschalnd', *Jahrbuch des Föderalismus 2004* (Baden-Baden: Nomos, 2004), p.166.

government is 'more concerned about the worries and desires' of the people in Germany. It shows very clearly that the federal government is not felt to be in touch with popular concerns; there is a parallel here with the image of a remote Westminster in Britain. But though Länder governments are felt to be much more in touch than the federal government, there has been a striking fall in positive endorsements of the Länder governments from 1995 to 2004, seemingly reflecting a more general disenchantment with a political system widely seen to be unwieldy and slow-moving.[34] That erosion of confidence in the Länder governments is most striking in the east, and would seem to capture broader east German dissatisfaction with the longer-term outcomes of unification. Also significant are the two parts of western Germany which returned more positive evaluations of the Länder governments in the 2004 survey: the 'south-west' (i.e. Baden-Württemberg and Hesse) at 40 per cent, and Bavaria at close to 50 per cent.[35] There appear in other words to be two dimensions of territorialisation at play: a stronger sense of confidence in Länder governments in southern Germany; and a broad sense of dissatisfaction across eastern Germany which is directed most strongly at federal government, but increasingly at Länder governments too. There is a strong echo here of a polarisation, as noted above, between the 'rich south' and the 'poor east'.

Notwithstanding these territorial nuances Länder governments across Germany remain six or seven times more likely to be judged as in touch with citizens' concerns as the federal government. That greater (if declining) confidence in Länder government does not mean Germans think the Länder should produce different policies in different places. Germans appear to emphasise proximity (*Bürgernähe*) of decision-making *alongside* uniform policy standards: 'The ideal situation for broad parts of the population would be a federal system that produces largely uniform regulations and outcomes in all Länder'.[36] Surveys in 1995 and 2004 showed that large majorities preferred uniform federal regulations on issues in education policy, law and order, social security and transport, including areas within the exclusive competence of the Länder. Where the federal system provides the possibility of variation, for example in education policy, there is clear disapproval (Table 6).[37] Despite federalism – but consistent with the traditions of the German welfare state – there is a clear preference for uniform living conditions, in Marshall's terms for a strong social component to German citizenship with a state-wide reach.

TABLE 6
IS IT AN ADVANTAGE OR DISADVANTAGE THAT EDUCATION POLICY DIFFERS FROM LAND TO LAND?

	Germany	East	West
Advantage	12	13	6
Disadvantage	84	83	90
Don't know	4	4	4

Source: W. Bürklin and C. Jung, 'Deutschland im Wandel. Ergebniss einer repräsentativen Meinugsumfrage', in K.-R. Korte and W. Weidenfeld (eds.), *Deutschland-Trendbuch* (Bonn: Bundeszentrale für politische Bildung, 2001), p.691.

How Important are Territorial Cleavages?

The discussion so far suggests that the post-war commitments to state-wide welfare provision captured in Marshall's conception of social citizenship continue to be endorsed by the British and German publics. People in Britain and Germany appear to want devolution/federalism as a guarantor of proximate government *as well as* uniform, state-wide policies. Public opinion would appear in that context to be a constraint on territorial variation in social rights.

Yet the discussion has also pointed to lines of territorial cleavage. The Scots and the Welsh clearly demarcate themselves from the English. And there is some evidence that southern Germans distinguish themselves from the rest of the Germans in the vigour of their support for proximate government (and in the Bavarian case in terms of territorial identity too), and east Germans from the west in their sense of dissatisfaction with the ability of the political system to meet a set of territorially distinctive concerns. There are in other words incipient territorial cleavages in both states.

Incipient cleavage is most obvious in Britain in the Anglo-Scottish relationship, though the issues at play apply in principle to the Anglo-Welsh relationship as well. Those issues are about representation and distribution. The implementation of devolution outside England, and the continued practice of centralised government in England, creates a representative anomaly commonly known as the 'West Lothian question'. This question is about the legitimacy of the situation in which, after devolution, a Scottish Westminster MP can still vote on policies for England in areas like health which in Scotland are now devolved while English MPs are excluded from devolved matters (Table 7). A majority in England (and a smaller majority in Scotland) think that the possibility of Scottish MPs voting on English laws after devolution is wrong. In related vein, and prompted by debate about Gordon Brown becoming Prime Minister after Tony Blair and the role of prominent Scottish cabinet ministers like Brown, John Reid and Alastair Darling, it appears that a majority of the English now think Scottish ministers running English business is becoming inappropriate, while a majority of Scots disagree.[38]

TABLE 7
ANGLO-SCOTTISH CONTENTIONS (%)

	England		Scotland	
	2001	2003	2001	2003
Scottish MPs no longer to vote on English laws				
Agree	57	60	51	51
Neither agree nor disagree	18	18	21	21
Disagree	14	11	24	24
Scottish Parliament to raise its own taxes				
Agree	73	74	52	51
Neither agree nor disagree	12	12	18	16
Disagree	12	10	28	29
Scotland's share of UK public spending				
More than fair	24	22	10	11
Pretty much fair	44	45	36	35
Less than fair	9	9	47	48

Source: J. Curtice, 'A Stronger or Weaker Union? Public Reactions to Asymmetric Devolution in the United Kingdom', *Publius. The Journal of Federalism* 36/1 (2006), p.106.

There are also distributional contentions. A large majority of the English (and a bare majority of the Scots) think the Scottish Parliament should be financed by taxes raised in Scotland, and not by the British (and therefore predominantly English) taxpayer. And around half of the Scots feel Scotland gets less than its fair share of public spending, while a little under a half of the English think the Scots' share is 'pretty much' a fair share. Devolution in other words has raised, or given new salience to resource distribution issues which play out differentl y on either side of the Anglo-Scottish border (Table 7).

Germany lacks asymmetries of constitutional structure, so there are no obvious equivalents to the West Lothian question. But what it has in much starker measure than the UK are economic disparities (Table 8). Variations above and below the German average on GDP per head and unemployment are high. All the east German Länder have well below average GDP per head and all have well above average unemployment. The west German Länder generally have above average GDP per head and they generally have under average unemployment. The worst-performing western Länder do better than the best-performing eastern Länder.

The reasons for these cleavages are long-standing and have to do with the separate development of the East and West German states and the terms of their unification in 1990. In many respects the situation in the east has improved massively since then, as east Germans acknowledge.[39] However, the continuing contrast of east with west creates divergent perceptions in the respective populations. In the east there is a sense that the inherited power relations of the society it joined in 1990 are loaded against them. East Germans are more likely to see their relationship with West

TABLE 8
ECONOMIC DISPARITIES AMONG THE GERMAN LÄNDER

Land	GDP/head (2005; €000)	Unemployment rate (2005; %)	Equalisation transfers (2004, €bn)
Baden-Württemberg	30.82	7.0	−2.1
Bavaria	32.41	7.8	−2.3
Berlin	23.47	19.0	+2.7
Brandenburg	18.76	18.3	+0.5
Bremen	36.93	16.8	+0.3
Hamburg	45.99	11.3	−0.6
Hesse	32.45	9.7	−1.5
Lower Saxony	23.53	11.6	+0.4
Mecklenburg-Vorpommern	18.26	20.3	+0.4
North Rhine-Westphalia	27.08	12.0	−0.2
Rhineland-Palatinate	24.01	8.8	+0.2
Saarland	26.09	10.7	+0.1
Saxony	20.03	18.3	+0.9
Saxony-Anhalt	19.38	20.3	+0.5
Schleswig-Holstein	24.38	11.6	+0.1
Thuringia	19.05	17.1	+0.5
Germany	*27.23*	*11.7*	*± 6.7*

Sources: GDP/head at http://www.vgrdl.de/Arbeitskreis_VGR/tab01.asp#tab07; unemployment at http://www.statistik-portal.de/Statistik-Portal/de_jb02_jahrtab13.asp; equalisation transfers at http://www.bundesfinanzministerium.de/lang_de/DE/Finanz__und__Wirtschaftspolitik/Foederale__Finanzbeziehungen/Laenderfinanzausgleich/
Vorl_C3_A4ufige_20Abrechnung_202004,templateId=raw,property=publicationFile.pdf.

TABLE 9
HOW STRONG IS CONFLICT BETWEEN EAST AND WEST GERMANS? (2000, %)

	Germany	West	East
Very strong	9	8	13
Strong	37	36	43
Not so strong	45	47	38
No conflict	5	5	4
Don't know	3	4	2

Source: W. Bürklin and C. Jung, 'Deutschland im Wandel. Ergebniss einer repräsentativen Meinugsumfrage', in K.-R. Korte and W. Weidenfeld (eds.), *Deutschland-Trendbuch* (Bonn: Bundeszentrale für politische Bildung, 2001), p.687.

Germans as one of conflict than is the case vice versa (Table 9). East Germans have different, and more pessimistic, evaluations of the 'provenness' of the German model of social market economy and the 'social justice' it delivers, and are less likely to favour market solutions to policy problems or to think the level of social policy expenditure is high enough.[40] And, as was noted above, these socio-economic concerns have a reflection in the perception that neither Länder governments nor, in particular, the federal government are responsive to east German concerns.

The economic weaknesses of the east create, in other words a strong sense of disadvantage in east Germany. That sense of territorial disadvantage creates claims on the system to treat east Germans better. That claim is institutionalised in the federal system by the fiscal equalisation process. Fiscal equalisation in Germany is intended to put all the Länder in a position, despite differences in economic structure and performance, to deliver uniform[41] living conditions on their territory. It is a powerful expression of commitment to a common, state-wide social citizenship. But as in the UK (Table 7) and elsewhere, the territorial distribution of resources is an inherently contentious issue, and has become all the more so since unification.[42] In 2004 €6.7 billion was transferred from economically stronger to economically weaker Länder. A small group of southern Länder – Bavaria, Baden-Württemberg and Hesse – accounted for 88 per cent (€5.9 billion) of that total transfer; 80 per cent (€5.4 billion) of the total transfer ended up in east Germany (Table 8).

The scale of these transfers provides a backdrop to Table 10, which records public attitudes in east and west on fiscal equalisation. Though at least two-thirds of Germans still think that the principle of equalisation is right, there has been a notable fall from the mid-1990s to the mid-2000s. And throughout west Germans have been less likely than east Germans to support the principle of equalisation; and once again survey respondents in the southern Länder stand out as least likely to support the principle of equalisation.[43]

There is here, as in the Anglo-Scottish case, an incipient weakening of inherited understandings of state-wide solidarity or, as some in the UK have termed it, 'territorial justice'.[44] Southerners in Germany appear to have begun to question the practice of solidarity with easterners, and on this and a range of other indices (identity, proximity of government) appear to be considering the narrower, territorialised frames of their Länder as more conducive to pursuing their interests. At the same time easterners appear to feel a sense of collective disadvantage which is tied to territory, though to

TABLE 10
SUPPORT FOR FISCAL EQUALISATION IN GERMANY (%)

	Germany		West		East	
	1995	2004	1995	2004	1995	2004
Right	78	67	76	64	88	79
Not right	11	17	12	19	5	9
Undecided	11	16	12	17	7	12

The full question asked was: 'There is a so-called fiscal equalisation between richer and poorer Länder. The richer Länder transfer money to the poorer Länder. Do you think it right that there is a fiscal equalisation between richer and poorer Länder or do you think it not right?
Source: N. Grube, 'Unverzichtbares Korrektiv oder ineffective Reformbremse? Wahrnehmungen föderaler Strukturen und Institutionen in Deutschalnd', *Jahrbuch des Föderalismus 2004* (Baden-Baden: Nomos, 2004), p.171.

the territory of the former German Democratic Republic as a whole rather than the six eastern Länder individually. That sense of distinctive territorial interest is again confirmed by multiple indices: identity; trust in government; the west as the 'other' in a conflict situation; the perception that the dice are loaded against the east. It serves to reproduce 'the east' as a frame for the mobilisation of social interests, opening up space for the post-communist Party of Democratic Socialism to present itself as an advocate for distinctive eastern territorial interests.[45]

These indices of social territorialisation in Germany, and their counterparts in Britain, challenge the commitments to a Marshallian social citizenship focused on state-wide equity that have been prioritised in both countries. They are still countervailed by strong trends in public attitudes which favour a state-wide frame for the pursuit of social interests, including: the apparent distaste in both Britain and Germany for territorial policy variation; the territorial evenness in Britain of social values and policy preferences; and the still high (if declining) endorsement of the principal of fiscal equalisation in Germany. But indices of territorialisation appear, at least potentially, to relax the constraints of those countervailing trends on territorial variation in social rights.

MARSHALL'S CITIZENSHIPS

This final section explores the circumstances in which a potential for the prioritisation of territorial diversity over state-wide equity might be realised. It does so by referring back to the guru of state-wide social citizenship, T.H. Marshall. Marshall distinguished three clusters of citizenship rights in Britain: civil rights, political rights and social rights. In their modern form these emerged in sequence, each the precondition of the next (Table 11).[46] Civil rights, protecting individual freedoms, emerged in something like the modern form in the eighteenth century in part as a set of defences of individual liberty versus the state, in part as a set of abolitions of restrictive practices which opened up the space for a market economy. Modern political rights – the right to participate in the exercise of political power through voting or standing as a candidate – emerged during the nineteenth century as the new social classes of the market

TABLE 11
THE EVOLUTION OF CITIZENSHIP IN BRITAIN

UK	18th century	19th century	20th century
Civil rights	√	√	√
Political rights		√	√
Social rights			√

economy exploited freedoms of speech and association to open up a political system dominated up to then by privileged groups of aristocrats, landowners and industrialists.

Social rights followed the final expansions of the franchise in the early twentieth century which, by 1945, had enabled a majority Labour government buoyed by the votes of the working class to come to power. Social rights consisted of minimum standards of welfare, guaranteed by the state, so that the working class in particular was protected from risks of ill-health, old age, unemployment and so on, paid for as an expression of state-wide social solidarity through taxation. In other words, state-wide social rights were guaranteed by the post-war welfare state.

This is a Britain-focused conception of the evolution of citizenship. In Germany the order of attainment of social rights and political rights was the reverse, with social rights introduced in the Bismarckian era, and political rights only enduringly secured after World War Two (though at that point the content of British and German citizenship fell broadly in line). But less important than Marshall's Britain-centric sequence is his notion of the relationship of one cluster of rights to another. Marshall clearly viewed citizenship as dynamic, ever-changing, its various components interacting to produce shifting outcomes. That view is often not reproduced in scholarship inspired by Marshall, in which there is a tendency to 'freeze-frame' Marshall on social rights to support a particular understanding of the welfare state that emerged after World War Two.[47] It is worth quoting Marshall on this point, from his celebrated lectures on citizenship delivered in 1949, shortly after the British National Health Service had been established, when he described his three clusters of citizenship rights as a kind of championship steeplechase extending over centuries: 'Before long they were spread far out along the course, and it is only in the present century, in fact I might say only within the last few months, that the three runners have come abreast of one another'.[48]

Of course, if the three clusters of citizenship rights only came abreast of one another in 1949, there is no reason that they should have stayed there in a synchronised canter ever since. And clearly they have not. Table 12 sets out the territorial location of Marshall's three sets of rights – as broadly applies to both Germany and Britain – for

TABLE 12
CITIZENSHIP IN THE EARLY TWENTY-FIRST CENTURY

	Decentralised	State	European Union
Civil rights		√	√
Political rights	√	√	
Social rights	√	√	√

the early twenty-first century. While the state is clearly still *a* location for the rights of citizens, it is not the only one. It was perhaps a near-exclusive location for those rights for a short period in the middle of the twentieth century, but more or less at the point when Marshall had lined up his three sets of rights as definitions of a *state-wide* political community, they began to diffuse to other territorial scales, both European and decentralised.

Marshall's civil rights included freedoms to trade without restrictive practice. The main framework for realising such freedoms has long been a European one, beginning with the first steps in European economic integration in the 1950s, and now significantly more important in regulating economic activity than state-level law. And should the European Constitution ever come into force, European citizens will have a constitutional charter of fundamental rights as a guarantee of their civil rights additional to state-level guarantees. While few yet see the EU as a primary arena for exercising their rights of political participation, there are plenty of ways in which social rights are beginning to take on a European dimension alongside their state-level ones, often – as Marshall might have suggested – as a consequence of EU-level civil rights such as freedom of movement, which have begun to make access to social rights portable across national borders within the EU.

As striking as these developments in the Europeanisation of citizenship has been a parallel territorial decentralisation of citizenship. This has to do in particular with the decentralisation of powers of government in Europe over the last 30 years or so – with Spain, Belgium, Italy, France and the UK emerging as regionalised states alongside the established federal states of Germany, Switzerland and Austria. As a result, political rights are now exercised at both state-wide *and* decentralised scales in these places. They are expressed through different patterns of interest aggregation, voting behaviour, party competition and government composition at those different scales. Those different patterns mean that both regional democratic processes – including those introduced by devolution in the UK and embedded by federalism in Germany – and state-wide democratic processes may produce their own, perhaps complementary, perhaps competing conceptions of social rights.

In other words, and again consistent with Marshall's understanding of the way different clusters of citizenship rights interact, social rights may become understood and delivered by decentralised government in ways which increasingly depart from the traditional imagery of the welfare state, with its emphasis on uniform public services across the whole state territory. The following sets out, in conclusion, two scenarios in which the incipient territorial cleavages discussed in the last section appear mobilisable to support a more territorialised understanding of citizenship.[49] They suggest that convergent processes of territorialisation are possible, or under way, in both states.

SCENARIOS

We Want Our Money Back!

The territorial distribution of resources has an obvious potential for political mobilisation. In most decentralised systems of government there are tensions about the distribution of resources. In Germany those tensions have become especially acute since unification. The 'over-levelling' effect of Germany's fiscal equalisation rules on the economically stronger contributor Länder has become one of the principal issues in the debate over the last decade on the reform of the federal system.[50] A much stronger discourse of 'our money' has emerged as a result. As one Bavarian minister put it in a remarkably candid statement of the end of solidarity, the aim is 'to make clear the causal relationship between the policies of a Land and their impact on its citizens.[51] Such views challenge older conceptions of a state-wide territorial justice and redefine 'justice' as something that happens within a narrower territorial frame. The data in Table 10 suggest that this problematisation of the costs of solidarity may be having an effect.

While the UK lacks an equivalent to Germany's fiscal equalisation system, there are parallels. For historical reasons Scotland has higher per capita public spending than England, yet that higher spending is funded by the British Treasury, and not financed by taxes levied by the Scottish Parliament. Periodically the Conservative Party, which is electorally weak in Scotland and strong in England, has flirted with the mobilisation of resentment about Scottish 'privileges' as a means of bolstering support in England.[52] That flirtation appears more serious at the time of writing in mid-2006, with a new Conservative leader, David Cameron, seeking to consolidate a growing popularity by playing on the Scottishness of his likely Labour opponent in a 2009/10 election, Gordon Brown. The data in Table 7 seem to show fertile ground for a tactic that draws dividing lines between the English and Scots and casts doubt on inherited assumptions of Anglo-Scottish solidarity.

Mobilising Territorial Identity

Distinctive territorial identity also has obvious potential for political mobilisation, especially if there is a perception that the system of government does not respond to the concerns of a particular territory whose inhabitants share a sense of distinctiveness. The obvious example was the devolution campaign in Scotland which was in large part a response to a crisis of representation in which the neo-liberal values of a Conservative British government were not felt to be shared in Scotland. Devolution has provided a context where it would be more difficult for a 'new Thatcher' to impose alien values on the Scots. There is a perhaps more intriguing example in post-devolution Wales, where Labour First Minister Rhodri Morgan has distanced his government's 'Welsh Labour' approach on health and education from the more market-oriented policy delivery mechanisms favoured by Prime Minister Tony Blair's 'new' Labour government in Westminster. Both examples are of forms of territorial protest about a state-level government which appeared to have moved beyond generally accepted values about the role of the state in guaranteeing the welfare of all its citizens. In both cases there is the claim to something like a right of territorial opt-out from the approach of the British government and to reassert traditional values, if necessary, within a narrower frame bounded by a sense of distinctive identity.

There is some scope to view in this light the situation in east Germany, a territory which has a sense of distinctive identity and whose citizens feel that the economic and political systems in Germany are loaded against them. The continued strength of the Party of Democratic Socialism, which styles itself as advocate for eastern interests, is a clear indicator of how that complex of territorial identity and perception of territorial disadvantage can be politically mobilised. The ease with which eastern Länder governments form pan-eastern coalitions irrespective of which political parties govern them – for example in the second wave of Solidarity Pact negotiations concluded in 2001[53] – is another. The options for responding to the territorial challenge in the east are intriguing. The controversies over resource distribution noted above suggest that the prospects of refashioning inherited territorial solidarity mechanisms for the post-unification era are anathema to the powerful southern Länder and are therefore slim. Rather more likely – not least because east Germany has become arguably the key federal election battleground – is the continuation of a trend begun in 1990 and now perhaps an enduring feature of the German political system: the consolidation of east Germany as a distinctive policy space funded by an asymmetrical dependence on federal government support on the one hand, and on the other a loosening of the commitment to uniform living conditions in a federal system increasingly shaped by the new territorialism of the rich south.

In both scenarios – territorialisation though money politics or identity politics – the spillovers from the exercise of political rights at the regional level into the terms on which social rights are realised is clear. If citizens understand themselves as a distinctive territorial community bonded either by identity, or some perception of territorial interest or disadvantage, or both, then it is possible for the existence of territorial political rights to become a platform for pursuing territorial policy diversity with sufficient vigour to outweigh even long-standing normative commitments to state-wide equity. Social citizenship may in other words become territorialised, *even if*, as is the case in Britain and Germany, there appears to be a broad, state-wide uniformity of policy values and a broad distaste for territorial policy variation.

Britain and Germany are not isolated examples. There are equivalent pressures for the territorialisation of social citizenship in other places, motivated either by territorial distributional conflict (Australia) or the assertion of territorial identities (Canada), or both (Italy, Belgium).[54] There is, in other words, a rather broader trend of convergence in the pressures faced by post-war welfare states, and, in varying intensities, the responses to them, which involve the political mobilisation of territorial cleavages. It would be difficult, though, to claim that these convergent responses are due to some process of cross-national learning. Neither the German federalism reform debate nor the design and implementation of devolution in Britain could be described as anything but highly insular and self-referenced. More important in this instance than any explicit or implicit learning process, and the key challenge for future research, is to build a fuller understanding of what Turner and Green call the 'problem pressure' which leads some places to prioritise narrower rather than wider identities and/or reduce their willingness to express solidarity with other places.

NOTES

1. C. Jeffery, 'Federalism: The New Territorialism', in S. Green and W. Paterson (eds.), *Governance in Contemporary Germany. The Semi-Sovereign State Revisited* (Cambridge: Cambridge University Press, 2005).
2. See for example J. Adams and P. Robinson (eds.), *Devolution in Practice. Public Policy Differences within the UK* (London: IPPR, 2002); J. Adams and K. Schmuecker (eds.), *Devolution in Practice 2006* (London: IPPR, 2006); M. Keating, 'Policy Making and Policy Divergence in Scotland after Devolution', *Devolution Briefings No. 21*, available at http://www.devolution.ac.uk/Briefing_papers.html

(2005); D. Wincott, 'Social Policy and Social Citizenship: Britain's Welfare States', *Publius. The Journal of Federalism* 36/2 (2006), pp. 169–88; A. Trench (ed.), *Devolution and Power* (Manchester: Manchester University Press, 2007 forthcoming).
3. See for example U. Münch, 'Konkurrenzföderalismus für die Bundesrepublik: Eine Reformdebatte zwischen Wunschdenken und politischer Machbarkeit', in *Jahrbuch des Föderalismus 2001* (Baden-Baden: Nomos, 2001); T. Fischer and M. Grosse Hüttmann, 'Aktuelle Diskussionsbeiträge zur Reform des deutschen Föderalismus – Modelle, Leitbilder und die Chancen ihrer Übertragbarkeit', in *Jahrbuch des Föderalismus 2001* (Baden-Baden: Nomos, 2001); R. Hrbek and A. Eppler (eds.), *Die unvollendete Föderalismus-Reform* (Tübingen: Europäisches Zentrum für Föderalismusforschung, 2005); A. Benz, 'Kein Ausweg aus der Politikverflechtung? Warum die Bundesstaatskommission scheiterte aber nicht scheitern musste', *Politische Vierteljahresschrift* 46/2 (2005); R. Sturm, 'Föderalismusreform: Kein Erkenntnisproblem, warum aber ein Gestaltungs- und Entscheidungsproblem?', *Politische Vierteljahresschrift* 46/2 (2005); C. Jeffery, 'Cycles of Conflict: Fiscal Equalisation in Germany', *Regional and Federal Studies* 13/4 (2003).
4. C. Jeffery, 'Devolution and Social Citizenship. Which Society, Whose Citizenship?', in S. Greer (ed.), *Territory, Democracy and Justice. Rethinking Territorial Politics* (London: Palgrave, 2006); C. Jeffery, 'Devolution and Divergence: Public Attitudes and Institutional Logics', in Adams and Schmuecker (eds.), *Devolution in Practice 2006*; J. Curtice, 'A Stronger or Weaker Union? Public Reactions to Asymmetric Devolution in the United Kingdom', *Publius. The Journal of Federalism* 36/1 (2006).
5. N. Grube, 'Föderalismus in der öffentlichen Meinung der Bundesrepublik Deutschland', in *Jahrbuch des Föderalismus 2001* (Baden-Baden: Nomos, 2001); N. Grube, 'Unverzichtbares Korrektiv oder ineffective Reformbremse? Wahrnehmungen föderaler Strukturen und Institutionen in Deutschalnd', in *Jahrbuch des Föderalismus 2004* (Baden-Baden: Nomos, 2004).
6. T.H. Marshall, 'Citizenship and Social Class', in T.H. Marshall and T. Bottomore, *Citizenship and Social Class* (London: Pluto Press, 1992).
7. For example: M. Lister, '"Marshall-ing" Social and Political Citizenship: Towards a Unified Conception of Citizenship', *Government and Opposition* 40/4 (2005); E. Rieger, 'T.H. Marshall: Soziologie, gesellschaftliche Entwicklung und die moralische Ökonomie des Wohlfahrtsstaates', in T.H. Marshall (ed.), *Bürgerrechte und soziale Klassen. Zur Soziologie des Wohlfahrtsstaates* (Frankfurt a.M.: Campus, 1992); K. Banting, 'Social Citizenship and Federalism: Is the Federal Welfare State a Contradiction in Terms?', in Greer (ed.), *Territory, Democracy and Justice*.
8. Jeffery, 'Devolution and Social Citizenship', esp. pp.82–9; N. McEwen and L. Moreno (eds.), *The Territorial Politics of Welfare* (London: Routledge, 2005); M. Keating and N. McEwen (eds.), 'Devolution and Public Policy: A Comparative Perspective', special issue of *Regional and Federal Studies* 15/4 (2005); N. McEwen, *Nationalism and the State. Welfare and Identity in Scotland and Quebec* (Brussels: Peter Lang, 2006).
9. For a recent overview of scholarship on federalism and the welfare state see H. Obinger, F. Castles and S. Leibfried, 'Introduction: Federalism and the Welfare State', in H. Obinger, F. Castles and S. Leibfried (eds.), *Federalism and the Welfare State. New World and European Experiences* (Cambridge: Cambridge University Press, 2005).
10. Wincott, 'Social Policy and Social Citizenship', p.169. See also P. Manow, 'Germany: Co-operative Federalism and the Overgrazing of the Fiscal Commons', in Obinger et al. (eds.), *Federalism and the Welfare State*.
11. R. Sturm, 'Der Föderalismus im Wandel. Kontinuitätslinien und Reformbedarf', in E. Jesse and K. Löw (eds.), *50 Jahre Bundesrepublik Deutschland* (Berlin: Duncker & Humblot, 1999), p.85.
12. See Fischer and Grosse Hüttmann, 'Aktuelle Diskussionsbeiträge zur Reform des deutschen Föderalismus'.
13. Jeffery, 'Cycles of Conflict', pp.34–5.
14. See C. Jeffery, 'From Cooperative Federalism to a "Sinatra-Doctrine" of the Länder?', in C. Jeffery (ed.), *Recasting German Federalism. The Legacies of Unification* (London: Pinter, 1998). The usage of the term is now becoming adopted elsewhere. See M. Knodt, 'Europäisierung à la Sinatra. Deutsche Länder im europäischen Mehrebenensystem', in M. Knodt and B. Kohler-Koch (eds), *Mannheimer Jahrbuch zur Europäischen Sozialforschung 2000* (Frankfurt: Campus, 2000); M. Knodt, 'Europäisierung regionalen Regierens. Mit Sinatra zum autonomieorientierten Systemwechsel im deutschen Bundesstaat', *Politische Vierteljahresschrift* 43/2 (2002).
15. S. Rokkan and D. Urwin, *The Politics of Territorial Identity* (London: Sage, 1982).
16. Cf. J. Mitchell, 'Evolution and Devolution: Citizenship, Institutions and Public Policy', *Publius. The Journal of Federalism* 36/2 (2006), pp.162–3.
17. With thanks to Daniel Wincott, the following draws on C. Jeffery and D. Wincott, 'Devolution in the United Kingdom: Statehood and Citizenship in Transition', *Publius. The Journal of Federalism* 36/2 (2006), p.12.

18. Cited in Mitchell, 'Evolution and Devolution', p.163.
19. G. Brown, Speech at the Smith Institute, 15 April 1999.
20. S. Greer, 'The Fragile Divergence Machine. Citizenship, Policy Divergence and Devolution', in Trench (ed.), *Devolution and Power*.
21. For example, see V. Bogdanor, 'Constitutional Reform', in A. Seldon (ed.), *The Blair Effect* (London: Little, Brown & Co, 1999), p.154; K. Woods, 'Health Policy and the NHS in the UK 1997–2002', in Adams and Robinson (eds.), *Devolution in Practice*, p.28; R. Hazell and B. O'Leary, 'A Rolling Programme of Devolution: Slippery Slope of Safeguard of the Union', in R. Hazell (ed.), *Constitutional Futures. A History of the Next Ten Years* (Oxford: Oxford University Press, 1999), p.46. This does not necessarily imply a reduction of welfare standards or a 'race to the bottom'. Where post-devolution Scottish and Welsh governments have debated or introduced divergences from England in social policy, they have often done so in the aim of re-introducing post-war commitments to universalism that more market-oriented Westminster governments have increasingly challenged over the last 25 years. See Jeffery, 'Devolution and Social Citizenship', pp.89–91; R. Simeon, 'Free Personal Care. Policy Divergence and Social Citizenship', in R. Hazell (ed.), *The State of the Nations 2003* (Thorverton: Imprint Academic, 2003).
22. Institut für Demoskopie Allensbach, IfD-Umfrage 6019 (Sept. 1995).
23. There is good data for all four UK nations. However, the focus here is on Scotland, Wales and England. Though the broad pattern of Northern Ireland data is similar to that of Scotland and Wales, identity issues excepted, the absence of devolved government there since the suspension of devolution in October 2002 provides a different and, arguably, less reliable context for the data.
24. Curtice, 'A Stronger or Weaker Union?', p.103.
25. Ibid., p.107.
26. Institut für Demoskopie Allensbach, IfD-Umfrage 6019, p.5.
27. Hanns-Seidel-Stiftung, *Generationenstudie 2003. Heimat und Heimatgefühl in Bayern* (Munich: Hanns-Seidel-Stiftung, 2003), p.49. Unfortunately the questions used were poorly designed, asking about autonomy and independence compared with the status quo in separate questions, and then allowing the rather odd option of supporting autonomy or independence 'in part'. In addition to the 24 per cent of unequivocal supporters of autonomy, another 33 per cent supported more autonomy 'in part'; and in addition to the 17 per cent supporting independence, another 21 per cent support 'partial' independence.
28. A. Heath, 'Is a Sense of British Identity in Decline?', *Devolution Briefings No. 36*, available at http://www.devolution.ac.uk/Briefing_papers.htm (2005).
29. P. Surridge, 'A Better Union?', in C. Bromley, J. Curtice, D. McCrone and A. Park (eds.), *Has Devolution Delivered?* (Edinburgh: Edinburgh University Press, 2006), p.35.
30. Mitchell, 'Evolution and Devolution', pp.165–6.
31. Scottish Constitutional Convention, *Scotland's Parliament, Scotland's Right* (Edinburgh: Scottish Constitutional Convention, 1995).
32. Jeffery, 'Devolution and Social Citizenship', pp.78–80.
33. Institut für Demoskopie Allensbach, IfD-Umfrage 6019, p.5.
34. Grube, 'Unverzichtbares Korrektiv oder ineffective Reformbremse?', p.166.
35. Ibid., p.166.
36. Institut für Demoskopie Allensbach, IfD-Umfrage 6019, p.14.
37. A similar picture was found by Institut für Demoskopie Allensbach, IfD-Umfrage 6019, pp.24–5, 28 in 1988 and 1995.
38. YouGov, *Voting Intention and Attitudes to Scotland*, available at http://www.yougov.com/archives/pdf/TEL060101009_1.pdf (accessed 1 Sept. 2006).
39. W. Bürklin and C. Jung, 'Deutschland im Wandel. Ergebniss einer repräsentativen Meinugsumfrage', in K.-R. Korte and W. Weidenfeld (eds.), *Deutschland-Trendbuch* (Bonn: Bundeszentrale für politische Bildung, 2001), p.683.
40. Ibid., pp.691–5.
41. Though the terminology of 'uniformity' of living conditions remains in the constitutional clause enabling federal intervention in areas of Länder legislative responsibility, 'uniform' was replaced by the notionally weaker term of 'equivalent' living conditions in the constitutional reform process conducted after German unification.
42. C. Jeffery, 'The Politics of Territorial Finance', *Regional and Federal Studies* 13/4 (2003), pp.189–91.
43. Grube, 'Unverzichtbares Korrektiv oder ineffective Reformbremse?', p.171.
44. J. Adams, P. Robinson and A. Vigor, *A New Regional Policy for the UK* (London: IPPR, 2003), p.7; K. Morgan, 'Devolution and Development: Territorial Justice and the North–South Divide', *Publius. The Journal of Federalism* 36/1 (2006), p.201.

45. Cf. D. Hough, *The Fall and Rise of the PDS in Germany* (Birmingham: Birmingham University Press, 2002).
46. Marshall, 'Citizenship and Social Class', pp.8–17.
47. See M. Zürn and S. Leibfried, 'Reconfiguring the National Constellation', in S. Leibfried and M. Zürn (eds.), *Transformations of the State?* (Cambridge: Cambridge University Press, 2005).
48. Marshall, 'Citizenship and Social Class', p.9.
49. These scenarios draw on Jeffery, 'Devolution and Social Citizenship', pp.83–9.
50. Jeffery, 'Cycles of Conflict', pp.30–35.
51. B. Stamm, 'Wettbewerbsföderalismus in der Sozialversicherung', in U. Männle (ed.), *Föderalismus zwischen Konsens und Konkurrenz* (Baden-Baden: Nomos, 1998), p.240.
52. M. Russell and G. Lodge, 'The Government of England by Westminster', in R. Hazell (ed.), *The English Question* (Manchester: Manchester University Press, 2006), p.84.
53. See U. Wachendorfer-Schmidt, *Politikverflechtung im vereinigten Deutschland* (Wiesbaden: Westdeutscher Verlag, 2003).
54. Jeffery, 'Devolution and Social Citizenship', pp.82–9; Jeffery, 'The Politics of Territorial Finance', pp.189–91.

Same Challenges, Diverging Responses: Germany, the UK and European Security

KERRY LONGHURST and ALISTER MISKIMMON

INTRODUCTION

The relationship between Germany and the United Kingdom is not as easy to categorise when compared to other bilateral relationships. As something less than a partnership, but more than *ad hoc* co-operation, political relations between the two governments have always been both fluid and ambiguous, especially when viewed against the standard set by the Franco-German partnership or the British–American special relationship. In the field of foreign and security policy, British and German positions have arguably pulled apart more often that they have pulled together, dynamics which have indelibly shaped developments in European and transatlantic security since the end of the Cold War. It is arguably the case that, in contrast to other policy sectors, in the area of foreign, security and defence policy there has been little in the way of actual policy convergence between the UK and Germany. In fact, we argue that policy divergence has, thus far, been the most pronounced characteristic in this bilateral relationship – a factor which does not mitigate against the two states seeing eye to eye on a range of contemporary foreign and security policy issues.[1]

The purpose of this study is to consider British and German policies and perspectives in the evolving context of European and transatlantic security. Differences and similarities in national policies on some crucial issues will be identified, such as the future of EU enlargement, the European Security and Defence Policy (ESDP) and longer-term strategic objectives. We intend to lay out and discuss where chief disagreements have occurred, but also where similar viewpoints are emerging, which may be giving rise to the potential for greater co-operation and synergies between the two states.

LOOKING BACK: THE *STILLE ALLIANZ*

Before moving onto a contemporary footing, it is worth revisiting the post-war history of British–West German relations and establishing the nature of security relations. John Roper and Karl Kaiser's conception of British and West German defence relations as a *Stille Allianz* accurately described the nature of this bilateral relationship at a time when security relations were conditioned by the Cold War.[2] Firmly anchored within the Atlantic Alliance and underwritten by the US security guarantee, West German and British defence and security thinking were aligned in the face of a common threat. Within this overarching framework, co-operation between the two governments was also shaped by relations with the US and France. Roper and Kaiser also noted that, although the British–German relationship was never as vibrant or visible as the Franco-German partnership or the US–UK 'special relationship', from the 1960s onwards, especially after the French withdrawal from North Atlantic Treaty Organisation (NATO)'s integrated command structure, the UK and West Germany emerged as the most significant European actors in the alliance working together to formulate common positions on a number of key strategic issues. This persistent yet discreet alliance became a close and effective bilateral relationship which endured until the end of the Cold War.

West German security and defence policy was a more complicated balancing act than British policy during the Cold War. German balancing was multi-dimensional– balancing Europeanist (France) and transatlanticist (USA/UK) commitments. In addition, there were pressures associated with balancing a self-limiting foreign policy to regain international trust and respectability with the need to pursue the important goal of German unification.[3] The UK's security and defence policy was exclusively wedded to the Atlantic partnership and in other ways to the Commonwealth, even after entry into the European Community in 1973. The presence of large numbers of UK troops in West Germany reinforced the military partnership between both states in light of the Soviet threat, but also reinforced the realities of the post-World War Two settlement and the abnormality of the 'German Problem'. Nonetheless, the Atlantic Alliance was a key consultative forum for both states which reinforced relations between the governments.

THE CHALLENGE OF GERMAN UNIFICATION

The fact that the UK government held a highly sceptical view of the prospect of German unification has been well documented and will therefore not be discussed at any great length here.[4] Briefly, four specific challenges to the United Kingdom's position and status were seen to arise from German unity. First, the increase in Germany's economic position, which would result from unification, questioned Britain's post-war status as a significant power. Second, the proposition voiced at the time that Germany should have a permanent seat on the UN Security Council was viewed as a challenge to the United Kingdom's global profile. Third, the American initiative to forge a new relationship with Germany as 'partners in leadership' in May 1989 was viewed as a clear indication that the United States expected the new Germany to play a more significant role in international affairs and was seen in London as a challenge to the United Kingdom's cherished special relationship with the United States. Fourth, the debates and discussions at the close of the Cold War concerning the future of security governance in Europe questioned the centrality of NATO, within which the United Kingdom had always been the main European player.[5] Liberal German thinking in the early 1990s about the notion of pan-European security structure, building on the Conference on Security and Co-operation in Europe (CSCE) and incorporating Russia, was an idea which rubbed particularly awkwardly against British perspectives.

Despite the frostiness at the time of German unification, when John Major became Prime Minister of the United Kingdom, the British–German relationship entered a slightly warmer period, which was greatly facilitated by the more congenial state of relations that emerged between the two leaders. Despite this, the United Kingdom's ambivalence towards Germany continued to be fuelled by developments in the EC, which were seen as detrimental to core British interests by most in the Conservative Party. Developments toward the deepening of integration, which were strongly supported by Germany, served to expose ever more acutely the contradictions between the British vision of European integration and what was actually happening on the ground, particularly with the moves to transform the EC into a European Union. The pro-deepening agenda pursued with great gusto by Chancellor Kohl at the time served to excite British Eurosceptic voices, which again were heavily tainted by an anti-German flavour. This was to peak in September 1992, when sterling was devalued and the United Kingdom forced out of the European Exchange Rate Mechanism in the wake of the Danish referendum on the Maastricht Treaty. The condemnation in the United Kingdom of the role of the Bundesbank served to illustrate that Euroscepticism was still being conflated with a fear and resentment of Germany inherited from the Thatcher years.

Convergence and Divergence in the Area of Security Policy

As already suggested, policy convergence is difficult to detect in security policy in British–German relations. One of the main reasons for this is that there is no template for policy adaptation within the EU, let alone between Berlin and London, but also because British and German strategic cultures remain inherently different – a point we shall return to later. Within the Common Foreign and Security Policy (CFSP) and the ESDP there remain a wide variety of perspectives and national preferences. EU foreign policy has resisted communitarisation – and importantly it lacks a substantive legal basis and enforcement mechanisms to ensure compliance to decisions taken by the Council of Ministers. Compounding this is the lack of clarity which still endures, to some degree, regarding the roles and division of labour between the EU as a security actor and NATO. Although a 'working relationship' has begun to emerge between the two organisations, the fact that there remains some ambiguity arguably serves to mitigate against a convergence of German and British perspectives and planning.

In terms of how the two countries have set about adjusting their security policies over time, in the case of Germany, Berlin's growing acceptance of the need to play a greater role in multinational military crisis management has resembled more of what Rose describes as 'lesson-drawing'.[6] Over the course of the late 1990s and early twenty-first century Germany has, more often than not, heeded calls from its key partners to play a greater international role and to utilise military force, when necessary. German foreign policy elites and the German Armed Forces have undergone significant adaptation, both in terms of the reform of the Bundeswehr and in security policy thinking more generally – in line with both EU- and NATO-level developments. In Germany, there has been a clear distinction between what is desirable and what is feasible in overseas military deployment (see Table 1). From the UK's perspective, whilst a growing embrace of CFSP and ESDP has certainly transpired in the course of the previous decade and is now a key characteristic of British security policy, 9/11 reinforced the need for a bolstering of UK–US defence relations.[7] In the British case, *lesson-drawing* has essentially focused on maintaining British–American military interoperability while not standing in the way of building further low-level military capabilities as part of the EU's ESDP. The following section will examine in greater detail developments in the 1990s, tracking how, in the course of the decade, the relationship shifted from divergence towards the potential for something closer to a partnership.

THE 1990S: A DECADE OF CHANGE

With the end of the Cold War the strategic context within which the *Stille Allianz* had operated transformed fundamentally. The removal of the Cold War overlay, as already noted, initially prompted divergent British and German responses to new security 'threats and challenges'. German unification and the acquisition of sovereignty presented an opportunity for German elites to construct a more active foreign and security policy, which occurred in a piecemeal fashion.

The early to mid-1990s witnessed the emergence of efforts to affect a greater collective European voice in security affairs. Germany's ability to play a bigger role in this was, in the early days, hampered by Hans Dietrich Genscher's concern to avoid a rapid expansion of Germany's military role and a further division of Europe, which, in his view, could occur if NATO and the EC prevailed as the only security institutions in Europe. The July 1994 decision of the German Federal Constitutional Court to allow Bundeswehr deployment outside the NATO area was an important step on the road to Germany's greater international engagement. Germany's tentative steps to widen its international role were anchored in the frameworks of NATO and the EU as a means to dispel fears, at home and abroad, of a newly confident unified Germany set on pursuing unilateral strategies.[8]

At this time British and German views on the emerging European security structures were in opposition. Tensions arose as a result of the emergence of the Common Foreign and Security Policy of the European Union after Maastricht, which in the eyes of the Conservative government in the UK threatened the transatlantic security relationship founded on NATO – and the USA's role in European security affairs. As a result, the British government showed great reluctance to develop CFSP, preferring to bolster the European influence within NATO through the European Security and Defence Identity (ESDI). Helmut Kohl's vision of the creation of Political Union, with foreign and security policy as components of the EU, ultimately clashed with John Major's preference for maintaining transatlantic structures and limited both the effectiveness of CFSP and the scope of co-operation between the two governments.

TABLE 1
GERMAN MILITARY DEPLOYMENTS OVERSEAS, 2006 (TOTAL: 7,674)

	ISAF Afghanistan Uzbekistan	KFOR Kosovo	EUFOR Bosnia and Herzegovina	UNMIS Sudan	AMIS Sudan	UNOMIG Georgia	UNMEE Ethiopia Eritrea	OEF Horn of Africa	EUFOR RD CONGO Congo Gabon	OAE Mediterranean	Troops stationed in Germany for the medical evacuation of troops (STRATAIR-MEDEVAC)
Total	2.756	2.890	881	36	0	12	2	262	770	23	42
Of which women	114	121	55	0	0	0	0	16	38	–	–
Of which reservists	244	191	84	1	0	0	0	6	17	–	–
Of which FWDL	137	338	70	0	0	0	0	31	16	–	–

Note: FDWL: *Freiwillig zusätzliche Wehrdienst Leistende* (Volunteer Conscripts).
Source: Figures from German Armed Forces Homepage (Figures correct as of 2 Aug. 2006), available at http://www.bundeswehr.de/ (accessed 10 Aug. 2006).

POST-1997: TOWARD AN ENDURING AFFINITY?

A critical juncture in British–German relations emerged in the late 1990s when in 1997 and then 1998 centre-left parties came to power in Germany and the United Kingdom. Crucially, changes of guard in both Germany and the United Kingdom opened up the prospect for a greater closeness of British and German perspectives on security issues.

The election to power of New Labour in the United Kingdom and the Social Democratic Party (SPD) in Germany signalled the emergence of a far closer ideological affinity between the two states, which was harnessed and nurtured under the mantle of the *Neue Mitte* or 'Third Way'. What Chancellor Gerhard Schröder and Prime Minister Tony Blair had in common, aside from belonging to the same post-war generation, was a desire to renew and realign some of the central tenets of social democracy, through a programme of modernization. Exhibiting this proximity, the so-called Blair–Schröder paper of 1999 entitled 'The Way Forward for Europe's Social Democrats' addressed such themes as social justice, civil society and citizenship, detailing points of convergence, a common political agenda, priorities and global visions shared between the British and German centre-left parties. Significantly, the new German–British meeting of minds, nestled within social democracy, also entailed a distant foreign policy element. At the core of this lay notions of fairness and justice in a call for an ethical foreign policy.

The junior coalition partner in the new German government in 1998, Bündnis '90/ Die Grünen, was an important player in developing Germany's new foreign and security policy position. Foreign Minister Joschka Fischer of the Greens outlined the moral and political responsibility for Germany to safeguard peace in the world, a position which was instrumental in paving the way for German involvement in the NATO operation in Kosovo. The shedding of the Greens' pacifist position was an important step in enabling the UK and Germany to co-operate on building EU military capabilities in the aftermath of the Kosovo operation in 1999. Indeed, Germany's Presidency of the EU/Western European Union (WEU) and the G8 enabled Germany to set the agenda on the emergence of the ESDP. For their part, the UK government smoothed the way for the EU's foray into military crisis management by forging agreement among NATO countries to consent to ESDP, as outlined in the Berlin Plus agreement of 1999.

The renewal of the Labour Party in the United Kingdom entailed a more proactive stance towards the issue of Europe, and in turn towards Germany, with a swift and decisive move away from the former obstructionist character of the United Kingdom's European policy.[9] Dubbed a 'step-change', this strategy placed great emphasis upon developing bilateral relationships and partnerships on key European issues, thereby taking the traditional form of 'multiple bilateralism' and assigning it a more strategic, less tactical, visionary mission.[10] The defence agreement signed between the United Kingdom and France in 1998 at St. Malo in France was one of the first and most sensational manifestations of this step-change; unsurprisingly, the realization followed after the federal election in 1998 that Germany, with Gerhard Schröder in power, would be a promising partner.

Greater convergence in British and German security perspectives in the late 1990s was further anticipated as Germany 'got to grips' with the use of force, a process which climaxed in Kosovo in 1999.[11] The SPD-Green government's decision to deploy the

Bundeswehr in a full combat role in Kosovo followed from Germany's previous deployments in the region, which began in the early part of the decade, during the Kohl era. Kosovo, as already mentioned, saw German soldiers play a full combative role – a fundamental shift which brought German policy more in line with other European allies, including the UK.

The evolution of German perspectives on the use of force, as seemingly manifest in Kosovo, meant that by the end of the decade British and German security policies were now less at variance than they were earlier in the 1990s. Convergence took place on both sides, with Germany accepting the need for a capabilities-led approach to ESDP and the UK accepting the need to bolster EU military capabilities as a means to strengthen transatlantic security relations.

By the end of the 1990s it seemed that the *Stille Allianz* had, to some degree, been recalibrated into an effective yet flexible partnership, with the UK and Germany seeing eye to eye on a number of strategic issues. Crucially, after St. Malo and in the light of Kosovo, Germany appeared to be evolving into the kind of security player UK policy could increasingly rely upon and, in turn, the UK government's more positive approach to the EU pointed to the potential for enhanced German–British partnership. A shared interest in EU and NATO enlargements also brought Germany and the UK closer on one of the most important foreign policy issues of the post-Cold War era, an effect of which was a loosening of the Franco-German partnership in the EU. These points notwithstanding, an enduring closeness between the UK and Germany based upon a commitment to social democracy proved to be elusive, largely as a result of diverging economic agendas, and contrasting positions towards a number of key foreign and security policy issues – ESDP and Iraq to name but two. However, the prominence of such divergences should not deflect from the achievements to which Britain and Germany both contributed. British and German positions were in accord on the two most important issues of the post-Cold War world, namely the enlargement of NATO in 1999 and of the European Union, which eventually transpired in 2004.

EMERGING CRACKS IN THE RELATIONSHIP: 9/11, AFGHANISTAN AND IRAQ

Despite the important areas of convergence mentioned above and despite Germany's deployment in Kosovo – which brought British and German policy into close proximity, diverging perspectives towards the US-led war on terror and the invasion of Iraq placed profound strains on the British–German relationship. These events exposed the fundamental differences between British and German strategic cultures, the limits to change in Berlin's approach to the use of force and the resilience of the UK's adherence to the special relationship with the United States.[12] The connection between British and German security perspectives that had transpired at the end of the 1990s was virtually swept away by the effects of 11 September 2001 and the subsequent radicalisation of US foreign policy. As the war on terror expanded and as Europe's common voice faltered and ultimately failed, the EU became polarised, with Germany and the UK in opposing camps.

The contrasting British and German positions reflected both deep-seated strategic cultures, threat assessments and in the case of Germany a recently acquired confidence and willingness to define and articulate German interests, which for the first time clashed dramatically with those of its original transatlantic mentor – the United States. Contrasting approaches to the use of force and the relative importance attached to multilateralism and international law, together with domestic and electoral pressures, which in Germany strongly militated against German involvement in 'America's war', gave rise to British and German discord after 2001, memorably characterised by Donald Rumsfeld as part of a broader European divide between 'old' and 'new' Europe.

The events of 11 September 2001 brought into sharp focus the underlying differences in British and German perspectives on the use of force, in particular, and the role played by national strategic cultures. As the Euro-Atlantic community ruptured, Germany and the UK faced stark and undesirable choices between Atlanticist and Europeanist solutions. In their own ways, both Germany and the UK got trapped by the stances of their own close allies – France and the USA respectively. In the end neither state had a substantial say in the outcome of the heated discussions within the United Nations Security Council. Germany's refusal to participate in any way on the ground in Iraq reinforced British–German divergence.

ENTER ANGELA MERKEL – HOPE FOR BRITISH–GERMAN CONVERGENCE?

Looking forward to 2005, there was more than the usual level of interest in the German federal election. From the perspective of the UK government, hopes were high for Merkel to carry out necessary economic reforms and to realign German foreign and security policy towards a more Atlanticist perspective – which had been negated under Schröder. Angela Merkel has sought to reduce Germany's dependency on the Franco-German 'core' of the EU, through attempting to repair relations with the UK and of course the US. In a rare show of positive British–German sentiment, *The Times* declared that, 'London and Berlin are on the cusp of a beautiful relationship', to mark Blair's first meeting with Merkel in Berlin on 18 February 2006.[13] Close co-operation on the issue of Iranian nuclear weapons, and greater common working on issues in the EU such as energy security, deregulation and efforts to connect more effectively with ordinary EU citizens have opened up avenues for partnership between Britain and Germany. Efforts to repair faults in British–German relations have also witnessed Blair actively praising Merkel's speeches at the World Economic Forum at Davos and the 2006 Munich Security Conference, whilst Blair's recent European speech to Oxford University received a positive appraisal from Merkel.[14]

Efforts to try and see more eye to eye on foreign policy issues between the British and German governments in London and Berlin have been helped by Chancellor Merkel's attempts to revive relations with Washington.[15] As something of a foreign policy novice, Merkel has been surprisingly well received for her engagement in international affairs. Clearly attempts to reduce tensions between Washington and Berlin will leave more space for improved relations between Germany and the UK. Furthermore, in the context of the enlarged EU of 25 states, Merkel appears to be open to pursuing a greater variety of alliances and partnerships within the EU and is thus less wedded to an exclusively Franco-German dialogue. Merkel's courting of George W. Bush in 2006, her more pragmatic approach to relations with Vladimir Putin, and her co-operation with Chirac in leading European Union Force République démocratique du Congo (EUFOR RD Congo) are signs of her efforts not to put all her diplomatic eggs in one basket.

EUROPEAN INTEGRATION: TOWARDS COMMON GROUND?

Behind much of the tension in British–German relations in the period during and after unity lay in the dramatically contrasting visions and strategies vis-à-vis European integration. Although on the fundamental issue of the future of the European Union, British and German perspectives remain poles apart, in some specific policy spheres and also in policy style a detectable closeness has emerged between the United Kingdom and Germany since 1997–98. As already noted, this synthesis of perspectives emerged when the UK's step-change in foreign policy matters gelled with the SPD–Green coalition's less reflexive, more considered approach to EU matters. Although many commentators had indicated that post-unification Germany's European policy might, or indeed should, take on a more British character, meaning a less unconditional form of support for integration, it was not until the arrival of the SPD–Green coalition government that it became apparent that the habitual, predictably reflexive German take on Europe had somewhat abated.[16] Demonstrating this, soon after becoming Chancellor, Schröder spoke of a new self-confidence in Germany and of the need for Germany to watch over its own interests.[17] Certainly the distance between British and German European policy has narrowed on a number of counts; this is seen in the synergy that has transpired in certain policy sectors, though, as mentioned above, on the issue of the future of Europe, national perspectives remain divergent.

EU AND NATO ENLARGEMENT AND THE WIDER NEIGHBOURHOOD

NATO and EU enlargements in 1999 and 2004 brought into the mix not only a larger number of states, but also rendered these institutions more internally diverse. In this context, the question of leadership and the role of big versus small states became prominent, with implications for the UK and Germany. The diminution of the Franco-German alliance within a more fluid EU brought the question of leadership in the enlarged EU to the fore. Within the area of foreign policy and diplomacy, a higher-profile role has been played by Germany, France and the UK, taking the EU foreign and security policy agenda forward. On the question of formulating a common response to Iranian nuclear ambitions, the cohesion of the trio derived not only from direct diplomacy on the ground, but also because it was underpinned, this time, by a coherent EU strategy which was distinct to the American approach to Tehran. Thus EU diplomacy towards Iran, though perhaps not as effective as desired, did illustrate the potential of CFSP and that on some crucial global strategic issues German and British perspective were in sync.

EU enlargement altered the foreign and security policy detail of the EU by challenging existing priorities and approaches to CFSP and ESDP, with direct implications for the UK and Germany. New member states from East Central Europe brought to the EU an overwhelming desire to bolster the EU's eastern policy. Ukraine's EU membership was brought onto the table and the need for a coherent EU as opposed to divergent national policies towards Russia was lobbied for. A recalibrated eastern policy finds resonance in both governments, which together with Poland, as the region's key power, potentially provides common ground for British–German co-operation in this particular field.

The UK remains pro-enlargement and is currently positive about Turkish membership, whilst Germany maintains a principled commitment but currently remains mute on questions of actual detail. What is clear from a German perspective, and this is where there is a clash with the UK, is that on the question of Turkish versus Ukrainian membership, it is the latter that is 'more like us' and therefore preferable. Crucially, Germany's enlargement policy is at a crossroads; the decision on which route to take will either weaken or inhibit the prospect of partnership with the UK.

In summary, enlargement brought into focus the question of future leadership in the EU. In an EU of 27 members, alongside other states, the UK and Germany will remain leading states, especially in the broader foreign policy field. Further EU enlargement presents an opportunity for closer British and German co-operation, although, on the crucial issues of candidates and timeframes, the two governments diverge.

THE EU AS A SECURITY AND DEFENCE ACTOR

Discord over the decision to go to war against Iraq continues to overshadow not only British–German relations, but EU foreign policy in general. After the failure of the EU's collective voice over Iraq, both Britain and Germany became committed to emboldening the EU's security and military capacities, in the form of European Security and Defence Policy. However, whilst Berlin and London have both supported a broad range of institutional and doctrinal developments, post-Iraq there is more that divides Britain and Germany on matters relating to ESDP than brings them together, especially in the context of an enlarged EU.

Both the UK and Germany are key players in European security and as such, along with other large states, are crucial for the further development of EU security policy and ESDP, though the prospects for an exclusive bilateral British–German dialogue is low. Not only do British and German perspectives diverge quite sharply, but also since enlargement there are a larger number of actors with a wider range of issues. This diversity has given rise to new and changing coalitions, as well as dyads, with implications for Germany, Britain and European security.

When the seeds of ESDP were sown in 1998 chiefly through a convergence of British and French perspectives, the expectation was that the EU's international voice would become more credible through the introduction of a military dimension. Despite the virtual negation of the EU's collective voice after 9/11 and the war on terror, ESDP was further developed 'on the ground' through a variety of missions in Europe and beyond.[18]

From both British and German viewpoints the further elaboration of ESDP was a welcome development. At this early phase, the two governments supported, contributed to and led EU missions. A shared perspective also held on the broad issue of the NATO–ESDP relationship, and the indispensability of the transatlantic partnership; NATO remained essential for wider combat missions, whilst EU forces should focus upon the Petersberg Tasks. America's 'war on terror' and the Iraq war in particular set British and German perspectives apart, bringing into greater focus fundamental differences and the complexities of British–German–French relations. The previous closeness that had prevailed in policy and perspectives between London and Berlin diminished as the broader *modus vivendi* amongst the large states waned on ESDP. Despite progress on ESDP 'in action', knotty questions of institutional arrangements and decision-making stalled advances and threw British and German perspectives into opposing camps on most fundamental issues.

Despite this distance between immediate British and German ESDP perspectives, as large states they share a fundamental goal of making ESDP work through the leadership of the large EU states. Not so much 'less America, as more Europe' is a view which brings British and German perspectives on CFSP/ESDP into proximity, a stance which tends to sideline France.[19] The UK and Germany also see eye to eye on Iran, where military force is not an option. Operation Althea, EUFOR RD Congo and the other ESDP deployments to date have gone well and will continue to forge operational co-operation.

Public opinion in both countries should encourage foreign policy-makers to pursue more co-operation on the EU level in CFSP. German public opinion remains fully behind Germany in the development of European security and defence policy, as Tables 2 and 3 demonstrate.[20] The tables also show that, on the same questions, British public opinion is less in favour, whilst signalling an improvement in favour of EU foreign and security policy over recent years. On the question of the EU's role in security and defence policy, public opinion in the UK has become more positive, settling at around 59 per cent support for the EU with around 27–29 per cent opposed to the EU's involvement in security and defence policy. With almost two-thirds of UK respondents to these *Eurobarometer* surveys viewing greater EU co-operation as a good thing, previous views that the UK is overwhelmingly pro-Atlanticist are losing credibility, particularly in light of concerns over recent US foreign policy.

However, despite public support in both countries for closer EU co-operation, what ultimately obviates against a longer term strategic partnership between the two states are the fundamentally different visions of ESDP within their governments. Whilst

TABLE 2
PUBLIC OPINION IN THE UK AND GERMANY ON EU COMMON FOREIGN POLICY
(PERCENTAGE VALUES)

	Germany			UK		
	For	Against	Don't know	For	Against	Don't know
EB60 (Winter 2003)	72	15	12	35	44	22
EB61 (Spring 2004)	74	16	9	39	39	22
EB62 (Winter 2004)	80	15	5	47	36	17
EB63 (Spring 2005)	78	17	5	44	38	18
EB64 (Winter 2005)	78	17	5	50	34	16

Survey Question: What is your opinion on each of the following statements? Please tell me for each statement whether you are for or against it? A common foreign policy among the member states of the EU towards other countries?
Source: Eurobarometer surveys, available at http://europa.eu.int/comm/public_opinion/index_en.htm (accessed 2 Sept. 2006).

TABLE 3
PUBLIC OPINION IN THE UK AND GERMANY ON EU COMMON DEFENCE AND SECURITY POLICY (PERCENTAGE VALUES)

	Germany			UK		
	For	Against	Don't know	For	Against	Don't know
EB60 (Winter 2003)	76	12	11	48	35	18
EB61 (Spring 2004)	80	12	8	52	28	20
EB62 (Winter 2004)	87	10	3	60	27	14
EB63 (Spring 2005)	85	10	5	59	27	14
EB64 (Winter 2005)	87	11	2	59	29	13

Survey Question: What is your opinion on each of the following statements? Please tell me for each statement whether you are for or against it? A common defence and security policy among EU member states?
Source: Eurobarometer surveys, available at http://europa.eu.int/comm/public_opinion/index_en.htm (accessed 2 Sept. 2006).

Germany seeks to 'Europeanise' ESDP with the ultimate goal of establishing a European Security and Defence Union, the UK position remains staunchly intergovernmentalist and disposed to a more *a la carte* approach – driven by capabilities, not institution-building. The 'reach' of ESDP, raising the thorny debate over the EU's global versus regional calling and the question of pre-emptive military force, also divide Berlin and London and are factors which will continue to dominate the European security agenda.

TENSIONS OVER DEFENCE SPENDING

The question of defence spending regularly crops up in discussions between the UK and Germany. Germany continues to maintain low levels of defence spending, despite the greater use of the Bundeswehr in military crisis management operations. The 2005 annual report by Reinhard Robbe, the *Wehrbeauftragte der Bundestag* (Parliamentary Ombudsman with responsibility for the German Armed Forces), was scathing in what he describes as the, 'long-term under-financing of the German Armed Forces' (see Figure 1).[21] This presents the German government with a significant challenge. With representatives of the Bundeswehr regularly criticising the lack of resources available to the German troops, it will be extremely difficult for the Grand Coalition to continue to participate in multinational crisis management.[22] Should Germany's allies sense that its inability to share an adequate amount of the burden of providing international security is due to underinvestment in the Bundeswehr, pressure on the German government will continue to increase. Lack of investment in the defence sector will also prevent Germany from taking advantage of emerging co-operation in European defence procurement, which France and the UK have been quick to capitalise on.[23]

Nowhere is this pressure on German military resources more pressing than in Afghanistan. British calls for greater support of UK forces from NATO partners in the south of the country have been resisted by the German government.[24] With Afghanistan a test case for NATO's new global engagement, it will be important for NATO partners to share the burden of the heavy fighting in the south of the country.

FIGURE 1
UK AND GERMAN DEFENCE SPENDING, PERCENTAGE OF GDP, 1985–2005

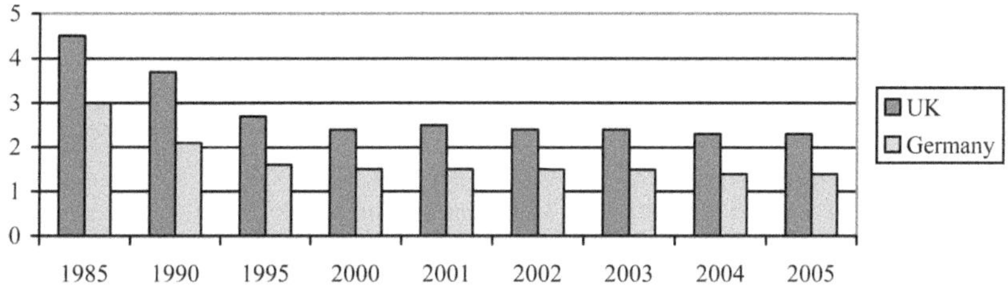

Source: NATO, *NATO–Russia Compendium of Financial and Economic Data Relating to Defence* (Brussels: NATO), available at http://www.nato.int/docu/pr/2005/p05-161.pdf (accessed 7 Sept. 2006).

German deployment to the south of Afghanistan would signal a readiness to consider more dangerous deployments of German troops. For the Bundeswehr to consider such high-intensity deployments, greater investment will be needed to equip German soldiers to operate alongside allied troops. Successful completion of the transformation of the Bundeswehr is an essential precondition for the international credibility of German troops operating in multinational missions. As the influence of European states grows within NATO, the expectations of a greater German role in burden-sharing will increase. With Germany only investing 1.4 per cent of its Gross Domestic Product (GDP) on defence, compared with 2.3 per cent GDP invested by the UK, Germany will struggle to equip the Bundeswehr for its future role (see Figure 1). If Germany wishes to maintain its influence within NATO and with the UK, Germany will need to invest further in its Armed Forces, despite the current budgetary challenges facing Berlin.

CONCLUSION: FROM *STILLE ALLIANZ* TO AN AMBIGUOUS RELATIONSHIP IN AN ENLARGING EU

The arrival of New Labour and the SPD–Green governments in 1997–98 seemed to herald a rebirth of British–German relations and with it the potential of a closer proximity of foreign and security policy perspectives. However, differences on the decision to go to war against Saddam Hussein and squabbles over EU policy forced Schröder back into the arms of his French partner, Chirac. Hopes of a less exclusive Franco-German core at the heart of the EU through greater UK involvement in European affairs were seemingly dashed and relations between Blair and Schröder were increasingly strained. Efforts to try and repair British–German relations were noticeable with the advent of Merkel's administration but a number of issues remain unresolved between London and Berlin, which will continue to restrict opportunities for substantive and enduring co-operation between the pair.

British and German perspectives on European security issues present a mixed picture. Numerous factors bring Germany and the UK together, but an equal number set them apart. Relations with the United States and with France bring further complexities to this bilateral relationship. In the search for solutions in European Security,

Britain and Germany may face similar challenges, especially in the age of global terrorism, sustained instability and uncertainty at Europe's borders. However, German and British starting points and long terms goals often differ – for example over the use of force in foreign policy.

For a more productive German–British dialogue within a broader EU context, much depends on Germany's willingness and capacity to modernise both German 'thinking' and capabilities for military action. In recent years, German security policy has lacked a strategy, leaving Germany vulnerable to the influence of other states and less able to influence the policies of its key partners. The 'resource crunch' in Germany's defence and security planning, a result of a near stagnant defence budget tarnishes Germany's image as a useful and reliable partner in both NATO and EU contexts. The modernisation of German security policy is necessary on every count. Without an upgrade of capabilities and political will, Germany's voice within European security will be limited and will run the risk of alienating the UK and France as well as the United States. An important decision which Germany needs to confront soon is the continuation of conscription. An indication that the draft will be abandoned sooner rather than later will enhance the perception of key allies that Berlin is ready to get serious in its commitment to European security. Essentially, by abandoning conscription, funds can be redirected towards research and development projects to aid the modernisation and operational efficiency of the Bundeswehr. However, recent remarks by Defence Minister Jung and the General Inspector of the German Armed Forces, General Wolfgang Schneiderhan, on the 50th Anniversary of the introduction of conscription, do not point to any plans for its removal any time soon.[25]

The role of the large states in taking foreign and security policy forward remains essential and is an issue upon which Germany and the UK agree. A meeting of minds between the UK, Germany and France is essential for success in this respect within an enlarged EU. Foreign, security and defence policy is an area where there is less potential and desire for an exclusive UK–German dialogue which could lead to concrete measures.

The notion of a *Stille Allianz* no longer finds resonance in British–German relations in the field of defence and security policy. The changing context of European security and the arrival of new actors and factors have brought ambiguity, rather than renewal, to this relationship. Such pessimism aside, scope for German–British collaboration will transpire on the broad question of EU enlargement and neighbourhood policy, a decisive area which may bring the governments into close collaboration with a range of new member states.

NOTES

1. D. Dolowitz and D. Marsh, 'Who Learns What and From Whom? A Review of the Policy Transfer Literature', *Political Studies* 44 (1996), pp.343–57; also D. Dolowitz and D. Marsh, 'Learning from Abroad: The Role of Policy Transfer in Contemporary Policy-Making', *Governance* 13 (2000), pp.5–24.
2. K. Kaiser and J. Roper, *Die Stille Allianz: Deutsch–britische Sicherheitskooperation* (Bonn: Schriften des Forschungsinstituts der Deutschen Gesellschaft für Auswärtige Politik: Europa Union Verlag, 1987).

3. H. Haftendorn, *Coming of Age: German Foreign Policy since 1945* (Lanham: Rowman & Littlefield, 2006).
4. W. Paterson, 'Britain and the Berlin Republic: Between Ambivalence and Emulation', in S. Padgett and T. Poguntke (eds.), *Continuity and Change in German Politics: Beyond the Politics of Centrality* (London: Frank Cass, 2002); Y. Klein, '"Obstructing or Promoting?" British Views on German Unification 1989/90', *German Politics* 5/3 (1996), p.407.
5. Klein, '"Obstructing or Promoting?"'
6. R. Rose, *Lesson-Drawing in Public Policy* (New Jersey: Chatham House Publishers Inc, 1993).
7. A. Miskimmon, 'Continuity in the Face of Upheaval – British Strategic Culture and the Impact of the Blair Government', *European Security* 13/3 (2004), pp.1–27.
8. J.S. Duffield, *World Power Forsaken: Political Culture, International Institutions, and German Security Culture after Unification* (Stanford, CA: Stanford University Press, 1998).
9. R. Holden, *The Making of New Labour's European Policy* (Basingstoke: Palgrave, 2003); R. Little and M. Wickham-Jones (eds.), *New Labour's Foreign Policy* (Manchester: Manchester University Press, 2000).
10. J. Smith and M. Tsatsas, *The New Bilateralism: The UK's Relations within the EU* (London: Royal Institute for International Affairs, 2002).
11. For more on this see K. Longhurst, *Germany and the Use of Force* (Manchester: Manchester University Press, 2004).
12. '... the strategic culture approach is interested in the subjective, nationally specific, aspects of security and defence policy and the ways in which collective historical experiences, channelled through pervading norms and values, play a role in defining interests and this shaping policy choices.' Longhurst, *Germany and the Use of Force*, p.1.
13. 'German Lesson: London and Berlin are on the Cusp of a Beautiful Relationship', *The Times*, 18 Feb. 2006, p.23, available at http://www.timesonline.co.uk (accessed 18 Feb. 2006).
14. H. Williamson, 'Berlin–London Links Thrive on Mutual Praise', *Financial Times*, 18 Feb. 2006, p.8; T. Blair, Speech on European Integration, St Anthony's College, Oxford University, 2 Feb. 2006, available at http://www.sant.ox.ac.uk/esc/BlairSpeechStAntonys.pdf (accessed 15 March 2006).
15. Szabo skilfully outlines the extent of the German–American falling out over the Iraq war which Merkel will need to redress should Germany wish to influence the USA once more. S. Szabo, *Parting Ways: The Crisis in German–American Relations* (Washington, DC: Brookings Institution Press, 2004).
16. A. Baring (ed.), *Germany's New Position in Europe: Problems and Perspectives* (Oxford: Oxford University Press, 1996).
17. A. Hyde-Price and C. Jeffery, 'Germany in the European Union: Constructing Normality', *Journal of Common Market Studies* 39/4 (2001), pp.689–718.
18. The EU's role in peacekeeping and crisis management has increased substantially as a result of developments kick-started by the Franco-British St. Malo agreement of 1998. The most significant expression of this is EUFOR's peacekeeping role in Bosnia-Herzegovina after taking over from NATO's Stabilisation Force (SFOR) mission in December 2004. From a German perspective, the EU's support of UN troops in the recent elections in the Democratic Republic of Congo was significant, as Germany played the role of 'lead nation' and set up operational command of the mission in Potsdam.
19. See Gerhard Schröder's speech to the 41st Munich Security Conference 2005, available at http://www.securityconference.de/konferenzen/rede.php?menu_2005 = &menu_konferenzen = &sprache = en&id = 143& (accessed 20 July 2006).
20. The following data can be found at Eurobarometer, available at http://europa.eu.int/comm/public_opinion/index_en.htm (accessed 20 May 2006).
21. Bundestag, 'Jahresbericht des Wehrbeauftragte 2005', *Bundestag Online*, available at http://www.bundestag.de/aktuell/archiv/2006/bericht_wb/bericht2005_kurz.html (accessed 20 July 2006); R. Robbe, 'Unterrichtung durch den Wehrbeauftragten – Jahresbericht 2005 (47. Bericht)', *Bundestagsdrucksache* 16/850 (2006). See also *Die Welt*, 'Wehrbeauftragter Robbe: Das Vertrauen der Soldaten ist erschüttert', 14 March 2006, available at http://www.welt.de (accessed 14 March 2006).
22. The Chairman of the *Bundeswehrverband*, Bernhard Gertz, repeatedly criticised the government for their lack of investment in the Bundeswehr, particularly during the debate over Germany's participation in the EU's mission in the Congo in 2006. His views were echoed in the statements of SPD defence expert Rainer Arnold and by Johannes Kahrs, spokesman for the SPD Seeheimer Kreis (the centrist faction within the party). See Deutschlandfunk, 'Widerstand gegen Kongo-Einsatz in der SPD-Fraktion' (2006), available at http://www.dradio.de/dlf/sendungen/interview_dlf/481339/.
23. See for example recent Franco-British plans to co-operate on building aircraft carriers. M. Aillot-Marie and J. Reid, 'Carriers Deal Signals Important Step in EU Defence Links', *Financial Times*, Asia edition, 6 March 2006, p.12; M. Jivkov, 'Britain and France to Share Carrier Programme', *The Independent*, 25 Jan. 2006, p.55.

24. 'NATO Allies Balk at Reinforcing UK in Afghanistan', *Financial Times*, 31 Aug. 2006, available at http://www.ft.com (accessed 31 Aug. 2006); 'Bundeswehr nicht nach Südafghanistan', *Frankfurter Allgemeine Zeitung*, 28 Aug. 2006, available at http://www.faz.net (accessed 28 Aug. 2006).
25. Bundesministerium der Verteidigung, '50 Jahre Wehrpflicht', 7 July 2006, available at http://www.bmvg.de (accessed 10 Aug. 2006). Jung stated, 'Ich glaube – nicht nur, weil ich selbst Wehrpflichtiger war – dass die Wehrpflicht einen entscheidenden Beitrag dazu geleistet hat, wie sich die Bundeswehr heute darstellt und wie sie in unserer Gesellschaft verwurzelt ist'.
26. Figures from German Armed Forces Homepage (Figures correct as of 2 Aug. 2006), at http://www.bundeswehr.de/ (accessed 10 Aug. 2006).

Divergent Traditions, Converging Responses: Immigration and Integration Policy in the UK and Germany

SIMON GREEN

INTRODUCTION

In the context of this volume on policy convergence in the UK and Germany, immigration and integration policy constitutes an obvious and in many ways ideal case study. There are three key reasons for this. First, for some decades now, these countries have been two of the most significant destinations for immigration in the European Union. In recent years, the two countries have received the highest volume of immigration and family reunification of all EU member states, as well as granting the highest numbers of naturalisations; in absolute numbers of non-national residents, Germany and the UK are first and third respectively. Between 1998 and 2002, these two countries took the top two places in the EU in terms of the number of asylum applications lodged; even since then, both have remained near the top.[1] Indeed, with the possible exception of France, no other EU member state can match the UK and Germany for both the sheer scale and diversity of immigration they have received, as well as for the long period of time over which this immigration has taken place. Some key indicators of immigration to the UK and Germany between 2002 and 2005 are given in Table 1.

Second, and as will be elucidated below, both countries are facing broadly similar challenges in this field, including skills and demographic shortages and, perhaps most importantly, in the integration of their non-national/immigrant minorities,[2] which has become a major political issue in Germany as well as the UK.[3] The third reason for undertaking such a comparison lies in the politics of New Labour and the SPD–Green government, which came to power in the UK and Germany in May 1997 and October 1998 respectively. Several other contributions to this collection draw on the 'Third Way' document,[4] and although it makes no direct mention of immigration, both the Labour and the SPD–Green governments, upon assuming power, explicitly

TABLE 1
IMMIGRATION AND CITIZENSHIP IN THE UK AND GERMANY, 2002–2005 (THOUSANDS)

	UK				Germany			
	2002	2003	2004	2005	2002	2003	2004	2005
Net foreign immigration	245	236	342	292	153	103	55	96
New asylum applications	103	60	40	30	71	51	36	29
Total non-national population	2,587[a]	2,760	n/a	n/a	7,336	7,335	6,717[b]	6,756[b]
Naturalisations	120	126	141	162	155	141	127	117

[a]2001.
[b]From 2004, the total is calculated on a different basis to previous years and is therefore not comparable.
Sources: UNHCR, Home Office, Office of National Statistics, Statistisches Bundesamt, Eurostat.

set out to 'modernise' immigration and citizenship policy from the essentially undifferentiated restrictive emphasis which had characterised the preceding conservative administrations.[5]

Together, this combination of common large scale immigration flows, similar challenges and the apparent ideological closeness of the two governments makes this area a prime example of where policy convergence might be expected. In this context, and drawing on Bennett's classification,[6] it is helpful to distinguish between convergence of *policy goals*, which refers to the issues which are to be tackled, and of *policy instruments*, which for the purposes of this discussion will refer to the actual policies adopted to address the policy goals. This contribution will show that both these elements are visible in varying degrees across this policy field.

At the same time, what makes this convergence all the more remarkable is that it has occurred against the backdrop of very different historical traditions in each of the two countries. The importance of history and traditions for understanding current politics and policy is of course widely acknowledged in political science, and the resulting 'path dependence' of initial political compromises or institutional configurations can be defined thus: 'When a government programme or organisation embarks on a path there is an inertial tendency for those initial policy choices to persist. That path may be altered, but it requires a good deal of political pressure to produce that change.'[7] In immigration and citizenship, as in several other areas covered in this collection, path dependence has been clearly identified by scholars in the cases of the UK and Germany.[8]

This analysis therefore begins by sketching out these historical traditions before examining a range of common pressures, both exogenous and endogenous, which have affected policy goals and instruments in the two countries. It also pinpoints membership of the EU and the gradual development of a common EU immigration policy as a key factor behind convergence in individual areas. The extent and nature of convergence is then discussed by drawing on examples from three main policy sub-fields: labour and dependant migration policy, integration and citizenship policy, and asylum policy. In addition, key exceptions to this pattern of convergence will also be outlined. The conclusion reviews the extent of convergence that has been identified and compares political and structural factors behind this.

HISTORICAL TRADITIONS IN IMMIGRATION AND INTEGRATION POLICY

One of the most striking factors of the convergence of policy is that where it has taken place in this field, it has occurred despite, and not because of, the very different prevailing traditions of immigration in both countries. And, as will be argued later on in this piece, in those areas where endogenous and exogenous pressures have not produced a degree of convergence, path dependence remains a central explanatory factor of policy responses in the UK and Germany.

In the case of the UK, immigration and citizenship policy has been significantly influenced by the country's colonial past.[9] Between the 1950s and 1970s, the vast majority of immigrants came from Commonwealth countries, primarily the Indian sub-continent and the Caribbean. Today, they constitute the majority of the immigrant population in the UK and its descendants, although there have been significant inflows of other nationalities since the late 1990s. These have occurred primarily via the asylum system, but also following the enlargement of the EU to central and eastern Europe in 2004.

Crucially, the fact that most immigration to the UK has been from Commonwealth countries has meant that access to citizenship, and in contrast to practically all other EU member states, has been sidelined as a political issue. For under the British Nationality Act 1948, British citizenship (or more properly, subjecthood) was defined in a particularly expansive and inclusive way, which for all intents and purposes equated Commonwealth and British nationals. Nor has dual citizenship, which has been particularly controversial in Germany, ever been a political factor the UK.[10] Indeed, the fact that the majority of the UK's non-EU residents (or third country nationals – TCNs) are Commonwealth nationals, who already possess most citizenship rights including voting rights, furnishes them with an enormously privileged position vis-à-vis other immigrant groups.

What does of course set the British case aside from other European countries is the more formal issue of how residence rights were gradually detached from nationality during the second half of the twentieth century.[11] Under the Commonwealth Immigrants Acts of 1962 and 1968, plus the Immigration Act 1971, access to residence in the UK was limited to 'patrials', or persons with direct family connections to the UK. This of course included most of the 'old' Commonwealth, specifically Australia, New Zealand and Canada, and excluded most people from 'new' Commonwealth countries such as India, Pakistan and Bangladesh. The situation was only partially resolved in the British Nationality Act (BNA) 1981, which drew a line under what had become the fallacy of a global Commonwealth subjecthood under the Crown,[12] but in doing so created new sub-sets of lesser citizenships in the form of British Dependent Territories Citizenship (BDTC) and British Overseas Citizenship (BOC). It also marked a departure from the pure application of the territorial principle in the ascription of British citizenship at birth (*ius soli*), in favour of the principle of descent (*ius sanguinis*) supplemented by a qualified form of *ius soli*. Significantly, though, and despite the clear tendency towards the restriction of the scope of British citizenship culminating in the BNA 1981, the UK retains one of the most liberal sets of rules concerning the acquisition of citizenship in the EU. In the future, this is likely to ease significantly the legal incorporation of new immigrants, especially TCNs and refugees.

The legacy of Commonwealth immigration has also affected a second area of difference between the UK and other EU member states, namely its approach to integration.[13] This has been based on the 'race relations' paradigm, in which an aspiration to strict immigration controls was combined with pragmatic and *'laissez-faire'* integration.[14] Throughout the second half of the twentieth century, the UK never attempted to pursue a joined-up integration policy; instead, its approach was characterised by the famous definition put forward by the then Home Secretary Roy Jenkins in a speech in 1966:

> I do not think we need in this country a 'melting pot', which will turn everyone out in a common mould, as one of a series of carbon copies of someone's misplaced vision of the stereotyped Englishman ... I define integration, therefore, not as a flattening process of uniformity, but cultural diversity, coupled with equality of opportunity in an atmosphere of mutual tolerance.[15]

In practice, this meant that each immigrant community group was encouraged to cherish and foster its own minority ethnic identity (Jenkins' 'diversity'). At the same time, 'mutual tolerance' was enforced through some of the most comprehensive anti-discrimination legislation in the EU, in the form of the Race Relations Acts 1965, 1968 and 1976.[16]

By contrast, Germany's historical legacy in immigration and integration policy can best be summarised by the statement 'Germany is not a country of immigration' (*Deutschland ist kein Einwanderungsland*), which punctuated government policy statements and documents throughout the 1970s, 1980s and up to the advent of the SPD–Green federal government in 1998. The rationale for this position dates back to the era of formalised labour recruitment (the so-called *Gastarbeiter* years), during which mainly young men were actively and formally recruited from Mediterranean countries, in particular Turkey, Italy and Yugoslavia, to work in West German factories and companies.[17] Their employment and hence residence was never considered to be anything other than temporary and, for that reason, few efforts were made to structure or promote their integration. However, when the SPD–FDP government called a halt to organised labour migration in 1973 (the *Anwerbestopp*), the perspectives of the remaining *Gastarbeiter* were swiftly transformed from a hitherto temporary group into a more permanent minority.[18] Accordingly, and against general expectations, the number of non-nationals in West Germany did not decrease after 1973 as the remaining temporary workers returned home: on the contrary, numbers increased due to new migration for the purposes of family reunification. Consequently, such secondary migration itself quickly became a policy priority in terms of restriction and actively divided the main parties for much of the 1980s and, to a lesser extent, the 1990s.

This migration alone would have justified rethinking the paradigm of the non-immigration country. But further large-scale primary immigration arose from the late 1970s onwards in the form of asylum seekers, and has continued ever since. Indeed, at its peak between 1990 and 1993, over 1.2 million persons claimed asylum in Germany. Furthermore, (West) Germany has also been the destination for one of the world's largest ethnic migrations, with over 4 million ethnic Germans, mainly from Poland, Romania and most recently the former Soviet Union, arriving between 1950 and 2004. Their right of entry was originally enshrined in the 1953 Refugees and Expellees' Law (*Bundesvertriebenen- und Flüchtlingsgesetz*), which, in a remarkable example of path dependence, continued until the end of the Cold War, when sharply rising numbers of arrivals rendered this entry mode unsustainable. Even now, any ethnic German born before 1993 can apply to be recognised as such, which, as well as right of entry to Germany, brings with it automatic citizenship and still comparatively generous help with linguistic, social and economic integration into German society.[19]

As early as 1980, this accumulation of immigration flows had transformed most large West German cities into permanent multi-ethnic, culturally pluralist spaces. Yet the political adjustment to this fundamentally changed reality has been slow.[20] The possibilities of permanent residence remained highly restrictive, and it was a decision by the Federal Constitutional Court in 1978, not a change in government policy, which opened up this avenue in the first place.[21] In particular, citizenship remained an elusive status, with no provision for *ius soli* at all, combined with very high requirements for naturalisation, including long periods of residence, eye-watering fee levels, a high degree of 'integration' (or, more properly, assimilation) into German culture and a rejection of dual nationality.[22] This also reflected the prevailing political view of integration, which, for instance in the debate over *Leitkultur* (or 'guiding culture') of 2000,[23] has consistently emphasised the duty of non-nationals in Germany to adapt to indigenous values, in whatever way these are defined. Indeed, until 1998 it was explicit government policy that naturalisation could only occur at the end of a successful integrative process, and not be considered a stepping stone towards this ultimate goal.

Moreover, despite the extent of immigration to West Germany, it was considered politically impossible to reform citizenship as long as the country remained divided. In an explicit attempt to undermine the German Democratic Republic, (West) Germany deliberately maintained Imperial Germany's 1913 citizenship law as the basis for its citizenship, since the law's pan-Germanic focus by definition included the citizens of the GDR.[24] Here too, then, the dynamics of path dependence are in evidence: it was not until 1999, almost ten years after unification and only once the government had changed, that enough political momentum could be generated to pass a new citizenship law at all.[25] Although the new law's provisions have meant some liberalisation, in particular through the introduction of partial *ius soli*, its overall impact has been much less than expected.[26] In consequence, access to full citizenship in Germany remains, even today, the exception rather than the rule.

Certainly, the historical traditions in the UK and Germany show considerable differences in the way the two countries have approached immigration and integration. Although both countries have emphasised their desire to restrict new immigration since the 1970s, the UK has generally been more relaxed about its status as a country of immigration than Germany. At the same time, that is not to say that immigration and 'race' have not been passionately contested issues in Britain – witness for instance the Notting Hill riots in 1958, the notorious 1964 election campaign in Smethwick,[27] Enoch Powell's apocalyptic 1968 vision of violent ethnic conflict, the Brixton riots of 1981 and the 1997 Macpherson report into institutional racism in the Metropolitan Police.

By contrast, Germany has only recently begun to acknowledge that it is an ethnically and culturally diverse society. Indeed, the extent to which this is the case has only become clear in the last few years: in 2005, the *Mikrozensus* revealed that over 15 million people in Germany, or almost one in five inhabitants, had some form of migrant background.[28] Much of this gradual transformation can be traced back to unification. This not only unleashed unprecedented migratory forces in the form of asylum seekers and ethnic Germans, but also rendered void one of the defining purposes of West Germany's citizenship policy: the undermining of the GDR.[29] Even so, the distinction between 'Germans' and 'others' remains largely intact, as illustrated by the party political focus on the perceived unwillingness of existing non-nationals (*Bestandsausländer*) to integrate into German society. In the UK, Tony Blair did make a similar call on immigrants to conform in a speech on 8 December 2006, but this was generally directed at new, not existing, communities – a fine but important distinction.[30]

As the remainder of this contribution will show, these broadly different starting points have nonetheless led to policy convergence in a number of areas, although some significant differences inevitably remain. Where convergence has taken place, it has done so as a result of a number of pressures, and it is to these that the discussion now turns.

PRESSURES TOWARDS CONVERGENCE

The pressures towards policy convergence in the UK and Germany can broadly be categorised under two headings: exogenous and endogenous pressures. In turn, under the rubric of exogenous pressures, two principal forces can be identified: asylum seekers and terrorism. Certainly, asylum is not a new political issue in Germany. As Figure 1 shows, (West) Germany has accepted large numbers of asylum seekers ever since 1980. Indeed, during the 1980s and early 1990s, asylum within the EU was in

FIGURE 1
ASYLUM APPLICATIONS IN EU-15, 1980–2005

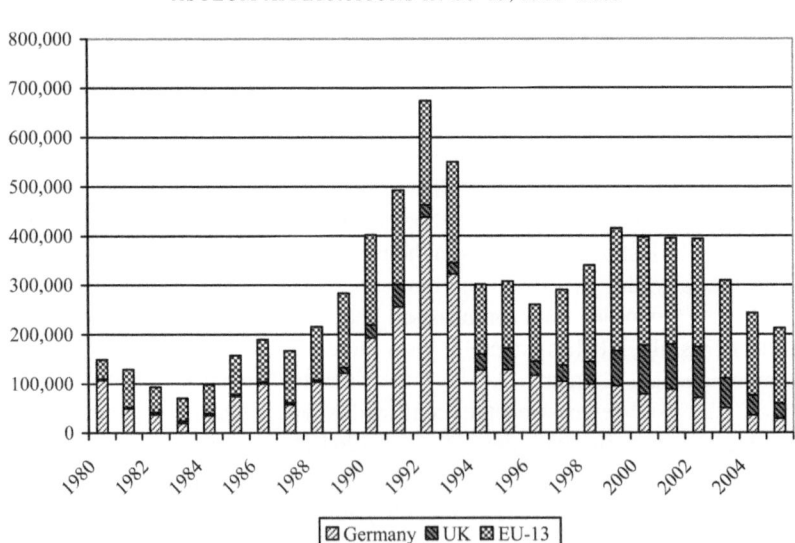

Note: The number of asylum seekers is not the same as asylum applications, as multiple persons can make one application in the UK.
Source: UNHCR; own calculations

effect a purely (West) German problem, as anything up to two-thirds of annual applications to EU-15 countries were made in Germany.

But Figure 1 also shows that, following the constitutional changes in 1993, the numbers of asylum seekers to Germany began to drop off; indeed, in 2005, just 29,000 applications were made in Germany, the lowest level for 20 years. Of course, the pressures for asylum themselves did not disappear (witness the rising number of total applications to the EU-15 from 1996 to 2002). Instead, applications were spread over a larger number of countries and, for the first time, asylum was no longer a *de facto* German problem.

In the first instance, it was in fact the UK which replaced Germany as the EU's primary destination for asylum seekers.[31] In 2000, the UK exceeded Germany's total asylum applications for the first time, and it has continued to do so in subsequent years too. From 2000 to 2003, the UK was in fact the favoured destination for asylum applications in the EU, although it was overtaken in 2004 by France. However, it must also be noted that the scale of asylum applications to the UK at all times remained far lower than in Germany during the early 1990s: even at their peak in 2002, the number of asylum seekers to the UK was lower than the 107,000 applications lodged in West Germany as early as 1980. But, crucially, the increase in numbers has raised much the same kinds of policy questions in the UK as it has done in Germany, as the existing 'liberal universalist' model of asylum has come under severe pressure.[32] It also opened up the possibility of both countries cooperating together in context of the EU to achieve EU-wide solutions, a point which will be returned to below.

The second key exogenous pressure, which has also taken on an endogenous dimension, especially in Britain, has been that of security generally, and terrorism more specifically. Although in both countries there has always been an internal security dimension to migration policy, this has taken on a much more dominant role in the aftermath of the terrorist attacks on New York and Washington DC on 11 September 2001, and the subsequent suicide bombings in London in July 2005.[33] Both countries have considered themselves in the front line against (radical Islamic) terrorism, due not only to the fact that both have large Muslim populations, but also because a considerable number of Islamic fundamentalists, such as the cleric Abu Hamza and Metin Kaplan were granted asylum or settled in Britain and Germany respectively after fleeing political persecution in their home countries. Unsurprisingly, following the suicide bombings in London in July 2005, this issue has been more explicit in the UK than in Germany. Overall, the spectre of terrorism has contributed both to the explicit 'securitisation' of immigration policy, especially at EU level,[34] as well as to a renewed emphasis on assimilatory elements of integration and citizenship, as the discussion below will argue.[35]

These two major exogenous pressures towards convergence are complemented by two further endogenous factors: demographic and skills shortages, and the persistence of apparent structural deficits in the integration of immigrants and non-nationals. Demographically, both countries are about to feel the full impact of long-term shifts in population structures, in particular the sharp reduction in the fertility rate most European countries have experienced at various stages since the early 1970s. In 2004, Germany's fertility rate was just 1.4 children per woman; in the UK, it was

1.8 – better, but nowhere near the 2.2 level needed for population stability.[36] What is more, this reduction in the number of children born in the UK and Germany has combined with increasing life expectancies to multiply the deleterious impact on support ratios between those of working age (15–64) and the remainder of the population. In this context, the UN Population Division in 2000 famously, albeit rather crudely, calculated that the number of immigrants required by the UK and Germany to keep support ratios at their 1995 levels, about 4:1 in both countries, was 1 million and 3.4 million respectively per annum.[37] Certainly, (non-EU) immigration is by itself not a viable solution to such structural developments, as immigrants of working age are destined to retire from the labour market themselves at a future stage. But, tellingly, the Office of National Statistics' prediction that the UK population will grow to 67 million by 2031 is largely predicated on continuing net immigration. By contrast, Germany's population is predicted to fall to around 73 million by 2050 *despite* assumed net immigration of 200,000 persons per annum.[38]

The UK and Germany's demographic problems are complicated by persistent skills shortages in key areas of the economy. In the UK, the Learning and Skills Council identified some 679,000 vacancies in the UK economy for 2003, principally in health and social work, business services and hotels and catering.[39] In Germany, too, skills shortages have persisted despite high levels of unemployment, with a survey of employers showing acute shortfalls in the pharmaceutical, engineering and information technology sectors.[40] Together, this combination of skills and demographic shortages has created strong pressure in both countries, especially from business interests, in favour of a more relaxed approach to labour migration.

The second endogenous factor towards convergence has been growing concerns about integration outcomes. In both countries, migrants and their descendants are, generally speaking, more likely than the indigenous population to suffer from lower educational outcomes, lower incomes and lower language skills.[41] In particular, their unemployment rates are often double those of the population as a whole.[42] Significantly, these integration problems are not spread equally across national or ethnic groups: in the UK, Pakistanis and Bangladeshis are particularly disadvantaged in terms of education and labour market outcomes, while in Germany, Turkish and ex-Yugoslav nationals are the most affected. Notably, ethnic German immigrants, who have already been granted citizenship on entry to the country, display strikingly similar patterns of exclusion to the non-national population. Overall, both countries are grappling with comparable problems of social cohesion within and between their respective immigrant and non-national communities.

One further pressure towards convergence needs to be considered at this point: the European Union. Over the past 15 years the EU's influence in this field has grown exponentially: its immigration policy has evolved from 'loose intergovernmental cooperation to a partially communitarised policy-making area' under the 1997 Treaty of Amsterdam, with an explicit aspiration of developing a common asylum policy for all EU member states.[43] Certainly, the process of 'Europeanisation' in this particular field is multifaceted, encompassing both the framing of issues and their governance, both of which have generated a rich body of academic literature;[44] the resulting implications of Europeanisation for policy convergence more generally are also examined in greater detail in the Introduction and in Simon Bulmer's contribution to this collection. But, essentially, Europeanisation can be considered to consist of both the 'uploading' of national policy preferences into the supranational policy-making process, and the 'downloading' of EU policy into the national policy arena, and it is these aspects which, within the spatial limitations of this discussion, will be the primary focus here.

Yet despite setting the goal of a common immigration and asylum policy, as well as its affirmation in the European Council meetings at Tampere in 1999 and at The Hague in 2004, progress towards fulfilling it has been painstakingly slow, for several reasons. For one thing, EU member states' interests are quite heterogeneous in this area. Although pressures of numbers in asylum now affect most European countries, they do not do so equally – of EU-15 states, Italy, Portugal and Spain all received less than 1 asylum application per 1,000 inhabitants during 2001–5, compared with 3.3 for Germany and 5.5 for the UK.[45] Second, because immigration is a classic 'high politics' area, concerns over loss of sovereignty are also clearly visible in this sector – witness the UK's refusal to participate in the Schengen Accord on border controls under the Treaty of Amsterdam, as well as in the EU's common visa policy. Lastly, the bar for achieving a communitarised policy is set higher in this policy field than in others: whereas the single market can operate according to the principle of 'mutual recognition' of standards and norms, a common immigration area cannot do so, and therefore requires full-scale harmonisation. Unsurprisingly, and given the first two factors, this has been difficult to achieve.[46] Key directives in this field on family reunification, asylum and the status of long-term resident third country nationals have only been agreed after literally years of negotiations.[47] Collectively, it can be argued that such directives have established something approaching an EU-wide immigration policy. Even so, in order to achieve agreement between member states, they have in part fallen back on principles such as mutual recognition, for instance in the conditions for granting long-term residence status to TCNs, as well as, in the case of family reunification, so-called EU-wide 'minimum standards'.[48] The extent to which the EU's immigration policy can be considered to be harmonised fully thus remains very much open to debate.

Nonetheless, the UK and Germany have both at different times been keen to use the EU in order to find solutions to their own national problems. During the height of asylum applications to Germany in the early 1990s, the CDU/CSU–FDP government under Helmut Kohl made it a political priority to seek an EU-wide asylum policy. However, given the widespread opposition to this from other, less affected member states, Germany had to content itself with the inclusion of asylum and immigration under the intergovernmental 'third pillar' of the 1992 Treaty of Maastricht.[49] Subsequently, the government reverted to a domestic solution in the form of the 1993 constitutional amendments, after which Germany became much less willing to support integration at all costs. This trend increased as it became apparent that the European Commission was pursuing a somewhat more liberal line on asylum than Germany was prepared to countenance.[50]

Similarly, the UK's discovery of the European arena coincided with the peak in its asylum applications between 2000 and 2003.[51] Despite having secured the possibility to 'opt in' to this area under the Treaty of Amsterdam, the UK signed up to all seven measures on asylum adopted by the EU between 1999 and 2004. Andrew Geddes therefore concludes that 'Britain has thus become a little more European in its migration management policies in the hope that Europe will become a little more British in terms of convergent policy preferences'.[52] At the same time, both countries also use their EU membership as a forum for informal coordination. Along with France, Italy and Spain and Poland, both are members of the so-called 'G-6' group of large member states, whose regular meetings, including in this policy area, have served as to coordinate policies and actions.

CONVERGENCE AND NON-CONVERGENCE IN POLICY AGENDAS AND RESPONSES

This, then, is the historical and topical background against which policy convergence can be considered. And, indeed, it is apparent that some convergence in policy goals, both domestic and European, as well as to some extent in actual policy instruments adopted, has taken place between the two countries, even though divergence persists in other areas. Without claiming to be exhaustive, especially with reference to EU initiatives, the following section draws on a range of examples from the domestic and supranational arenas to illustrate this argument. It is subdivided into three substantive areas, each of which illustrates increasing levels of convergence: labour and dependant migration, citizenship and integration policy, and asylum policy.

Labour and Dependant Migration

Initially, labour migration represented one of the core elements of the process of modernisation in immigration policy to which New Labour and the SPD–Green governments aspired. Instead of maintaining their predecessors' ultimately undeliverable promises to prevent (non-ethnic) immigration altogether,[53] the centre-left governments in the UK and Germany resolved instead to structure migration to the respective countries' advantage. This change in perspective coincided not only with demographic and skills issues returning to the fore, but also with the boom of the 'New Economy', with its seemingly insatiable demand for new ideas and skills in information technology. And it was this sector which proved to be the catalyst to new labour migration in both countries.[54] In February 2000, Chancellor Schröder, to widespread acclaim from business leaders, announced the introduction of the so-called 'Green Card' scheme, under which up to 20,000 IT specialists would be allowed to work for up to five years in Germany. Despite its limited scope, this proposal helped redefine the terms of the debate, by emphasising for the first time in almost 30 years that new immigration could actually benefit Germany.[55] This principle was carried forward in 2001 into the discussion over the form a possible comprehensive immigration law (*Zuwanderungsgesetz*), the first in Germany's history, might take. The so-called Süssmuth Commission, which was set up by Interior Minister Otto Schily to develop reform proposals, even suggested a points-based system to attract an annual quota of high-skilled migrants, plus additional migration in shortage sectors.[56]

In the end, though, the Commission's recommendations proved too radical a change in political terms. Faced with an electorate which remained deeply sceptical about immigration, not least in times of record unemployment, the opposition

CDU/CSU dropped its initial support for the government. Ultimately, the new law, which did not come into force until 1 January 2005, failed to go beyond providing limited entry possibilities to individual high-skilled migrants from outside the EU. Tellingly, the Green Card programme itself proved not to be a great draw either: not even the initial, distinctly modest quota could be fulfilled.[57] What is more, holders of Green Cards quickly came up against ingrained administrative patterns of implementation, which continued to view their very presence as undesirable.[58] Yet, despite such setbacks, the issue of new labour migration remains very much on the political agenda and, during 2006, the CDU/CSU–SPD Grand Coalition began to explore once more the possibility of introducing a points-based entry system for high-skilled migrants.[59]

In the UK, the policy response to demographic and skills shortages was similar, although it went much further than in Germany. In contrast to its German counterpart, the Home Office from the outset went on the offensive in terms of framing labour migration, both skilled and unskilled, as indispensable to the UK economy; crucially, and in direct contrast to Germany, it met with little resistance, due no doubt also to the continued buoyant economic situation in Britain.[60] Thus, in early 2002, the UK government introduced the Highly Skilled Migrants Programme (HSMP), which aimed to attract non-EU professionals, principally in finance, information technology and medical services, and which sat alongside a range of entry schemes for both high-skilled and lesser skilled migrants.[61] But in the UK, too, the HSMP has not been seen as a success, due to its cumbersome process and perceived inflexibility.[62] Since then, the UK government, in its five-year strategy for migration published in 2005, has outlined plans to consolidate all existing entry schemes into a single, points-based system of recruitment.[63]

In labour migration, then, there has been a certain degree of convergence around the overall policy goal of facilitating the immigration of skilled labour. There has also been convergence around the policy instruments for facilitating such migration, in the form of a points system. That said, the UK has been prepared to countenance a much wider definition of labour migration than Germany, to include lower and even unskilled migrants. Clearly, along with more favourable public opinion, the strength of the UK labour market compared to Germany's (see the contribution by Funk to this collection) is a major factor behind the UK's hitherto more liberal approach.

Indeed, this constitutes the principal dimension of divergence between the two countries, which became most clearly visible in their responses to the 2004 accession of eight central and eastern European countries to the EU. Germany, together with Austria, imposed a seven-year delay in the implementation of free movement of labour for these states, whereas the UK, Ireland and Sweden opened their labour markets immediately. However, despite its restrictions, Germany has been grappling with formally self-employed tile-layers and abattoir workers from accession states undercutting existing labour. Even the UK government has been taken by surprise by the extent of labour migration from these countries: between May 2004 and June 2006, a total of almost 447,000 workers, mainly from Poland, were registered in the UK.[64] This has been far more than the government originally estimated and has prompted the Home Office to limit access to the UK labour market to self-employed workers from Bulgaria and Romania following these countries' accession on 1 January 2007.

Dependant migration constitutes a further area of divergence in both policy goals and instruments between the UK and Germany.[65] In Germany, this has been one of the most protracted areas of dispute in immigration policy, and the subject of party conflict since the early 1980s. The single most recurrent issue has been the age limit for children to immigrate to join their parents, which has been set at 16 since 1981, but which the CDU/CSU has periodically attempted to lower to 12, 10 or even 6. By contrast, although family reunification has been recognised as an important issue, it has rarely been politicised in the UK in the same way as in Germany, and certainly not around the same totemic issue. Indeed, when the 2003 Directive on Family Reunification set a minimum age of 12 for any limitation of the immigration of dependant minors, this represented a direct 'uploading' of the debate at that time in Germany (which was being held in the context of the discussions over the *Zuwanderungsgesetz*); other member states could of course choose to diverge upwards in setting this limit. In the UK, by contrast, family reunification has never been as polarised as in Germany; indeed, the UK chose not to opt in to the EU Directive. Here, then, is a further example of the power of path dependence: because the German discussion about family reunification has been framed for over 20 years around the specific issue of the maximum age of dependant minors, this not only continues to affect contemporary policy-making (witness the discussions about the *Zuwanderungsgesetz* between 2000 and 2004),[66] but has even shaped policy instruments for the EU as a whole.

Citizenship and Integration Policy

The second area where policy convergence can be identified is in citizenship and integration policy. As was noted above, this policy area has grown in importance within this sector as a result of the persistence of structural integration problems in both countries. An additional catalyst in this respect has also been the impact of 9/11, which not only moved security considerations into the spotlight, but also raised public expectations of immigrants to identify actively with, and to assimilate more explicitly into, their countries of residence.[67] This convergence in policy agendas has generated specific convergence in three principal areas.

First, the formal provisions for naturalisation are converging, not only in the UK and Germany but also across other EU member states.[68] Indeed, the direction of convergence is interesting: whereas Germany, like most other EU countries, tended to liberalise its citizenship provisions during the 1990s, the British Nationality Act 1981 actually represented a restriction. In both cases, this can be put down to respective historical traditions: thus, Germany started from an almost completely exclusive position in the 1970s, while the main policy challenge for the UK during the 1960s and 1970s was to manage the retreat from the expansive definitions of the British Nationality Act 1948. But, certainly, a degree of convergence is crystallising in citizenship policy, with both countries employing a mixture of *ius soli* and *ius sanguinis* in the ascription of citizenship at birth, and both countries as a rule requiring between five and ten years' residence for naturalisation.

Second, these baseline requirements have been supplemented in recent years by additional criteria aimed at raising the symbolic value of obtaining British and German citizenship. In the Nationality, Immigration and Asylum Act 2002, the UK introduced both citizenship tests and ceremonies, which themselves drew heavily on the practises of countries such as Canada and Australia.[69] Germany followed suit in mid-2006, with the Länder collectively agreeing on the inclusion and organisation of naturalisation tests and a formal ceremony, both of which had hitherto been implemented only on an *ad hoc* basis.[70]

In fact, the introduction of integration courses and tests generally is emerging as an area of convergence between the two countries. However, this was not always the case. Germany was first to introduce integration and language classes in the 2004 Zuwanderungsgesetz and in doing so explicitly modelled these on the Netherlands, where such courses were set up in 1998. Accordingly, they were linked to permanent residence and not nationality, while the opposite was true for the UK. But now, not only is Germany making naturalisations subject to tests, but in his speech of 8 December 2006 Tony Blair also announced that the UK would introduce a language requirement for permanent residence.[71] Even though the two countries' respective philosophies of integration persist (see above), it is clear, therefore, that integration policy as structured by government is starting to show distinct signs of convergence. Significantly, this convergence is not limited to the UK and Germany, but encompasses other member states too.[72]

Third, following the inclusion of an anti-discrimination provision in Article 13 of the Treaty of Amsterdam, which came into force in 1999, a Racial Equality Directive and an Employment Equality Directive were passed only one year later in 2000.[73] Of these, the content and aims of the former bears close resemblance to the UK model of race relations legislation (see above). At first sight, this therefore appears to be a clear example of an 'uploading' to the EU and subsequent diffusion to other EU member states of existing UK norms and practices. But, as Andrew Geddes and Virginie Guiraudon show in a fascinating study, the full picture is more complex.[74] They argue that the very adoption of Article 13 at Amsterdam was contingent on the victory of centre-left governments in both France and the UK in early 1997, both of which, albeit for different reasons, favoured its inclusion in the Treaty. Furthermore, the SPD–Green government in Germany, having won the 1998 federal election, then also committed itself to formulating Germany's first anti-discrimination law in its subsequent coalition agreement.[75] This meant that when the European Commission tabled the first draft of the Race Equality Directive in late 1999, the broad policy goals of the governments of three key EU member states had already converged, although this was due less to ideological factors than to an independent alignment of national positions. However, ideology did come into play in the adoption of the policy instrument in the form of the Directive itself, which was completed by June 2000, just seven months after being introduced. Although Geddes and Guiraudon also acknowledge the role of the Portuguese Presidency in this process, they pinpoint one factor in particular: the formation of the new Austrian government in early 2000 to include the extremist Freedom Party under Jörg Haider. This prompted other member states, mainly with centre-left governments, to back this Directive, even in cases where, as in France and Germany, the country's traditional interpretation of the role of anti-discrimination legislation did not match with the focus of the policy instrument.[76] The Directive was finally transposed into German national law during 2006.

The case of the Race Equality Directive highlights how convergence in policy instruments can occur. Certainly, the EU played an indispensable role in this; but at the same time, the independent convergence of national positions was a vital precondition for the success of the Commission's initiative.[77] Interestingly, the question of an ideological convergence of governments appears only to have played a subsidiary role, principally in determining the response to Austria's new government. Yet, in this area, the Directive arguably represents the start of convergence, not its conclusion, as both national courts and the European Court of Justice are likely to guide its implementation.

Even so, areas of divergence remain in citizenship and integration policy, and they are areas in which the historical legacies in both countries are arguably most clearly visible. First, there is clear divergence in the status of nationality as a policy goal. In the UK, as noted above, the acquisition of nationality is not politically contested in any real way. This is due also to the fact that the UK's (Commonwealth) immigrants already possess voting rights, which is itself a clear historical legacy and one which affects the structure of British citizenship in a path dependent fashion. In Germany, by contrast, the incorporation of non-nationals, over 20 per cent of whom were actually born in Germany, has continued to be sluggish. Correspondingly, access to citizenship rights remains a substantive political issue which is hotly contested, not least for electoral reasons: ethnic German immigrants tend to vote overwhelmingly for the CDU/CSU, while naturalised immigrants, for instance of Turkish origin, support the SPD and Greens by a comparable margin.[78] Similarly, the question of to what degree dual citizenship should be tolerated in Germany, although latent, remains highly salient; conversely, there is no real prospect of it being politicised in the UK.

Asylum Policy

The third area to be considered, and the one which shows the greatest degree of convergence, has been asylum policy.[79] In two key respects, convergence in fact took place long before the election of New Labour and the SPD–Green coalition to government: during the 1980s, both the UK and West Germany used visa requirements and carrier sanctions for undocumented immigration to prevent asylum seekers from even being able to lodge a claim in the country. Nonetheless, the fact that for most of the 1980s and 1990s asylum was a 'German problem' (see above) meant that there was little direct convergence beyond the general desire in both governments to keep claims for asylum as low as possible. However, this changed in the late 1990s with the sharp increase in asylum applications to the UK. Faced with record numbers (and record costs), the UK government drew on a range of ideas first developed in the German context.

First and foremost, in 2000, the UK introduced a formal system of 'dispersal' for asylum seekers, in order to spread their accommodation around the country, as opposed to London and the South East (in particular Kent), which had hitherto borne the brunt of this task.[80] This instrument drew obvious comparisons with Germany, where the Länder have been allocated fixed proportions of the total number of asylum applications since the late 1970s. Although the two countries' systems of dispersal in fact differ in key respects,[81] it is the similarity in their aims, a more-or-less formal system of 'burden-sharing', which is of relevance here.

Second, and linked to this, the UK in 2000 replaced its cash payments to asylum seekers. Under the new system, asylum seekers received the bulk of their welfare payments via vouchers, which could be used to purchase goods in shops and supermarkets. This too drew on German practices, in which welfare is mostly provided 'in kind', for instance in the form of food parcels, but where some municipalities also use a voucher system.[82] However, in the UK the system was heavily criticised for the fact that the retailers would not be required to give change on the vouchers. Unhelpfully for the government, the French company Sodexho, which had run the German version and which was now operating the British scheme, issued promotional literature in which retailers were urged to sign up in order to exploit the 'revenue-making opportunities' this presented.[83] In 2002, the vouchers were dropped for asylum seekers in favour of a return to cash payments, thereby actually marking a divergence from German policy instruments.

Third, the UK has, in the Nationality, Immigration and Asylum Act 2002, introduced a so-called 'White List' of countries from which asylum applications are not accepted. Again, this draws on the 'Safe Country of Origin' category introduced in Germany as early as 1993, although the countries listed notably do not coincide. In Germany, non-European countries on the list are limited to Ghana and Senegal, while the UK in November 2006 considered Brazil, Ecuador, Bolivia, South Africa, India, Jamaica, Mongolia and Sri Lanka to be safe, as well as Ghana and Nigeria for male applicants only.

Overall, then, in those areas where a broad convergence in domestic asylum policy has taken place, the UK has tended to follow, and on occasion even exceed, the German example. Curiously, an almost reverse picture emerges in the case of debates at EU level, due largely to Germany's growing reluctance to integrate further in this policy area. For instance, in the 2004 Qualifications Directive,[84] Germany finally accepted the principle of recognition of non-state agents of persecution in asylum; hitherto, this question had been one of the most visible and contested elements of divergence between several EU member states, including the UK and Germany. A second example concerns the processing of asylum seekers: in the run-up to the 2003 European Council meeting in Thessaloniki, the UK proposed that 'regional protection areas' (in areas of origin) and 'transit processing areas' (in neighbouring countries to the EU) be set up, with the aim of preventing asylum seekers from even arriving in the EU. While these proposals were roundly rejected by Germany at the time, Interior Minister Otto Schily performed a remarkable volte-face just one year later, by supporting similar Italian proposals.[85]

But the EU has also served as a vehicle for informal cooperation in areas of mutual interest. Key among these has been the sensitive area of the repatriation of failed asylum seekers: in both countries, numbers of removals have been low in recent years, and both countries' governments have grappled with the practical issues surrounding repatriation.[86] In this context, the Interior Ministers of the UK and Germany, along with their counterparts from France, Italy and Spain, agreed in 2005 to operate joint repatriation flights to countries of origin. In May 2006, this initiative was adopted by all 25 member states.[87]

As the previous examples show, the extent of convergence, both in the overall policy goals and some of the actual instruments adopted, is considerable, and greater than in labour migration and citizenship and integration policy. This development is certainly linked to the fact that asylum has constituted an explicit common policy challenge to both countries, encouraging common responses. Indeed, the pressures have been such that policy divergence is now effectively limited to individual policy instruments, but not policy goals.

CONCLUSION

The preceding analysis has argued that there is notable convergence between the UK and Germany in a number of goals in immigration policy, as well as in a range of specific policy instruments adopted. This convergence is most evident in asylum policy, but also in citizenship policy and, to a lesser extent, labour migration policy. The extent of convergence in this sector is summarised in Table 2.

Most significantly, where convergence has occurred, it has done so despite the very different historical traditions of response to immigration in both countries. It has also done so despite differences in public opinion and differences in the political system, which after all affects the way in which policy goals are articulated and negotiated. This testifies to the strength of the endogenous and exogenous pressures identified – the demographic rationale for new labour migration, the sheer pressures of numbers in the asylum system and the politicisation of integration deficits, real or otherwise. In particular, and despite the UK's *de iure* opt-in, the EU stands out as a key vehicle towards convergence, especially in the field of asylum policy, where harmonisation is most advanced. The EU has not only acted as a source of policy initiatives in its own right, but has also afforded both countries the opportunity to 'escape to Europe' in seeking solutions to their national asylum problems. In addition, EU membership has as provided a forum for Germany and the UK to coordinate policy instruments, for instance in the context of the G-6 group of member states.

Nonetheless, divergent goals and instruments remain in a number of areas and their persistence can largely be explained historically. This is certainly the case for approaches to integration and family reunification, and arguably labour migration too. Even if overall German unemployment levels were much lower, it is a moot point whether new non-EU labour migration would be tolerated politically and electorally. Path dependence thus remains an important factor in understanding particularly policy goals in this field.

Neither this convergence nor the instrumental nature of their relationship with the EU is limited to the UK and Germany. Other EU immigration countries, principally France, the Netherlands, Austria and Sweden share many of the same pressures; they also share at least some of the policy goals and at least some of the policy instruments in at least some of the areas considered here. Indeed, membership of the EU itself represents one of the central pressures towards convergence in a global context.[88] But equally, it is fair to conclude that, within EU member states, the UK and Germany show a high degree of convergence across a range of fields.

TABLE 2
POLICY CONVERGENCE IN IMMIGRATION AND INTEGRATION POLICY

	Labour and dependant migration	Citizenship and integration	Asylum policy
Convergence in goals	Yes	Yes	Yes
Convergence in instruments	No	Partial	Partial
Key aspects of divergence	Unskilled labour migration; dependant migration	Philosophies of integration; dual citizenship	Limited to individual elements

How much of this is due to the purported ideological closeness of the Labour and SPD–Green governments? Apart from the general and abstract desire to shape labour migration in the respective country's interests, as well as the example of the adoption of the 2000 Race Equality Directive, a common ideological purpose, as put forward in the Third Way document, is difficult to distinguish. Instead, where convergence has taken place, it has generally been in response to the various pressures outlined here, refracted through the prism of national political priorities.

To conclude, the extent of policy convergence established here is likely to increase in coming years. Not only will the pressures identified above persist in at least the medium term, but the EU is expanding into new areas of activity, as laid down in the 2004 Hague Programme.[89] One of these is the management of economic migration, on which the Commission published a Green Paper in 2005.[90] Therefore, in immigration and integration policy, not only in the UK and Germany but across the EU, convergence appears to be very much the order of the day.

NOTES

The author would like to thank Insa Nolte, Thomas Saalfeld and Ed Turner for comments on an earlier version of this piece.

1. See comparative data in Beauftragte der Bundesregierung für Migration, Flüchtlinge und Integration, *Daten – Fakten – Trends: Deutschland im Europäischen Vergleich* (Berlin: Beauftragte der Bundesregierung, 2005).
2. Strictly speaking, a differentiation needs to be made between immigrants (i.e. foreign-born residents) and non-nationals (residents without the nationality of their country of residence), where the former term is more common in the UK, and the latter is preferred in Germany.
3. C. Boswell, *European Migration Policies in Flux: Changing Patterns of Inclusion and Exclusion* (London/Oxford: Royal Institute for International Affairs/Blackwell, 2003), pp.74–5.
4. T. Blair and G. Schröder, *Europe: The Third Way*, available at http://www.socialdemocrats.org/blairandschroeder6-8-99.html (accessed 20 September 2006).
5. D. Flynn, 'New Borders, New Management: The Dilemmas of Modern Immigration Policy', *Ethnic and Racial Studies* 28/3 (2005), pp.463–90; S. Green, *The Politics of Exclusion: Institutions and Immigration Policy in Contemporary Germany* (Manchester: Manchester University Press, 2004), pp.95–7.
6. C. Bennett, 'Review Article: What Is Policy Convergence and What Causes It?', *British Journal of Political Science* 21 (1991), pp.215–33.
7. G. Peters, *Institutional Theory in Political Science: The New Institutionalism* (London: Pinter, 1999), p.63.
8. See for instance R. Brubaker, *Citizenship and Nationhood in France and Germany* (Cambridge, MA: Harvard University Press, 1992); R. Hansen, *Citizenship and Immigration in Post-War Britain* (Oxford: Oxford University Press, 2000).
9. Z. Layton-Henry, 'Citizenship and Nationality in Britain', in Z. Layton-Henry and C. Wilpert (eds.), *Challenging Racism in Britain and Germany* (Basingstoke: Palgrave, 2003).
10. R. Hansen, 'The Dog that Didn't Bark: Dual Nationality in the United Kingdom', in R. Hansen and P. Weil (eds.), *Dual Nationality, Social Rights and Federal Citizenship in the US and Europe* (Oxford: Berghahn, 2002).
11. For a magisterial discussion of this process and the politics which surrounded it, see Hansen, *Citizenship and Immigration*.
12. See Hansen, *Citizenship and Immigration*, pp.250–53.
13. Cf. Boswell, *European Migration Policies*, pp.77–9.
14. A. Favell, *Philosophies of Integration*, 2nd edition (Basingstoke: Palgrave, 2001); see also S. Glover et al., *Migration: an Economic and Social Analysis*, RDS Occasional Paper No. 67 (London: Home Office, 2001).
15. Cited in Favell, *Philosophies of Integration*, p.104.
16. Cf. C. Munro, 'Race Laws and Policy in the United Kingdom', in Layton-Henry and Wilpert, *Challenging Racism*; see also C. Joppke, *Immigration and the Nation-State* (Oxford: Oxford University Press, 1999), pp.223–59.

17. On this era in Germany, see K. Schönwälder, *Einwanderung und ethnische Pluralität. Politische Entscheidungen und öffentliche Debatten in Großbritannien und der Bundesrepublik von den 1950er bis zu den 1970er Jahren* (Essen: Klartext, 2001); U. Herbert, *Geschichte der Ausländerpolitik in Deutschland* (München: C.H. Beck, 2001), pp.191–230; J. Motte, R. Ohliger and A. Von Oswald (eds.), *50 Jahre Bundesrepublik: 50 Jahre Einwanderung* (Frankfurt a.M.: Campus, 1999).
18. See D. Bischoff and W. Teubner, *Zwischen Einbürgerung und Rückkehr. Ausländerpolitik und Ausländerrecht in der Bundesrepublik Deutschland* (Berlin: Hitit Verlag, 1991), pp.113–17.
19. Cf. Green, *The Politics of Exclusion*, pp.31, 84–8.
20. S. Green, 'Immigration and Integration Policy: Between Incrementalism and Non-Decisions', in S. Green and W. Paterson (eds.), *Governance in Contemporary Germany: The Semisovereign State Revisited* (Cambridge: Cambridge University Press, 2005).
21. Joppke, *Immigration and the Nation State*, p.73.
22. Green, *The Politics of Exclusion*, pp.39–41.
23. Cf. D. Klusmeyer, 'A "Guiding Culture" for Immigrants? Integration and Diversity in Germany', *Journal of Ethnic and Migration Studies* 27/3 (2001), pp.519–32.
24. On the question of how the 1913 citizenship law came to form the basis of citizenship in West Germany, see Brubaker, *Citizenship and Nationhood*, pp.168–71; also P. Hogwood, 'Citizenship Controversies in Germany: The Twin Legacy of *Völkisch* Nationalism and the *Alleinvertretungsanspruch*', *German Politics* 9/3 (2000), pp.125–44.
25. The formulation of the new citizenship law was itself accompanied by one of the most polarised controversies of recent years in Germany, which revolved around the proposed acceptance of dual citizenship. See Green, *The Politics of Exclusion*, pp.79–109.
26. Numbers of naturalisations have fallen every year between 2000 (the first year of operation of the new law) and 2005. See S. Green, 'Between Ideology and Pragmatism: The Politics of Dual Nationality in Germany', *International Migration Review* 39/4 (2005), pp.921–52, here pp.944–6; also S. Green, 'Beyond Ethnoculturalism? German Citizenship in the New Millennium', *German Politics* 9/3 (2000), pp.105–24.
27. In which the Conservatives infamously ran campaign posters bearing the slogan 'If you want a nigger neighbour, vote Liberal or Labour'. Quoted in Hansen, *Citizenship and Immigration in Post-War Britain*, pp.132–5.
28. 'Deutschland: 15 Mio. Einwohner mit "Migrationshintergrund"', *Migration und Bevölkerung* 5(2006), available at http://www.migration-info.de/migration_und_bevoelkerung/artikel/060502.htm (accessed 5 September 2006). Persons with 'Migrant background' are defined as those who have migrated themselves, or whose parents or grandparents have migrated to Germany.
29. S. Green, 'Immigration, Asylum and Citizenship in Germany: The Impact of Unification and the Berlin Republic', *West European Politics* 24/4 (2001), pp.82–104.
30. Tony Blair, 'The Duty to Integrate: Shared British Values', 8 December 2006, available at http://www.prime-minister.gov.uk/output/Page10563.asp (accessed 8 December 2006).
31. Although not, it must be noted in relative terms, where smaller EU member states, especially Belgium, Ireland, Austria and Sweden, have much higher levels of applications per 1,000 population than either the UK or Germany. See UNHCR, *Asylum Levels and Trends in Industrialized Countries 2005* (Geneva: UNHCR, 2006), available at http://www.unhcr.org (accessed 12 September 2006).
32. C. Boswell, 'European Values and the Asylum Crisis', *International Affairs* 76/3 (2000), pp.537–57.
33. Cf., for instance, N. Choucri, 'Migration and Security: Some Key Linkages', *Journal of International Affairs* 56/1 (2002), pp.97–122; T. Faist, 'Extension du Domaine de la Lutte: International Migration and Security before and after September 11, 2001', *International Migration Review* 36/1 (2002), pp.7–14.
34. Cf. J. Huysmans, 'The European Union and the Securitization of Migration', *Journal of Common Market Studies* 38 (2000), pp.751–77.
35. See C. Joppke and E. Morawska (eds.), *Towards Assimilation and Citizenship* (London: Palgrave, 2003).
36. See Eurostat, *Key Figures on Europe: Statistical Pocketbook 2006* (Luxembourg: Office for Official Publications of the European Communities, 2006), p.43, available at http://epp.eurostat.ec.europa.eu/cache/ITY_OFFPUB/KS-EI-06-001/EN/KS-EI-06-001-EN.PDF (accessed 12 September 2006).
37. United Nations Population Division, *Replacement Migration: Is it a Solution to Declining and Ageing Populations* (New York: United Nations Population Division, 2000), available at http://www.un.org/esa/population/publications/migration/migration.htm (accessed 12 September 2006); see also S. Green, 'Immigration to the UK and Germany: A Panacea for Declining Labour Forces?', in. L. Funk and S. Green (eds.), *New Aspects of Labour Market Policy* (Berlin: Verlag Wissenschaft und Forschung, 2002).

38. Animated population pyramids for Germany and the UK, which include assumptions of net immigration, are available, respectively, at http://www.destatis.de/basis/d/bevoe/bev_svg_var.php (accessed 12 September 2006) and http://www.statistics.gov.uk/populationestimates/svg_pyramid/default.htm (accessed 12 September 2006).
39. Cited in Institute for Public Policy Research, *Labour Migration to the UK: An IPPR Factfile* (London: IPPR, 2004), p.12.
40. Deutscher Industrie- und Handelskammertag, *Ruhe vor dem Sturm. Arbeitskräftemangel in der Wirtschaft* (Berlin: DIHK, 2005), available at http://www.dihk.de/inhalt/download/studie_arbeitskraeftemangel.pdf (accessed 12 September 2006); cf. A. Reinberg and M. Hummel, 'Fachkräftemangel bedroht Wettbewerbsfähigkeit der deutschen Wirtschaft', *Aus Politik und Zeitgeschichte* B28 (2004), pp.3–10; also 'Mittelständler beklagen Fachkräftemangel', *Die Welt*, 1 December 2006.
41. See for instance data in Beauftragte der Bundesregierung für Migration, Flüchtlinge und Integration, *6. Bericht der Beauftragten der Bundesregierung für Migration, Flüchtlinge und Integration zur Lage der Ausländerinnen und Ausländer in Deutschland* (Berlin: Beauftragte der Bundesregierung, 2005), available at http://www.bundesregierung.de/Webs/Breg/DE/Bundesregierung/BeauftragtefuerIntegration/Service/service.html (accessed 1 September 2006); OECD, *Die Arbeitsmarktintegration von Zuwanderern in Deutschland* (Paris: OECD, 2005), available at http://www.oecd.org/dataoecd/62/12/35796774.pdf (accessed 12 September 2006); R. Berthoud, *The Incomes of Ethnic Minorities*. ISER Report 98-1 (Colchester: University of Essex, Institute for Social and Economic Research, 1998); G. Bhattacharyya, L. Ison and M Blair, *Minority Ethnic Attainment and Participation in Education and Training: The Evidence*, Research Topic Paper RTP01 03 (London: DfES, 2003), available at http://www.dfes.gov.uk/research/data/uploadfiles/RTP01-03.pdf (accessed 12 September 2006).
42. Beauftragte der Bundesregierung, *6. Bericht*; Commission for Racial Equality, *Employment and Ethnicity*, Factfile 1 (London: CRE, 2006), available at http://www.cre.gov.uk/downloads/factfile01_employment_and_ethnicity.pdf (accessed 12 September 2006).
43. J. Monar, 'Justice and Home Affairs: Europeanization as a Government-controlled Process', in K. Dyson and K. Goetz (eds.), *Germany, Europe and the Politics of Constraint, Proceedings of the British Academy 119* (Oxford: Oxford University Press, 2003), p.309; see also A. Geddes, *Immigration and European Integration: Towards 'Fortress Europe'?* (Manchester: Manchester University Press, 2000).
44. See, for instance, Monar, 'Justice and Home Affairs'; S. Lavenex, 'Shifting Up and Out: The Foreign Policy of European Immigration Control', *West European Politics* 29/2 (2006), pp.329–50; V. Guiraudon, 'European Integration and Migration Policy: Vertical Policy-making as Venue Shopping', *Journal of Common Market Studies* 38/2 (2000), pp.251–71; Huysmans, 'The European Union'; V. Guiraudon, 'The Constitution of a European Immigration Policy Domain: A Political Sociology Approach', *Journal of European Public Policy* 10/2 (2003), pp.263–82. See also the Introduction to this collection.
45. UNHCR, *Asylum Levels and Trends in Industrialized Countries 2005*, p.9. Notably, the highest application rates in EU-15 during this period were in Sweden (14.2 applications per 1,000 population) and Austria (18.2).
46. Cf. Lavenex, 'Shifting Up and Out', pp.336–7.
47. Council Directive 2003/86/EC, OJ L 251, 3 October 2003, p.12 (family reunification); Council Directive 2003/109/EC, OJ L 16, 23 January 2004, p.44 (long-term resident third country nationals); Council Directive 2004/83/EC, OJ L 304, 30 September 2004, p.12 (asylum qualifications); Council Directive 2005/85/EC, OJ L 326, 13 December 2005, p.13 (asylum procedures).
48. Cf. Article 3 Section 5, Council Directive 2003/86/EC.
49. P. Henson and N. Malhan, 'Endeavours to Export a Migration Crisis: Policy Making and Europeanisation in the German Migration Dilemma', *German Politics* 4/3 (1995), pp.128–44.
50. M. Bösche, 'Trapped inside the European Fortress? Germany and the European Union Asylum and Refugee Policy', in G. Hellmann (ed.), *Germany's EU Policy on Asylum and Defence: De-Europeanization by Default?* (London: Palgrave, 2006).
51. M. Gibney, *The Ethics and Politics of Asylum* (Cambridge: Cambridge University Press, 2004), p.129.
52. A. Geddes, 'Getting the Best of Both Worlds? Britain, the EU and Migration Policy', *International Affairs* 81/4 (2005), pp.723–40, here pp.724, 734.
53. The so-called 'gap hypothesis'; see W. Cornelius and T. Tsuda, 'Controlling Immigration: The Limits of Government Intervention', in W. Cornelius, T. Tsuda, P. Martin and J. Hollifield (eds.), *Controlling Immigration: A Global Perspective*, 2nd edition (Stanford: Stanford University Press, 2004), pp.4–15.
54. A. Caviedes, 'The Social Partners and the Changing Face of German and British Labor Migration Policy', paper presented at the annual conference of the American Political Science Association, Washington DC, 1–4 September 2005.

55. Cf. H. Kolb, 'Die Green Card: Inszenierung eines Politikwechsels', *Aus Politik und Zeitgeschichte* B27 (2005), pp.18–24.
56. Green, *The Politics of Exclusion*, pp.110–32.
57. Beauftragte der Bundesregierung, *6. Bericht*, pp.81–2.
58. See *Der Spiegel* (2 September 2002), '"Lasst uns hier abhauen"', pp.138–42.
59. 'Deutschland: Debatte um Zuwanderung von Fachkräften', *Migration und Bevölkerung* 7 (2006), available at http://www.migration-info.de/migration_und_bevoelkerung/artikel/060704.htm (accessed 5 September 2006).
60. Boswell, *European Migration Policies*, pp.37–40.
61. Cf. IPPR, *Labour Migration to the UK*, pp.7–11.
62. See 'Immigration and the Labour Market: Demand, Recruitment and Integration', Search for Solutions Briefing Paper No. 2 (Birmingham: University of Birmingham, 2004), available at http://www.igs.bham.ac.uk/searchforsolutions/Immigration%20Briefing%20Paper.pdf (accessed 3 June 2006).
63. Home Office, *Controlling our Borders: Making Migration Work for Britain*, CM 6472 (London: HMSO, 2005).
64. Home Office, Department for Work and Pensions, HM Revenue and Customs and Department for Communities and Local Government, *Accession Monitoring Report May 2004–June 2006* (22 August 2006), available at http://www.ind.homeoffice.gov.uk/6353/aboutus/Revised_data_MT.final.pdf (accessed 12 September 2006).
65. For a discussion of this area, especially in the UK, see E. Kofman, 'Family-related Migration: A Critical Review of European Studies', *Journal of Ethnic and Migration Studies* 30/2 (2004), pp.243–62.
66. K. Hailbronner, 'Reform des Zuwanderungsrechts. Konsens und Dissens in der Ausländerpolitik', *Aus Politik und Zeitgeschichte* B43 (2001), pp.7–19, here pp.12–14.
67. R. Brubaker, 'The Return of Assimilation', *Ethnic and Racial Studies* 24/4 (2001), pp.531–48.
68. R. Hansen and P. Weil (eds.), *Towards a European Nationality? Citizenship, Immigration and Nationality Law in the EU* (London: Palgrave, 2001).
69. The substantive basis of UK citizenship tests is outlined in Home Office, *Life in the United Kingdom: A Journey to Citizenship* (London: The Stationery Office, 2004).
70. 'Deutschland: Neue Einbürgerungsrichtlinien', *Migration und Bevölkerung* 5 (2006), available at http://www.migration-info.de/migration_und_bevoelkerung/artikel/060503.htm (accessed 12 September 2006).
71. Blair, 'The Duty to Integrate'.
72. C. Joppke, 'Beyond National Models: Civic Integration Policies for Immigrants in Western Europe', *West European Politics* 30/1 (2007), pp.1–22.
73. Racial Equality Directive: Council Directive 2000/43/EC, OJ L 180, 19 July 2000, p.22; Employment Equality Directive: Council Directive 2000/78/EC, OJ L 303, 2 December 2000, p.16.
74. A. Geddes and V. Guiraudon, 'Britain, France and EU Anti-discrimination Policy: The Emergence of an EU Policy Paradigm', *West European Politics* 27/2 (2004), pp.334–53.
75. 'Aufbruch und Erneuerung – Deutschlands Weg ins 21. Jahrhundert. Koalitionsvereinbarung zwischen der Sozialdemokratischen Partei Deutschlands und Bündnis 90/Die Grünen' (Bonn, 20 October 1998), Article 9; available at http://www.datenschutz-berlin.de/doc/de/koalo/index.htm (accessed 1 October 2006).
76. Geddes and Guiraudon, 'Britain, France and EU Anti-discrimination Policy', pp.346–7.
77. This therefore echoes Andrew Moravcsik's explanation of the formulation of the Single European Act. See A. Moravcsik, *The Choice for Europe: Social Purpose and State Power from Messina to Maastricht* (London: Routledge, 1998).
78. A. Wüst, 'Das Wahlverhalten eingebürgerte Personen in Deutschland', *Aus Politik und Zeitgeschichte* B52 (2003), pp.29–38.
79. For a general discussion of this area in a British–German context, see L. Schuster, *The Use and Abuse of Political Asylum in Britain and Germany* (London: Frank Cass, 2003).
80. In fact, dispersal of immigrants had been practised previously, albeit intermittently and on a much smaller scale. See V. Robinson, 'Dispersal Policies in the UK', in V. Robinson, R. Andersson and S. Musterd (eds.), *Spreading the 'Burden'? A Review of Policies to Disperse Asylum Seekers and Refugees* (Bristol: The Policy Press, 2003).
81. C. Boswell, 'Burden-sharing in the European Union: Lessons from the German and UK Experience', *Journal of Refugee Studies* 16/3 (2003), pp.316–35.
82. C. Boswell, *Spreading the Costs of Asylum Seekers: A Critical Assessment of Dispersal Policies in Germany and the UK* (London: Anglo-German Foundation), p.21, available at http://www.agf.org.uk/pubs/pdfs/r1314e.pdf (accessed 12 June 2006).
83. 'Keep the change, refugee voucher stores are told', *The Guardian*, 10 March 2000.
84. Council Directive 2004/83/EC.

85. See 'EU: Entwicklungen in der Asyl- und Einwanderungspolitik', *Migration und Bevölkerung* 6 (2003), available at http://www.migration-info.de/migration_und_bevoelkerung/artikel/030607.htm (accessed 5 September 2006); also 'Deutschland: Schily schlägt Asyllager in Afrika vor', *Migration und Bevölkerung* 7 (2004), available at http://www.migration-info.de/migration_und_bevoelkerung/artikel/040701.htm (accessed 5 September 2006).
86. Cf. C. Phuong, 'The Removal of Failed Asylum Seekers', *Legal Studies* 25/1 (2005), pp.117–41; M. Gibney and R. Hansen, *Deportation and the Liberal State: The Forcible Return of Asylum Seekers and Unlawful Migrants in Canada, Germany and the United Kingdom*, UNHCR New Issues in Refugee Research Working Paper No.77 (Geneva: UNHCR, 2003); 'Alias aus Angeblichstan', *Der Spiegel*, 6 November 2000, pp.72–85. See also National Audit Office, *Returning Failed Asylum Applicants*, HC76 (London: The Stationery Office, 2005), which explicitly draws on the German experience of this issue.
87. 'EU: Gemeinsame Abschiebungen und Anhebung der Visa-Gebühren', *Migration und Bevölkerung* 4 (2006), available at http://www.migration-info.de/migration_und_bevoelkerung/artikel/060406.htm (accessed 12 September 2006).
88. Cornelius and Tsuda, 'Controlling Immigration', p.18.
89. COM(2005) 184 final.
90. COM(2004) 811 final.

Convergence in Employment-Related Public Policies? A British–German Comparison

LOTHAR FUNK

INTRODUCTION

In contrast to Britain and despite recent efforts, Germany is still seen as being in need of institutional reform. The symptoms of Germany's problems include persistently high and apparently ever-increasing unemployment, low employment growth, as well as slow economic growth over the past decade.[1] In terms of these indicators, the German economy has lagged behind those of most other EU member states since the early 1990s.[2] By contrast, British economic growth and labour market performance has been quite good recently, which stands in contrast to its past performance, and also the performance of other EU member states over the same time period, especially Germany (see Table 1). Whereas in the 1970s Britain was regarded as the 'sick man of Europe', this has changed considerably since the mid-1990s, when Germany, rather than Britain, was unable to decrease (standardised) unemployment rates. In fact, unemployment has risen steadily to its current level of just over 9 per cent in Germany, as opposed to the steadily falling unemployment rate in Britain, which has been below 5 per cent for some years. In general, Britain's superior performance can largely be explained by institutions that are better adapted to current structural changes than is the case in Germany.[3] The early sections of this paper will explain – in a stylised way – the general background of the relevant institutions and labour market developments in both countries since the mid-1970s, when symptoms of crisis first emerged in western Europe.

TABLE 1
A BROADER PICTURE OF LABOUR MARKET-RELATED INDICATORS

	Britain	Germany	EU-15
Employment – percentage change from previous period			
Average 1993–2003	1.1	0.3	1.1
2004	1.0	0.4	0.9
2005	1.0	−0.2	0.9
Unemployment in OECD countries – percentage of labour force			
Average 1993–2003	7.0	7.6	8.8
2004	4.7	9.2	8.1
2005	4.8	9.1	7.9
Growth of real GDP – percentage change from previous period			
Average 1993–2003	3.0	1.6	2.3
2004	3.1	1.1	2.0
2005	1.8	1.1	1.5

Source: OECD, *Employment Outlook* (Paris: OECD, 2006), pp.17, 19, 21.

Based on these results, the question arises whether there has been any convergence of labour market-related policies below the level of the macro-economy in Britain and Germany in recent years. On the one hand, any such convergence could be due first and foremost to adjustments in common economic pressures faced by both countries. On the other hand, the so-called Blair–Schröder paper, in which the British Labour Prime Minister Tony Blair and the then German Chancellor Gerhard Schröder set out their 'Third Way' ideas on a modernised programme for a social democratic movement in Europe, may have played a role in shaping the policies of both countries as a result of cross-national policy learning since the late 1990s.[4] This paper appeared to highlight a shift towards convergent public policies in work and welfare, based on sound macroeconomic policies. One of the key ideas was the proposal to increase the adjustment capacity of labour markets, allowing them to adapt to constantly changing circumstances as a result of, above all, common shocks, experienced in spite of cross-national differences in policy settings and problems in both countries. These common shocks require a reallocation of resources across qualifications, sectors and regions in order to mitigate against the resulting short-term increase in unemployment, as well as a further fall in employment in the medium term. Highly regulated markets are, in general, less able than markets with low levels of regulation to lead to the desired outcomes, at least in terms of (un)employment.

In order to analyse systematically the question of convergence in employment-related public policies, we first of all need to consider the traditional labour market-related systems in both countries, as well as the reforms which were introduced prior to the advent of the centre-left governments in Britain and Germany in 1997 and 1998 respectively. Secondly, we have to examine the policy response of the centre-left governments to current labour market problems in both countries and see whether convergence can be found. Thirdly, this article will discuss Germany's 'Agenda 2010' reforms in relation to the earlier proposals made by Blair and Schröder, and reform proposals made by mainstream economists. Related to this the essay will try to explain Germany's disappointing record in terms of labour market outcomes and suggest potentially superior alternative policies. Finally, some policy lessons for Germany will be outlined.

THE CONTEXT: ALTERNATIVE MARKET ECONOMIES AND NEW STRUCTURAL CHANGES

From the early post-war years until the 1970s, western European countries were able to consolidate systems of economic, labour market and social policy governance which differed significantly from country to country.[5] In this period, countries prospered to a greater or lesser degree irrespective of the structure of their work and welfare systems. While during this so-called 'golden age' between the 1950s and early 1970s protective barriers of capital exchange controls, fixed but adjustable exchange rates, and optional barriers to trade existed, these were gradually dismantled in the ensuing period, when these systems were challenged by increasing pressures on their systems of economic governance from a range of factors.

Two approaches during this period highlighted alternative ways of managing economic systems in the West. Germany and Britain were often regarded as the paradigm European cases of the *coordinated market economy* and the *liberal market economy* respectively.[6] In the traditional German 'coordinated market economy', business cooperated with one another through mutually reinforcing networks, as well as with organised labour through a central role of collective bargaining negotiations above the firm level. Welfare in this continental-conservative model was hardly redistributive compared to the British system, as both (quite hefty) insurance-based contributions and social benefits, as well as social assistance, were dependent on the individual's level of income. The social insurance-based system was connected to the contract of employment, based on employment history, and provided by the state and intermediary groups, with a comparatively high level of benefits but not of services. Further features of this so-called conservative welfare state in (west) Germany were strict employment protection laws, and considerable expenditure on active and passive labour market policies.[7]

Compared to West Germany, the state had a hands-off approach to both labour and business in the traditional post-war British liberal market economy. In their relationships, businesses were more individualistic, and industrial relations were often adversarial. In Britain, welfare was assumed to be a matter of individual responsibility provided by the state on the basis of needs, not rights, and primarily for the poor, with a comparatively low level of benefits and services. Additionally, the countries' monetary policies differed considerably. Whereas the political independence of the Bundesbank was characteristic of German monetary policy, until the 1990s the British Chancellor of the Exchequer had always refused to pass monetary policy independence to the Bank of England.[8] The latter was an important difference between the countries as the British combination of strong trade unions and a lack of monetary credibility caused the 'stop/go' cycles of disinflationary and expansionary macroeconomic policies as a reaction to unsound wage demands by trade unions characteristic of Britain during the 1970s. In turn, this led to rising unemployment, inflation and public debt. In contrast, (west) Germany could deal with inflation more effectively, but labour market, social security and product market regulations were not flexible enough to adapt quickly to the new conditions without causing high unemployment, from the mid-1970s, when the Bretton Woods system of fixed exchange rates collapsed, followed by the two oil crises.[9]

Pressures on the models were exacerbated in the 1980s and 1990s by a transition to a post-industrial service-oriented economy, coupled with high levels of technological change and a rising internationalisation of national markets for goods, capital and services ('globalisation') as well as the challenges of Europeanisation. The latter involved the integration into a single market of the national markets for goods, capital, services and labour, as well as eliminating national currencies in favour of a single currency, the Euro, in 12 of the then 15 European Union countries (including Germany but not Britain). The countries responded at different times, in different ways and with differing outcomes to the effects of these new mega-trends, which now included labour market pressures stemming from changes in family structure and an ageing population.[10]

Due above all to these developments, the stable labour market of the post-war 'golden age' no longer exists in contemporary western Europe. Notably, the new structural trends have led to labour market shifts that reduce opportunities for low-skilled workers in all countries. Low-skilled workers are most exposed to the risk of long-term unemployment (particularly in Germany) and poverty (especially in Britain). As a result of a lack of adequate adjustment capacities in the respective economies, the standardised unemployment rates rose to unprecedented levels: over 11 per cent in Britain and over 7 per cent in West Germany in 1985, albeit for fundamentally different institutional reasons, as will be explained below. High unemployment levels and the parallel, weak employment performance strained government budgets and increasingly became a constraint on economic growth. In response to these pressures, Britain and Germany (as well as the rest of western Europe) had no choice but to adjust their systems of labour market-related institutions.

LABOUR MARKETS IN THE 1980s AND 1990s

The Conservative government in Britain (1979–97) was keen to tackle unemployment by a reduction in business regulation in general, and the deregulation of labour market institutions and improving incentives to take work, in particular, for example, by weakening the power of trade unions and cutting benefits, tightening eligibility and imposing enhanced work requirements.[11] Although the level of unemployment benefit was already one of the lowest in Europe, the Conservatives reduced it by a further 25 per cent. In 1987 the 'restart programme' provided closer monitoring of job-seeking activities and more intensive counselling and job placement for the long-term unemployed. As a result, the average duration of individual unemployment decreased. National insurance unemployment benefit was replaced by the 'Jobseeker's Allowance' in 1996, conditional on approved job-seeking activities. Recipients had to accept low-paid jobs. This policy, which aimed to avoid long-term benefit dependency, was based on the view that benefit receipt should be viable only if certain job search obligations were met.

Even though Conservatives stressed the 'sticks' by questioning benefit receipt if approved ways of finding work were not met, some 'carrots' were also introduced. To strengthen work incentives, the 'family credit', which was introduced in 1988, provided in-work benefits for low-wage earners and families with low income. In summary, the Conservatives' reforms increased incentives to supply labour and had the effect of reducing job security for many employees by making it easier for employers to terminate contracts. Even lower levels of employment protection and unemployment benefits in the hitherto already comparatively lightly regulated British economy (which relied substantially on targeted social assistance to decrease poverty, with hardly any maintenance of previous income), had the effect of making labour markets even more flexible and helped to improve labour market performance. All this served to liberalise an already deregulated environment even further; but it only very slowly helped to solve British macroeconomic problems, as the credibility of monetary policy was still missing, despite Margaret Thatcher's radical overhaul of the British collective bargaining system, which limited the trade unions' previous ability to disrupt the workings of the economy.[12] As Pissarides argues,

> In the 1970s and early 1980s the public could not believe that the inflation bias in British monetary and fiscal policy was taken out of the system. The Treasury refused to change the institutional rules of monetary policy and monetary policy was discretionary and completely under Treasury control. The Thatcher disinflation lacked credibility. It took a massive recession and a large increase in unemployment to bring inflation down, and it took four years to do it.[13]

Therefore, only two factors in combination can explain the superior British experience of some of the lowest unemployment and inflation rates in many years simultaneously since the 1990s, and especially the start of the twenty-first century, according to mainstream economists.[14] The first was the high level of labour market flexibility, which greatly increased in the 1980s under the Conservative government, above all by curbing trade union power. The second was the fact that Britain followed the German tradition of pursuing a goal of low inflation from 1992 onwards and granted operational independence to the Bank of England on the second day of the incoming Labour government in 1997. As a result, ministers of either party no longer had the option of using expansionary monetary policy in a bid to curry favour with voters before a general election, which would of course have most likely led to higher inflation in the medium-term. The consequence was a lower expected inflation, which in turn led to more moderate wage claims in the economy as well as affecting the price setting of firms. In other words, the move helped create a 'virtuous circle'.

The essence of the British adjustment is summarised in Table 2. The arrow highlights the adjustment path from the 1970s of low monetary policy credibility and strong trade union power, which has economically similar effects to strongly regulated markets, the 1980s, during which Britain still lacked monetary policy credibility despite the decline in trade union power; and the shift towards the 'Goldilocks' environment of low inflation and unemployment since the 1990s.

By contrast, the Christian Democratic/Christian Social Union (CDU/CSU) coalition with the Free Democratic Party (FDP) in Germany between 1982 and 1998 was only able to maintain its appeal with a majority of voters because it hardly touched the former policies of 'growth with redistribution' of its predecessor, the Socialdemocrat-led SPD–FDP coalition under Helmut Schmidt. The German 'salami slicing tactic' of making small cuts in social security and in some parts of labour market regulation and active labour market policies over many years without destroying the main pillars of the traditional systems, appeared to be a step in the right direction. Amongst other things, the policies included, for example, relaxing

TABLE 2
INTERACTIONS OF MONETARY POLICY FRAMEWORKS AND REGULATORY ENVIRONMENTS SINCE THE MID-1970S

		Inflationary expectations due to monetary policy institutions	
		low	rather high
Regulations / trade union power	low	British economy since about the mid 1990s → simultaneously low unemployment/high employment and low inflation	British economy in the 1980s → very slow labour market improvement only as a result of missing credible monetary policy
	rather high	(west) German economy since the mid 1970s → rather low inflation and persistently high and rising unemployment	British economy in the 1970s → stop-go cycles with disastrous labour market consequences and high inflation

Source: based on C. Pissarides, 'Unemployment in Britain: A European Success Story', in M. Werding (ed.), *Structural Unemployment in Western Europe* (Cambridge/London: The MIT Press, 2006), pp.209–35.

restrictions on fixed-term contracts and temporary work agencies through several consecutive reforms from 1985 onwards. However, the strong provisions protecting workers from redundancy remained largely intact over this period. Minor reforms increased and decreased the size threshold for enterprises to be exempt from restrictive redundancy protection, without questioning the general system. The (dis)incentive structure for unemployed workers to re-enter the labour market, which saw generous unemployment benefits compared to Britain of 63 or 67 per cent of former net earnings depending on the nature of the household, which was followed by an indefinite period of tax-financed unemployment assistance at a lower rate, was largely left intact. Even worse, the maximum benefit duration was increased in the mid-1980s so that older workers could receive earnings-related benefits for up to 32 months. Until 1984, all unemployed people were entitled to receive insurance based benefits for 12 months, independent of age age.[15]

On the whole, this 'salami slicing reform tactic' proved detrimental to the economy, as it was not implemented sufficiently comprehensively to solve labour market problems; West Germany, in contrast to Britain, delayed many microeconomic reforms until the 1990s, when the impact of reunification heralded a significant increase in the already substantial labour market problems.[16] In the final analysis, the centre-right-led government was unable to break one of the important unwanted side-effects of a coordinated market economy with a conservative welfare state: on the one hand, the availability of both social security and wage increases for protected insiders, which raise their labour costs at the expense of job cuts, and, on the other hand, the exclusion of 'outsiders' as the chances of (re-)entering the labour market diminish, particularly for the long-term unemployed and the low-skilled. In other words,

> even in periods of low economic activity, the employed (insiders) try to increase wages without considering the situation of the unemployed (outsiders). The aim of the insiders is to obtain wages that are as high as possible, but not so high that the outsiders can offer their work under more favourable conditions. In fact, the premium that can be exploited by insiders is limited by the costs of job turnovers (hiring, firing and search costs), investments in human capital, and costs of training on the job, among other factors. As a result of the premium received by insiders, lower levels of production and employment are optimal for firms, compared with the competitive environment. As a consequence, the workers remain employed, but the unemployed only have a low probability of finding work again. Unemployment is going to persist over time, once a job is lost. The actual power of insiders is closely linked to the institutional framework. In particular, generous systems of unemployment benefits will relieve the insiders' position.[17]

In sum, the piecemeal reforms in the labour market during the Kohl era, above all, eased regulation of flexible jobs whereas stronger benefit cuts and bold deregulation of the core labour market dominated by the insiders was avoided. This approach proved insufficiently substantial to adapt the German economy to the emerging structural changes and the challenges of German unification, as was demonstrated by the long-term rise in unemployment and the fall in employment mentioned earlier. As the root causes of these labour market problems were not fundamentally addressed, Germany proved unable to leave the inferior quadrant of Table 2, characterised by persistently high and rising unemployment, and shift to the favourable British upper quadrant, in spite of prudent monetary policy during the years of the Kohl government.

The labour market problems which Kohl's government was unable to solve worsened later on, due at least in part to the inadequate flexibility of labour market institutions to adjust to the structural changes which have increasingly demanded even greater sensitivity of labour to adjust to new situations. Since the mid-1990s at the latest, when technology-driven structural change dominated, fuelled by new information and communication technologies and further globalisation as a result of new opportunities due to lower relocation costs for firms, these new structural changes were regarded as the driving forces for change towards supply-side-dominated policies in all economically advanced countries, as they appeared to impose a neo-liberal logic of the market. There seemed to be little alternative even in Germany, as stability-oriented monetary policy cannot solve such problems alone. In other words, as in Britain, inflation expectations were clearly low in Germany as the Bundesbank (superseded by the European Central Bank) enjoyed independence in the conduct of monetary policy and aimed at low inflation, roughly similar to Britain. In contrast to Britain, however, labour market and business regulations were much higher in Germany and were regarded as the main explanatory factors behind Germany's persistently poor labour market performance. A sufficient condition for an improved employment and economic growth situation, therefore, would be less regulation in labour and product markets as well as less generous social security systems, that is, a shift towards the current British situation (vertical arrow in Table 2). Did the German centre-left-led government deliver?

THE POLICY-RESPONSE OF THE CENTRE-LEFT-LED GOVERNMENTS IN BRITAIN AND GERMANY AND THE QUESTION OF CONVERGENCE

The supply-side-oriented paradigm change had strong repercussions on many left-wing parties, which had tended to put a more active response to unemployment at or near the centre of their successful electoral programmes. In 1997, when New Labour entered government in Britain, followed by an SPD–Green coalition in Germany (from 1998 until 2005) and several other left-wing parties in Europe, the majority of left-wing-dominated governments in Europe appeared to have understood, at least in principle, that the current structural problems and changes prescribed a much larger role for supply-side policies and proscribe certain other policies in order to solve lasting (un)employment and social exclusion problems.[18] This included Germany – after a very brief period of old-style macroeconomic policy by the German Finance Minister Oskar Lafontaine, an enthusiastic supporter of Keynesian demand management. This supply-side model meant giving up, above all, high taxes and generous welfare spending as well as strong governmental interventionism in labour and other markets, at least if such interventions are implemented ineffectively and inefficiently, and a prominent role for expansionary demand-side management. It includes, particularly in our context, the demand for more flexible labour markets and the retrenchment of welfare states combined with low government deficits, debts and inflation.[19] Sound monetary and fiscal policies belonged to the most important measures by the New Labour government to earn credibility among business and investors during their first term (in stark contrast to the first term of the SPD/Green government in Germany).[20]

In addition to these more or less traditional liberal market instruments, however, among the measures advocated by the left were, in particular, the introduction of targeted programmes for certain groups of workers, for example the long-term unemployed, the assessment of all benefit recipients for their potential to earn, and the reform of governmental employment services in order to assist those capable of work in finding appropriate jobs. The aforementioned 'Third Way', which tried to combine new policy tools from a left-wing perspective ('more market elements instead of strong state interventionism' cushioned by targeted help by the state for job seekers) with the eternal values of the left (e.g. a strong role for 'social justice and fairness') became the buzzword for a few years in Britain and, at least for a short while, in Germany as well.

According to the Blair–Schröder paper, which supported 'a new supply-side agenda for the left', public policy responses to the contemporary structural changes should be quite similar despite the radically different starting positions in Britain and Germany.[21] But the paper, which generated little interest in Britain as it merely highlighted New Labour's prevailing approach to economic, labour and social reforms, caused such controversial discussions within the SPD and was criticised by most Germany trade unions, so that a direct implementation of most of the proposals suggested in the paper was unthinkable, at least in 1999 or in the following few years. The existing German arrangements appeared to reflect a political equilibrium: the inefficient features for the economy and society as a whole were fiercely defended by vested interests.

As a result, the first years of the SPD–Green government were more or less lost for fighting unemployment and improving employment due to inconsistent 'stop/start' policies during Schröder's first term. Each step to promote supply-side policies including corporate and individual tax cuts, an austerity budget, greater investments in high technology, limited pension reform and the reduction of non-wage labour costs, was accompanied by rolling back the modest supply-side policies of the preceding CDU/CSU–FDP government. Examples include restoring decreased sick pay and re-regulating job protection or increasing the costs and bureaucratic blockages for the expanding number of minor jobs. Additionally, instead of following the new supply-side agenda, the government built new hurdles for firms by expanding co-determination rights in small firms and, finally, halting further economic reforms in order to placate trade unions, a traditional ally of the SPD.[22] Therefore, with reasonable simplification, it can be argued that at the beginning of the twenty-first century the Anglo-Saxon 'liberal' model in Britain not only provided lower employment protection legislation but also lower levels of out-of-work benefits and less active labour market policies than in coordinated market economies with a conservative welfare state as, for example, Germany.

The obvious fate of the Blair–Schröder paper as a provocative reaction to the prevailing mega-trends was a lack of short-term influence on policies. This experience demonstrates that at least in the short-to-medium term, a convergence of policies in countries based on different 'varieties of capitalism' like Britain and Germany is by no means a necessity, despite apparently similar economic pressures to market-enhancing reforms.[23]

The theoretical academic hypotheses highlighted in the introductory article of this collection do not allow an unequivocal positive or negative answer with respect to policy convergence. In terms of empirical evidence on labour market systems, however, it currently appears undisputed that the current mega-trends of structural change have led at least in a medium-term perspective to a gradual restructuring of the systems of work and welfare in all west European countries including Britain and Germany. The changes concern, amongst other things, a retrenchment of many aspects of the traditional welfare state programmes, especially with regard to availability, duration and replacement rates of unemployment benefits (which have become stricter, on average), as well as the promotion of new welfare schemes and policies to enhance job creation, including lower labour market regulations and the measures affecting the 'employability' of workers, including training, employment subsidies, in-work benefits and new forms of labour contracts.[24]

A recent Organisation for Economic Co-operation and Development (OECD) study shows considerable efforts in Britain and Germany with regard to changing labour market-related incentives during the period of the predominance of centre-left governments in western Europe.[25] This includes in Britain, above all, further cuts in the unemployment benefit system, increased redistribution through the tax-benefit system as well as better incentives to participate in New Deal welfare-to-work programmes for problem groups in the labour market; the introduction of a national minimum wage with reduced rates for certain groups in order to increase the supply

POLICY CONVERGENCE IN THE UK AND GERMANY 125

of labour during a period of comparatively high economic growth; and a sustained expansion in childcare provision in order to improve the compatibility of work and family life.

Whereas the early reforms of the SPD–Green government in Germany, which increased the level of labour market regulation, proved to be counter-productive or ineffective, economic experts regard more recent changes as steps in the right direction. Most important was a fundamental reform of the benefit system for the long-term unemployed and other non-employed individuals living on general welfare benefits. Unemployment assistance merged with social assistance into a new tax-funded and means-tested flat-rate unemployment assistance (*Arbeitslosengeld II, ALG II*) topped up, for example, by social allowances for children below the working age (*Sozialgeld*) and by regionally differentiated housing rents as well as during the first two years under certain conditions by temporary supplements replaced the earnings-related but also means-tested former unemployment assistance (*Arbeitslosenhilfe*) for people capable of working by January 2005. In this system, employed persons are also entitled to *ALG II* if their earnings are not sufficient to safeguard the socially accepted basic income. Additionally to the implementation of this new basic income scheme for needy jobseekers (*Grundsicherung*), means-tested and tax-funded social assistance (*Sozialhilfe*) was restricted to those working age people who are unable to work and for persons below basic incomes above 65 years. As a result of these changes, amongst other things, the number of *ALG II* recipients strongly increased compared to the former programmes for transfer-recipients outside the insurance-contribution based unemployment systems.[26] Benefit duration of the contribution-funded and earning-related unemployment benefit (*Arbeitslosengeld I*) was harmonised for all age groups under 55 to 12 months in 2004. From 2006 onwards it was lowered to 18 months for persons aged above 54, cutting entitlement periods by up to 14 months for many older age groups. Moreover, the rejection of any job offer entails benefit sanctions for recipients of the new unemployment assistance benefit since 2005. Further reforms included the restructuring of the Federal Labour Office (now Agency) involving a re-organisation of the placement of job-seekers by, for example, intensifying counselling and increasing the use of private employment agencies, the establishment of temporary work agencies for the previously unemployed (Personnel Service Agencies), stronger incentives to work in low-paid employment, cuts in top and entry level statutory tax rates, reductions in pensions, increases in the maximum duration for contracts through work agencies and the raising of the company size limit for redundancy protection from five to ten employees (a deregulation that was reversed in 1999 and re-introduced with only slight changes in 2004).

As both countries started from very different frameworks in 1997/98, we must now ask whether the measures taken since then imply policy convergence. In employment protection, for example, Britain offered, in contrast to the strongly regulated German economy, the lowest provisions among the (pre-enlargement) EU member states, and expenditures on active labour market policies were low in Britain compared to Germany. Were these gaps closed in recent years?

As Table 3 shows, despite all changes listed above, the specific mixes of labour market-related instruments used in Britain and Germany are still rather different. In other words, the convergence of the relevant policy measures, which may include changes in the UK towards the coordinated market economy model, has still been rather weak. Therefore, one should not be too surprised that despite certain, limited liberal policy adjustments in Germany in terms of labour market-related instruments, the policy outcomes in terms of (un)employment and economic growth between Britain and Germany (see Table 1 above) have not converged up until 2006.

TABLE 3
CONVERGENCE OF INSTITUTIONAL VARIABLES BETWEEN 1997 AND 2002–2004

Year	Germany 1997	Germany 2003	Britain 1997	Britain 2003	Convergence?
Unemployment benefits: [a,b] *net replacement rates (NRR) and duration of unemployment benefits*					Dominance of divergence
NRR average long-term 67% APW	75.3	77.7[c]	84.1	68.8[c]	No
NRR average initial 100% APW	66.1	75[c]	57.1	56.2[c]	No
Maximum benefit duration of regular unemployment benefits (in months)	12, but up to 32 for older workers	12 months for workers aged up to 54, maximum 18 months for workers aged above 54 (effective only in 2006)	6	6	Very partial
Direct tax wedge average [a]					Dominance of divergence
Single 2 children 67% APW	32.3	30.1	15.1	−12.1	No
Couple no child 100% APW, 0% APW	43.6	43.0	30.5	29.5	No
Active labour market policies (ALMPs)					Partial convergence to a higher level
ALMPs spending per unemployed person, constant US$ PPP)	5720.6	7107.6	2556.1	3868.1	Increasing role in both countries, however very different starting levels
Employment Protection Legislation					Very limited convergence to the middle
Temporary[d]	2.3	2.0	0.3	0.4	Very limited convergence
Permanent[d]	2.7	2.7	0.9	1.1	Very limited convergence
Early retirement – implicit tax on continued work [e]					Limited tendency towards convergence to the middle
55 years to 60 years early retirement	49.0	32.3	21.6	23.2	Partial convergence
Working time flexibility					Tendency towards convergence to British levels
Percentage of part-time workers	15.8	19.6	22.9	23.0	Particularly rising in Germany

(Continued)

TABLE 3 CONTINUED

	Germany		Britain		Convergence?
Year	1997	2003	1997	2003	
Wage formation and industrial relations					Very partial
Coordination[d]	4.0	4.0	1.0	1.0	No
Centralisation[d]	3.0	3.0	1.0	1.0	No
Union density (%)[b]	27.0	23.2	32.1	30.4	Convergence to a lower level
Union coverage (%)	80+	68	40+	30+	Convergence to a lower level

[a]Earnings are calculated with reference to the earnings of an average productivity worker (APW); 0 per cent, 67 per cent and 100 per cent concern previous earnings in work. In case of tax wedges different current percentages of APW earnings are used. For couples, earnings are reported for first and second earners respectively. NRR or net replacement rates are post-tax measures of benefit generosity. NRR are an average of cases of a single person and one-earner married couple and an average of cases with no children and with two children. Only few cases are reported here but a range of others reported in the original study also point to divergence with regard to unemployment benefits and direct tax wedge averages in Britain and Germany.
[b]2003 = 2002
[c]2003 = 2004
[d]Figures based on different OECD indices. Higher figures show stronger degrees of EPL, coordination and centralisation.
[e]Implicit taxes on continued work for persons aged 60 to 65 in early retirement or old-age pension also show partial convergence only.
Source: N. Brandt, J.-M. Burniaux and R. Duval, *Assessing the OECD Jobs Strategy: Past Developments and Reforms – Annexes* (Paris: OECD Economics Department Working Paper No. 429, 2005), pp.48 and 127; and http://www.oecd.org/els/social/workincentives. Updates of figures were only made where comparability of data to the late 1990s is still possible.

Only limited tendencies of convergence between Britain and Germany can be found with regard to activation policies, employment protection policies, early retirement incentives and working time flexibility as well as wage and industrial relations systems when looking at the indicators for which cross-national data are available, collected recently by the OECD.[27] British expenditure on active labour market policies remains comparatively low despite the fact that it rose considerably as a result of the new programmes implemented by New Labour, which stressed activation as the centrepiece of its employment policy. Thus New Labour retained some Conservative policies, but also stressed positive activation programmes for various vulnerable groups of unemployed people, to improve skills and incentives. The low expenditure compared to Germany can be explained by the very positive general employment performance in Britain and because, throughout the period, British policy was dominated by a concern with flexibility. Participation in active schemes was also used as an effective work test. German expenditure has been rising from a much higher level than in Britain, partly as a result of increasing unemployment, and partly due to new methods of activation. Nevertheless, one may speak of a partial convergence towards a higher level as the percentage increase in Germany between 1997 and 2003 was considerably lower than in Britain. The increasing role of activation policies in both Britain and Germany as well as in other countries might be interpreted as a limited hybridisation of the original models.[28] In spite of some new labour market-related regulations since 1997 in Britain, which resulted in a small increase of the

Employment Protection Legislation (EPL) indicator of the OECD, the United Kingdom still offers amongst the most limited provisions of the member states of the EU.[29] Only partial reforms with regard to temporary employment relationships resulted in a fall in the EPL index for Germany. On the whole, therefore, just a very limited convergence can be detected in this field, as major political barriers to any substantial reduction in the degree of protection of labour market insiders still appear to exist in Germany.

Early retirement incentives measured as implicit taxes (that is disincentives) on continued work after the age of 54 appear to be converging between Britain and Germany, as incentives to stay in employment are increased in Germany, whereas the implicit tax barriers for the employment of older workers are rising in Britain. Nonetheless, the remaining disincentives to work after 54 remain generally higher in Germany when evaluated by this indicator. An increase in working time flexibility in Germany is confirmed when looking at one important indicator of working time flexibility, part-time work, which is converging upon the somewhat higher British level. This may partly be the result of the partial deregulation and subsidy of minor jobs and also because employees have obtained the right to transform a full-time job into a part-time job unilaterally under certain conditions since 2001. Other evidence points in the same direction of increased working time flexibility in Germany compared to Britain, where no action was taken: in Germany, working time 'accounts' and increases in working time without additional pay have increasingly been adopted by German social partners in recent times.

Despite the fact that union densities and coverage rates of bargaining with unions are decreasing in both countries, the general assessment of the industrial relations systems with regard to centralisation and coordination has not changed during the period under investigation. Market elements in the German bargaining system have risen a little, however, as social partners have increasingly used the existing possibilities to negotiate at the plant level during the 1990s (partly illegally) and as they have increasingly deployed existing possibilities to make use of opt-out clauses, which speeded up aggregate wage adjustments a little in Germany. Therefore, one may speak of a very limited tendency of convergence upon a more liberal bargaining model in Germany, even in the absence of new legislation.

Regarding unemployment benefits and direct tax wedges, a divergence between the two countries developed between 1997 and 2003/04. Whereas the net replacement rates as post-tax measures of unemployment benefit levels were roughly similar in both countries in 1997 for an average of different family-related categories, and in part even more generous in Britain than in Germany, this changed considerably in 2004. In Germany, the net replacement rates increased. At the same time they decreased in Britain, amounting to rather different incentives to re-enter the labour market in this respect. The longer duration of insurance-based unemployment benefits in Germany made labour supply incentives even worse in 2004 compared to Britain. Nonetheless, it has to be acknowledged that the scrapping of the open-ended German unemployment assistance scheme in 2005 marks progress towards more 'employment friendly' income support. The new scheme seems to be associated with lower replacement ratios for those unemployed the longest, who would have been eligible for unemployment assistance in the former system. Additionally, means testing for this group has become stricter. Drawbacks of the new system are, however, amongst other things, higher income replacement rates for a large proportion of people who would have received social assistance or unemployment assistance in the old system, due to the integration of certain supplementary 'top-ups' that were not paid automatically under the previous system. Moreover, a significant number of beneficiaries now appear to receive income replacements that are close to or exceed market wages. All these factors explain why the new measures have done little up until now to improve the German labour market situation.[30]

Divergence also characterises the average levels of direct taxation for different categories of families or single people. Very slight decreases in these taxes characterise the German situation between 1997 and 2003 and result in positive net levels of taxation and hardly any improved labour supply incentives for earners with children in the low wage sector. Better tax incentives to supply labour for such people in Britain compared to Germany even in 1997 were, meanwhile, further improved by the British government's decision to make the working tax credit much more generous, in particular in the government's first term of office. To strengthen work incentives for the low-skilled unemployed and to reduce poverty in work resulting from high wage inequality in the strongly decentralised system of wage bargaining in Britain, the paradigm of strict activation with intensive monitoring of job search activities was complemented by very effective increases in tax-based in-work benefits.[31] In other words, divergence dominated in this respect, at least until recently. Alternatively, however, critics may argue that the enormous expansion of the British welfare state that paralleled these and other recent welfare reforms made the British model less liberal, which may raise concerns about the medium- and long-term sustainability of the new balance between rights and responsibilities in Britain.

In summary, despite the fact that national government policies of work and welfare as well as bargaining in industrial relations systems have become more similar and more market-reliant in recent years, as a result of the pressures of current mega-trends, they are far from the same in both countries.

THE BLAIR-SCHRÖDER PAPER REVISITED IN THE LIGHT OF POLICY CONVERGENCE

Indirectly, the spirit of the Blair–Schröder paper resurfaced, especially when Gerhard Schröder announced his 'Agenda 2010' reforms, even if both the paper, and the 'Third Way', went unmentioned. However, quite a few of the elements of the 1999 paper that supported, amongst other things, a fruitful combination of microeconomic flexibility and macroeconomic stability including sound public finances, a reduction in non-wage labour costs, tax cuts and social security reforms as well as welfare-to-work programmes and the promotion of a low wage sector, were part of the Agenda 2010 blueprint for German labour market and social reforms which Schröder announced on 14 March 2003. Due to a combination of growing economic problems and political defeats in the first months of the SPD–Green government's second term (including the loss of the majority in the first chamber to the CDU/CSU in February 2003, which made major legislation against the will of the opposition in the second chamber difficult) as well as the failure of the 'Alliance for Jobs' as a method of fighting unemployment, Schröder finally appeared persuaded that further 'stop/go' policies or the temporary halting of economic reforms as in his first term would not help to stimulate growth and employment sufficiently to reduce registered unemployment.[32] Moreover, such a strategy would almost certainly have been punished by voters at the next federal election.[33]

Therefore, from a political economy perspective, it was quite logical for Schröder to suggest a comprehensive reform programme which emphasised greater individual responsibility and less state support, as the Blair–Schröder paper had done four years earlier.[34] Amongst other things, the Agenda 2010 package contained proposals to relax job protection legislation, decrease unemployment benefits, increase the retirement age, and to cut back on the requirements for masters' certificates for craft professions. It also included proposals to cut health care coverage, reduce subsidies for some industrial sectors, increase the number of all day schools, and invest in public day care in order to improve the incentives for women to work. Several of the proposed reforms were passed by the legislature in the autumn and winter of 2003 and took effect on 1 January 2004, and were followed by further labour market and social reforms.

It is true that some of the proposals were watered down in order to satisfy left-wing members of the SPD and trade unions as well as to win approval of the opposition parties in the Bundesrat. Nonetheless, at the time it was widely recognised that the SPD-led government's ability to pass many of the Agenda 2010 measures was noteworthy, for three reasons in particular – all of which can be traced back to the Blair–Schröder paper:[35]

1. Those reforms which focused on reducing disincentives in unemployment-related benefits to accept employment and better activation strategies for the unemployed marked a notable change in Germany's policy-making process, as the German chancellor introduced a reform agenda similar to the Blair–Schröder declaration, without seeking consensus from the various vested interest groups within the country; this may be regarded as a convergence upon British policy-making.[36]
2. These reforms marked a significant, path changing departure from the SPD's traditional policies of collective responsibility and the expansion of workers' rights and social benefits; in particular, it included a replacement of the two-tier system of benefits based on former net wages to the long-term unemployed, which had proven harmful to employment, with one flat-rate payment defined by the subsistence level of income of a given household (and, as, mentioned, certain supplements); such a measure signals the acceptance of the fact that the level of benefits has a negative effect on the transition from unemployment to employment because high benefits are connected with high reservation wages, which may cause and prolong high unemployment, especially in low-productivity jobs. This measure may in practice help to 'transform the safety net of entitlements into a springboard to personal responsibility', as the Blair–Schröder paper stated; moreover, as the Blair–Schröder paper did, it marked a recognition of the changed economic circumstances that limit governmental ability to use monetary and fiscal tools and re-distributional interventions to stimulate employment and growth.
3. These reforms also reflected, as did the Blair–Schröder paper, the political desire of the SPD to draw support from centrist voters in the quest for re-election.

Two further parallels of the Agenda 2010 reforms to the Blair–Schröder paper also deserve mention. First, both approaches were notable steps in the right direction, but both packages for reform probably underestimated Germany's key deficiencies, in particular the rigidity of the labour market, by, above all, shying away from effectively breaking up the 'insider–outsider' mechanisms of the German labour market. The government instead confined itself to a rather ineffective appeal to unions and employers to allow 'opening clauses' in wage contracts instead of legislating for them to be binding in all collective agreements. Further measures demanded by mainstream economists to improve the labour market performance, such as, for example, the elimination of most dismissal restrictions, increases in the regular retirement age by two years to 67, substantial lowering of additional labour costs, or a further liberalisation of shop opening hours, proved too controversial for the Schröder government to implement. In other words, whereas the Agenda 2010 reforms were a substantial change for the Social Democrats, they proved to be a still rather modest change to Germany's employment and social welfare systems and were not enough significantly to improve Germany's economic performance in the short or medium term, as they did not do enough to reduce social insurance costs or stimulate employment. In the words of Lars Calmfors, a well-known Swedish economist, 'one should not expect very large effects from these measures alone. To put it rudely and only with a slight exaggeration, Germany may be moving from *very bad* active labour market policies to *bad* such policies. If so, it is an improvement, but not a very impressive one'.[37]

Second, both approaches became victims of Germany's problematic political system. As mentioned before, the Blair–Schröder paper led to such an outcry by certain vested interests in Germany that for several years a consistent reform policy from a centre-left party appeared impossible. The measures begun by Agenda 2010 reforms partly also became victim to Germany's clogged political decision-making system, which has been characterised by overlapping competences of the Bundestag and Bundesrat. Until recently, only a few crucial reform measures could be passed without agreement of both houses.[38] Especially in turbulent times, when controversial and painful reforms needed to be launched by the federal government, the upper house tended to be dominated by the national opposition parties and reform legislation could then only be passed when consensus was reached. The need for a consensus among the parties in government and opposition in a 'grand coalition by stealth' had proved to be a serious roadblock to meaningful economic reform. On the one hand, this is because policy formulation was often subject to complex and opaque 'concession bargaining' between the federal government and the states and communities even when federal legislation does not formally require the approval of states. On the other hand, this is because legislation coming out of the mills of the mediation committee was often a mere shadow of the original policy programme, suffering from inconsistencies and formal errors. Moreover, the opposition parties who had been partly responsible for the inconsistent results were usually quick to point out that the measures taken were insufficient to boost the economy, thereby undermining any positive confidence effects that may have come from the implemented measures. Important reform packages including labour market-related reforms implemented by the SPD–Green government fell victim to this system.[39] One example is the outcome of a compromise in the Bundesrat not to concentrate all responsibilities for benefit and employment policies at one level of administration, which proved disastrous for the effectiveness of parts of the reform package due to the resulting inefficiencies.[40] Partly as a result of such problems and because, in spite of higher costs than in the former unemployment benefit system, the financial incentives for welfare recipients to pick up work (particularly full-time jobs) often remained low, the implemented reforms did not decrease unemployment in the short term or increase employment and, therefore, contributed to an unprecedented series of defeats in regional elections.[41] Annoyed, as well, by traditionalist anti-reform criticism from his own party's ranks, Schröder had set the scene for an early departure from power and opened up the way for new elections in September 2005 which he, surprisingly, failed to win only by a slim margin. Even though his party gained power as the junior partner in a CDU/CSU–SPD grand coalition, Schröder himself left office.

When trying to explain Chancellor Schröder's labour market reforms since his Agenda 2010 announcement, he appears to have been clear that, after the failure of the importation of the Dutch model of an 'Alliance for Jobs' to Germany, some convergence towards more effective employment and labour market policies pursued in Britain (which itself was partly inspired by Scandinavian activation policies) was needed to improve the labour market record. It may also have been important that at least parts of Schröder's policy package had repeatedly been proposed and promoted by supranational institutions like the European Commission, the International Monetary Fund (IMF) or the OECD.

Politically, Schröder had to find a strategy to implement both the economically necessary and politically viable reforms in order to fight unemployment. This proved particularly difficult, as Germany's persistent long-term high unemployment rate was, on the one hand, mainly structural and, therefore, could clearly not be solved by expansionary demand-side policies alone. On the other hand, the rather slim support for painful structural reforms in Schröder's own party and the reform-blockage power of the existing political governance systems made the political viability of the reforms extremely difficult. He finally failed to find one of the few coherent policy packages which could have led to both a lasting improvement in Germany's labour market and the re-election of the reformers (potentially the interface of economic necessities and the political viability of reforms can be zero at certain times). In short, as a result of 'too little, too late', the labour market reforms, although they were certainly a step in the right direction, led neither to political nor economic success for Schröder. They were 'too little' as the reform package was insufficient to achieve a considerable and lasting improvement in the labour market situation, and 'too late' as the urgently required reforms would have been needed immediately after the presentation of the Blair–Schröder paper in order to achieve a lasting fall in unemployment (similar to Britain) to under 3.5 million, as was announced by Schröder before he was elected Chancellor in 1998. It is true, however, that, as in Britain, more thought is needed in Germany on the question of whether there are ways to use potential synergies between structural labour market reforms and supporting macroeconomic policies, as the feasibility of labour market reforms can be hindered by the fact that they entail short-term costs, while their benefits typically take more time to materialise.[42]

CONCLUSION

This article has attempted to shed some light on the question of whether Britain and Germany showed tendencies of policy convergence with regard to their labour markets. It has argued that apart from an important shift of British monetary policy towards the German tradition of an independent central bank, and despite a few tendencies towards convergence with regard to labour market-related instruments used, convergence with regard to labour market results has remained low up until now.

Despite the shared rhetoric in the Blair–Schröder paper, the reform strategies since the publication of the paper differed between the two countries, as one might have expected when taking into account the differences in economic models and the political systems. In line with these alternative environments, the labour market-related reform process was narrowly targeted on specific areas (labour taxes and activation policies), where deep reforms were undertaken in Britain. This reflects the favourable British position in many other areas of labour market policy. By contrast, despite the fact that Germany introduced many labour market-related reforms, including some bold ones in recent years, their effects have been comparatively limited and the country still experienced a rise in structural unemployment. According to the OECD, 'this may reflect the fact that the key reforms in this country were not directed at the most important barriers to improved performance or that reforms were not sufficiently intensive. The long-lasting aftermath of the reunification shock may also have been a contributing factor'.[43]

Radical economic reforms, as occurred in Britain during the Thatcher era, are one possible way of fighting persistently high unemployment and low growth, but they have been limited by institutional and political constraints in Germany in recent years. These constraints normally included (at times without a federal grand coalition) the need to gain the opposition in the Bundesrat, the need to maintain support for the party from ptoential losers of much needed reforms, and the limited authority of the German Chancellor when compared with the British Prime Minister.[44]

It remains to be seen whether the recently enacted, much needed reform of German federalism, which constitutes a step towards the disentanglement of cooperative federalism, will lead to the necessary reforms of the labour market (even bolder than the ones implemented by Gerhard Schöder's coalition, which still have to be regarded as important steps in the right direction compared to the earlier system, despite their initial and current implementation problems).[45]

The minimum reforms that are required to generate a long-term improvement in the German labour market situation and thus to contribute to a convergence of outcomes in terms of (un)employment rates and growth in Britain and Germany include, amongst other things, further improving the activation strategies for the unemployed and the present tax and transfer system which still implies significant disincentives for labour supply. This is particularly true in the presence of children or a non-working partner as the social minimum threshold increases with household size. In other words, the income from work required to pass this threshold also increases and potentially weakens, therefore, labour supply. Furthermore, if there is no earner in a household who provides substantial income, part-time work in low-paid jobs can replace the need to work full-time in such jobs as it may lead to similar earnings because the wage income in minor employment can currently be topped up by ALG II in order to safeguard the social minimum income. Moreover, the efficiency of Germany's employment protection system needs to be raised and provisions should be made to allow for a higher degree of wage flexibility across qualifications and regions by breaking up still important insider-outsider problems. These reforms will be more effective in generating new employment if they are combined with regulatory reforms that reduce barriers to entry for new firms and impediments to the growth of enterprises. In other words, 'a comprehensive reform strategy is required to fully exploit [sic] the benefits from policy initiatives and raise their acceptability among the electorates'.[46]

Unfortunately, from an economist's point of view it remains unclear whether the present grand coalition will be able to implement such a reform package that would, at least partially, lead to more convergence upon some of the success factors of the British model. Despite some important reform successes and proposals (some stricter activation provisions through amendments of passive labour market policies, reform of federalism and the governmental announcement of the increase in the general retirement age from 65 to 67), some of the 'hot spots' that will ultimately lead to a much better performance in Germany remain more or less untouched or will become worse. To give but one important example: several proposals were put forward during the 2002–05 legislative period which aimed to make the German industrial relations system more supportive of employment, by, for example, increasing the role of 'opening clauses' imposed by the legislator. According to the coalition agreement, however, it is highly unlikely that such proposals will make it on to the statute book as no actions are planned by the grand coalition in this regard. For the time being decentralisation of wage bargaining is left entirely to the partners of collective bargaining, despite the fact that they have proved unable to contribute sufficiently to solving Germany's unemployment problems in the last decade. The current government will only step in when social partners utterly fail, that is if they fail to stop a further rise in unemployment.

NOTES

The author would like to thank the editors of this special issue for comments on an earlier version.

1. See, for example, L. Funk, 'Economic Reform of Modell Deutschland', in R. Harding and W. Paterson (eds.), *The Future of the German Economy: An End to the Miracle?* (Manchester: Manchester University Press, 2000). According to the OECD, 'unemployment has been drifting upward since the first half of the 1970s ... with unemployment rising when adverse shocks to economic activity occurred and falling only partially as the shocks subsided'. See OECD, *Germany: OECD Economic Surveys 2006* (Paris: OECD, 2006), p.23.
2. Due to the still very different real incomes and problems in the new member states of the European Union of 25 members since 1 May 2004 (27 Since 1 January 2007), the paper will compare Britain and Germany with the European Community of 15 members only. This will be denoted EU-15.
3. The root causes of Germany's poor economic growth performance in recent years compared to Britain and the EU-15 include a negative growth contribution of employment and low labour productivity growth which was unable to offset the impact on growth of the weak labour inputs. Both factors can be traced back to structural rigidities. See OECD, *Germany*, p.26. By contrast, since the beginning of the twenty-first century Britain has experienced low unemployment and inflation rates in many years simultaneously.
4. I. Blair and G. Schröder, The Third Way/Die Neve Mittle, *Dissent* 2 (2000), pp.51–56.
5. See for the following paragraphs the excellent chapter by V. Schmidt, 'The European Economy, 1954 to 2004: The Miracle of Growth and the Sources of Wealth', in R. Sakwa and A. Stevens (eds.), *Contemporary Europe*, 2nd edition (Basingstoke: Palgrave Macmillan 2006), pp.160–85, particularly pp.173–9.
6. P. Hall and D. Soskice, 'An Introduction to Varieties of Capitalism', in P. Hall and D. Soskice (eds.), *Varieties of Capitalism* (Oxford: Oxford University Press, 2001), pp.1–68. The approach is also discussed in the introduction to this volume.
7. G. Esping-Andersen, *Three Worlds of Welfare Capitalism* (Princeton, NJ: Princeton University Press, 1990).
8. See W. Eltis, 'The Lessons for Britain from the Success of German Counter-Inflation Policy', *Britain and Overseas* 25/4 (1995), pp.3–9.

9. C. Pissarides, 'Unemployment in Britain: A European Success Story', in M. Werding (ed.), *Structural Unemployment in Western Europe* (Cambridge/London: The MIT Press, 2006), pp.209–35.
10. For further discussion see L. Funk, 'Current Structural Changes: Challenges for the German Labour Market and Collective Bargaining', in J. Hölscher (ed.), *Germany's Economic Performance: From Unification to Euroisation* (Basingstoke: Palgrave Macmillan, 2006), pp.175–95; L. Funk, 'Current Structural Changes: Risks and Opportunities for German Trade Unions', *International Journal of Comparative Labour Law and Industrial Relations* 21/1 (2005), pp.59–76, here pp.64–6; and particularly on the service economy, see C. Annesley, *Postindustrial Germany: Services, Technological Transformation and Knowledge in Unified Germany* (Manchester: Manchester University Press, 2004).
11. W. Eichhorst and R. Konle-Seidl, 'The Interaction of Labor Market Regulation and Labor Market Policies in Welfare State Reform', *IAB Discussion Paper No. 19/2005* (Nuremberg: German Federal Employment Agency, 2005), pp.18–19
12. The implemented legislation limited wide immunity enjoyed by unions from civil suit to those immediately involving industrial action. Unions were also forced to elect their officials in secret balloting. During the 1990s, union membership in Britain declined by more than 20 per cent and union density declined from above 50 per cent to about 40 per cent.
13. Pissarides, 'Unemployment in Britain', pp.222–3.
14. See in particular C. Pissarides, N. Mankiw and M. Taylor, *Economics* (London: Thomson, 2006), pp.759–60.
15. Eichhorst and Konle-Seidl, 'Interaction of Labour Market Regulation', pp.31–2.
16. L. Funk, 'Towards a Transformed Federal Republic of Germany? Structural Change and the Renewal of Social Democratic Economic Policy', in M. Stierle and T. Birringer (eds.), *Economics of Transition: Theory, Experiences and EU Enlargement* (Berlin: VWF, 2001), pp.17–36, here pp.20–24. More specifically on Britain, see A. Daguerre and P. Taylor Gooby, 'Adaptation to Labour Market Change in France and the UK: Convergent or Parallel Tracks?', in P. Taylor-Gooby (ed.), *Making a European Welfare State: Convergences and Conflicts over European Social Policy* (Oxford: Blackwell Publishing, 2004), pp.84–97, here p.90. On the specific problems of German unification not discussed here, see J. Leonhard and L. Funk (eds.), *Ten Years of German Unification: Transfer, Transformation, Incorporation?* (Birmingham: Birmingham University Press, 2002).
17. European Commission, *The Contribution of Wage Developments to Labour Market Performance* (Luxembourg: European Commission, 2005), p.28.
18. In 1999, there were social democrats either in government or prominent in ruling coalitions in Britain, Germany, France and nine further member states of the European Union. Additionally, social democrats were in the majority in the European Council and the European Parliament.
19. See Schmidt, 'The European Economy', p.174.
20. See S. Driver and L. Martell, *New Labour*, 2nd edition (Oxford: Polity Press, 2006), pp.67–85.
21. See ibid., pp.196–202.
22. See Funk, 'Economic Reform of Modell Deutschland', pp.31–3, and P. Camerra-Rowe, 'Agenda 2010 and the Dilemmas of Economic Reform', in Robert Bosch Stiftung (ed.), *Building a new Transatlantic Generation* (Stuttgart: Robert Bosch Stiftung, 2004), pp.58–66, here p.61.
23. See P. Hall and D. Soskice, *Varieties of Capitalism: The Institutional Foundations of Comparative Advantage* (Oxford/New York: Oxford University Press, 2001).
24. See Daguerre and Taylor-Gooby, 'Adaptation to Labour Market Change', p.86.
25. N. Brandt, J.-M. Burniaux and R. Duval, *Assessing the OECD Jobs Strategy: Past Developments and Reforms – Annexes* (Paris: OECD Economics Department Working Paper No. 429, 2005), pp.46–7 and 125–6.
26. See for further details W. Ebbinghaus and W. Eichhorst, Employment Regulation and Labor Market Policy. in Germany, 1991–2005, *IZA Discussion Paper No. 2505* (Institute for the Study of Labor, 2006), pp. 20–26.
27. See Brandt *et al.*, *Assessing the OECD Jobs Strategy*, pp.46–7 and 125–6.
28. In this respect, one may speculate that a reduction of differences among regime types might thus be going on. However, the 'common active measures label hides differences in terms of the content of their measures, their philosophy etc. Nevertheless, the activation principle is nowadays widely shared. One of the success factors of these measures is that they can be interpreted in very different ways: as a mean to favour labour market reintegration for the unemployed, as a mean to accelerate reintegration, as a mean to control unemployed persons etc. This ambiguity assures a wide political support to ALMPs'. Quoted from F. Bertozzi, 'Reforming Labour Market Policies in Europe: Towards Increasingly Similar National Policies', Paper presented at the *ESPAnet Conference European Social Policy: Meeting the Needs of a New Europe*, University of Oxford, 9–11 Sept. 2004, p.20.
29. See D. Coats, *Who's Afraid of Labour Market Flexibility?* (London: The Work Foundation, 2006), pp.10–11. According to Coats, the present government has introduced measures that constitute a

significant re-regulation of the British labour market. This includes, for example, the extension of standard employment rights to part-time workers, more extensive information and consultation obligations for employers, a reduced period for unfair dismissal protection and increased compensation as well as a national minimum wage. Despite the fact, however, that no national minimum wage in Germany exists, the collectively bargained actual minimum wages in several low wage sectors are still typically set at a higher level (relative to the average wage) in Germany than in Britain, which is part of a possible explanation why unemployment is higher in Germany than in Britain. See L. Funk and H. Lesch, 'Minimum Wage Regulations in Selected European Countries', *Intereconomics – Review of European Economic Policy* 41/2 (2006), pp.78–92.
30. See OECD, *Germany*, p.91.
31. 'In 1999 more generous tax benefits for low-wage earners with dependent children (Working Families' Tax Credit) were introduced. In 2003, the new Working Tax Credit addressed single low-wage earners for the first time. The New Deals fit into a long-term strategy for make non-employment less attractive for working-age persons and to not only increase work incentives but also employability through activating labour market policies.' Quoted from Eichhorst and Konle-Seidl, 'Interaction of Labour Market Regulation', p.19.
32. An alliance for jobs is certainly neither necessarily a 'dead end', as is argued by many German economists, nor a 'miracle cure', as some journalists suggested. In truth, such a pact is always ambiguous for solving labour market problems. See L. Funk, 'The German Alliance for Jobs: Dead End or Miracle Cure?', *German Politics* 10/1 (2001), pp.217–24. Unfortunately, the German Alliance was implemented and steered in a way by the government that failed to help solve Germany's labour market problems and, therefore, ended in February 2002 without success. See on the background K. Dyson, 'Binding Hands as a Strategy for Economic Reform: Government by Commission', *German Politics* 14/2 (2005), pp.224–47, here pp.229–34.
33. In 1998, Schröder had declared that if he had not had reduced unemployment to 3.5 million, the SPD did not deserve re-election. He obviously failed in this respect and knew that it was only because of his response to the devastating floods in eastern Germany in August 2002 and his public opposition to the war in Iraq that the Social Democrats were able to come to power again and not because of a turn-around in the labour market. In summer 2002, registered unemployment nearly reached the level of four years earlier, again rising above the psychologically unsettling 4 million mark. In autumn 2005, when Schröder left office after losing the elections, the unemployment situation was even worse.
34. For an overview, see L. Funk, 'Chancellor Proposes Agenda 2010 to Revive Economy', *European Industrial Relations Observatory online*, available at http://www.eiro.eirofound.eu.int/print/2003/03/feature/de0303105f.html (accessed 12 June 2006), and L. Funk, 'Lower House Approves Key Elements of Agenda 2010 Reforms', *European Industrial Relations Observatory online*, available at http://www.eiro.eirofound.eu.int/print/2003/11/inbrief/de0311101n.html (accessed 12 June 2006).
35. See Camerra-Rowe, 'Agenda 2010', pp.63–6.
36. According to the OECD, 'the thrust of reform are important steps in the right direction. However, reform is incomplete yet'. See OECD, *Germany*, p.85,
37. L. Calmfors, 'Activation versus Other Employment Policies – Lessons for Germany', *CESifo Forum* 4/2 (2004), pp.35–42, here p.39.
38. Nearly two-thirds of legislation passed by the Bundestag during Schröder's terms was blocked by the Bundesrat, which was most of the time controlled by opposition parties. See J. Dempsey, 'Germany Takes Step to Ease Federal Tangle', *International Herald Tribune*, 1– 2 July 2006, p.3. See the related debate on German reform blockage in S. Green and W. Paterson, 'Introduction: Semisovereignty Challenged', in S. Green and W. Paterson, *The Semisovereign State Revisited* (Cambridge: Cambridge University Press, 2005), pp.1–19, here pp.10–11.
39. See T. Mayer, 'Germany is Fading', *Focus Europe: Deutsche Bank Global Markets Research*, 9 Feb. 2004, p.12; OECD, *Germany*, pp.53–5.
40. See OECD, *Germany*, p.96.
41. See W. Streeck, 'A State of Exhaustion: A Comment on the German Election of 18 September', *The Political Quarterly* 77/1 (2006), pp.79–88, here p.80.
42. Such a question needs to be asked since evidence shows that European Monetary Union may cause a reform problem particularly for a rather large country like Germany, as in a large country structural reforms seem more likely to be undertaken if it has an independent monetary policy. See Brandt *et al.*, *Assessing the OECD Jobs Strategy*, p.65.
43. See ibid., p.66.
44. See Camerra-Rowe, 'Agenda 2010', p.66.
45. See Dempsey, 'Germany Takes Step', p.3.
46. See OECD, *Germany*, pp.85–6.

The Unmovable Elephant: Germany and the UK's Competitiveness Jungle

REBECCA HARDING

INTRODUCTION: THE POLICY CONTEXT

The debate on economic policy in Germany and the UK over the past ten years has focused on competitiveness. In the UK, the New Labour administration, puzzled by the productivity gap with its major European and US counterparts, has focused on policy mechanisms to facilitate endogenous growth. On an assumption that the economy is actually lean and efficient, substantial policy effort has been put behind leveraging the drivers of productivity in the micro-economy through skills, innovation, enterprise, business investment and the competitive environment.[1] Alongside this, the Treasury has placed enormous emphasis on macroeconomic stability, first by making the Bank of England independent and interest rates the domain of the Monetary Policy Committee and, second, by staying outside of the Eurozone.

Interestingly, much of German economic policy over the past ten years has been similar in emphasis but without the intellectual underpinning of the approach to endogenous growth that has been taken by the UK government. Policy makers and analysts since 1990 have been concerned, variously, with 'Reunification', 'Europeanisation' and 'Globalisation', all of which are presenting threats to the institutional and competitive structure of the German economy and calling its adaptiveness into question.

Since Römer's seminal work in 1990, the importance of the internal, or endogenous, capacity of an economy to adapt to change through its innovation *system* (broadly, the skills, financial and institutional structures and market conditions that generate the propensity of an economy to innovate), has been understood as a core driver of competitiveness.[2] Competitiveness is measured using Total Factor Productivity: the unexplained 'residual' in economic growth equations that can be attributed to innate efficiencies or 'intangibles' in a particular system after all labour and capital allocations are taken into account. Around 15 per cent of the UK's productivity gap with Germany, France and the US is attributable to this 'systemic' residual.[3]

It is enlightening, therefore, to look at the debate in Germany from a UK perspective and this is the focus of this paper. It looks at the debate in Germany and argues that the focus on *Modell Deutschland* misses the real 'elephant' in the debate about competitiveness through wealth creation, or productivity. It demonstrates, using an endogenous growth model around the productivity drivers identified by the UK government (skills, investment, enterprise, competitive markets and innovation), that Germany's endogenous growth capacity is still strong, and stronger than that in the UK. A forecast based on a *ceteris paribus* assumption that there are no changes to policy and no exogenous shocks suggests that Germany's endogenous growth will slip slightly over the next five years leaving Germany placed sixth in the world rather than fifth. In contrast, on the same assumptions, the UK will see its position slip from its current sixth to twelfth.

This is a wake-up call to policy makers in both countries: in Germany the perpetual focus on the sustainability of *Modell Deutschland* is masking the imperatives to strengthen the endogenous growth drivers. In the UK, the focus on the endogenous growth drivers without understanding the need for a systemic approach undermines the effectiveness of policies to make the 'system' work as a coordinated whole. This point is made all the more clearly by focusing on the debate in Germany, and it is with this that the discussion begins.

WHERE IS THE ELEPHANT?

The usefulness of *Modell Deutschland* as an analytical tool for understanding German political economy has become an epistemological elephant in the middle of the debate about alternative models of capitalism. Everyone knows that that we may need to change our terms of reference as the pressures of economic, technological and organisational change destroy the habitat in which this legendary animal once flourished. Yet there is a degree of comfort in assuming that our orthodoxy will help us interpret the way in which it will adapt to its new, and global, environment.

Within the parameters laid down by Katzenstein in 1987, protagonists in the debate highlight the mutualistic relationships between actors in the industrial system that will either guarantee, or equally undermine, its sustainability.[4] For example, the 'optimists' broadly feel the model is adapting successfully albeit slowly.[5] For these authors, *Modell Deutschland* is based on networked linkages between the economic and social institutions of the state, civil society and political outcomes and is intrinsic to industrial society in Germany. As Annesley and Harding argue, these networks are just as important, if not more important in an economic era defined by science, innovation and knowledge transfer.[6] Instead of rendering Germany uncompetitive, the competitive, but equally collaborative, relationship between institutions and economic actors creates an underlying dynamic to the system, or *symbiotic tension*, that allows it to adapt progressively to the inevitable process of exogenous, and inevitable, change.[7]

In contrast, the 'pessimists' are those who look at the macroeconomic facts against the background of a fiercely competitive 'Anglo-Saxon' era of globalisation, and argue that the model is being swept away by the inevitability of global market forces.[8] The heavy, statist structures, the high costs of the welfare system and the intractable unemployment problem make the Rhineland Capitalist model intrinsic to *Modell Deutschland* incapable of evolving with sufficient speed to catch up with the more adept US or UK economies.

Perplexed by the apparent paradox of disturbing macroeconomic performance alongside strong export performance and a vibrant, and innovative, business sector, some are beginning to hint at the need for some kind of intellectual metamorphosis to create a hybrid that can survive even when faced with the inevitability of change. Thus, for Dyson the economic crises of reunification and subsequent 'Europeanisation' and 'Globalisation' have created 'tipping points' that have required strengths of the system to come to the fore.[9] By focusing on the consensus-based elements of the system, the role of contest within the institutional framework has been ignored. Similarly, for Dyson and Padgett the underlying continuity in the system has meant that it can cope incrementally with external change.[10] There is little doubt that, as Czada points out, many of the 'interfirm networks, co-operative labour relations and an enabling industrial state will not just disappear. The push towards a more competitive profile of the political economy might be fully compatible with a renewed pattern of managed capitalism'.[11]

What underpins all of these perspectives is that change is inevitable.[12] Our understanding of Germany's response to that process of change, therefore, must be based on a real understanding of the latest phase of globalisation if we are to discover how useful *Modell Deutschland* is as a means of understanding change in Germany itself. However, despite the uniformity of agreement on this simple fact, the debate has become stuck. Put simply, either one believes the system is changing supported by the inherent strengths of the 'model', or one believes it is not changing swiftly enough and is therefore not 'competitive' in the current economic era.

The elephant, however, is not *Modell Deutschland* itself. Rather, it is the definition of what makes a nation state 'competitive'. To say that 'competitiveness' is a fiercely contested concept in the economics profession is something of an understatement. For some, the role of the nation state is redundant in a global era since it is businesses that compete rather than governments.[13] For this first group, competitiveness means the supremacy of the firm as an organisational entity, able to make and implement decisions swiftly and easily globally with little or no need for the structures of the state. Companies locate where productivity (measured by output per worker hour) can be most effectively maximised, with the logical conclusion that low cost locations around the world provide real competitive advantage, especially if the taxation and regulation thresholds are low.

Conversely, for others, the role of the nation state becomes paramount in providing the frameworks within which businesses can compete through access to finance, the science and technology base, skills and capabilities acquisition and investment opportunities.[14] For these authors, the latest phase of globalisation represents a visible paradigm shift in the basis on which businesses compete. No longer do firms compete in terms of a rather linear view of productivity, but instead compete not just to minimise costs, but also to maximise the acquisition of unique value-adding skills and networks: in short, to acquire capabilities and intangible assets.[15] These authors take the 'national systems of innovation' approach to competitiveness that starts from the basis of unique and evolving systems at the national level that evolve (or 'learn' in different and distinct ways to allow adaptation to exogenous change as it happens.[16] That is, there is no *one* system. Companies, in order to maximise their strategic advantage as they internationalise, locate in order to take advantage of the competitive advantage that a specific national environment can give. Competitiveness, therefore, is in the symbiotic set of relationships between the public and the private sector that build endogenous growth.[17]

The logical consequence for policy from the first set of authors is that costs, especially in the form of real wages, regulation and tax have to be kept as low as possible in order to attract inward investment and to retain investment from indigenous firms. Germany has fared relatively badly under this view of the global economic order with the well-documented high rates of unemployment, labour market inflexibility and high social, real wage and regulatory costs relative to other 'competitor' nations.[18] The Schröder reforms to the labour market in particular, which limit social security payments to the long-term unemployed, make 'hiring and firing' easier and encourage self-employment, were a reaction to this rigidity in the macro-economy.

The remainder of this essay, however, argues that if we examine more closely the endogenous performance of the German economy over the past 20 years then we can step outside the politics of *Modell Deutschland* and begin to understand how it functions as an economic model. Germany's economy has been historically weak in terms of exogenous growth.[19] However, the results of an endogenous growth model that produces a country competitive ranking presented here illustrate the intrinsic strength of the inter-relationships between its innovation, enterprise, macroeconomic and investment structures.[20] On the basis of the forecasting potential in the model, the paper goes on to argue that Germany's competitive position is unlikely to slip by much, if at all. In other words, if we assume that there are nationally specific characteristics that affect its long-term competitiveness, the German economy has indeed been adapting, and more effectively than the UK! Some policy mechanisms, such as innovation networks at a regional level, have been particularly successful in accelerating change in the last ten years and transforming the heavy, statist structure of *Modell Deutschland* into something that represents a paradigm in the latest phase of globalisation.

So we have been ignoring the very real elephant in the middle of the debate: that the sustainability of *Modell Deutschland* is not the most interesting issue. In the global era, there is no one model of capitalism, or even two. The US economy has networks and linkages within its technology system very similar to Germany's, not least because the German innovation system was translated into an American context at the beginning of the twentieth century.[21] Moreover, Germany's largest firms have been as global as their US counterparts, if not in terms of market capitalisation, then in terms of sales, personnel and research and development.[22] Similarly, in the early twenty-first century the US economy, despite the much-proclaimed productivity miracle, creates jobless growth just as the German economy does.

The issue, then, is not whether or not Germany's structures can adapt to an era in which adeptness and flexibility are drivers of competitiveness. Rather, we should focus our discussion on what sort of a state Germany actually needs to generate competitiveness.[23] The debate about *Modell Deutschland* has become mired in politics but the economics of it are quite clear. The inter-relationships between the economic infrastructures of innovation, investment, enterprise and the macroeconomy represent a strong and adaptive base. The political economy of the debate now should focus on just how this strength can be harnessed with the market correcting mechanisms that accelerate flexibility and dynamism.

COMPETITIVENESS AND SEEING THE ELEPHANT

Our elephant is sitting in the middle of a debate on economic competitiveness. In essence, competitiveness in economic terms, whether at a business or a national level, is the capacity to add value, in other words to create wealth. The very word 'wealth' is loaded with connotations of inequality (wealth creation may imply that some get richer relative to others) that are unpalatable to a civil society that cherishes *Gerechtigkeit*. Yet if we look at wealth as standards of living and of the propensity of the economy to raise those standards of living through the performance of its businesses, then wealth creation arguably takes centre-stage irrespective of political persuasion.

There are several approaches to measuring competitiveness when one assumes it to be synonymous with wealth creation but all work on the basis that wealth creation is endogenous to the system and can therefore be measured in terms of the 'new economy' drivers of productivity.[24] These include innovation potential (propensity to patent, university–industry links and citations) and entrepreneurial propensity (such as access to capital, private equity investments, costs to start up and levels of entrepreneurial activity), all of which can be directly linked to increases in productivity.

Since productivity and wealth creation are often used synonymously, it stands to reason that any model created to rank the competitiveness of an economy must do two things:

1. It must measure productivity in a way that indeed indicates added value creation rather than simply increased income per capita. In other words, it must measure the intangible elements of wealth creation rather than the rather blunt instrument of output per worker or per hour worked.
2. It must measure productivity in a way that provides a clear link with the business base of the economy. That is, it must have the potential to capture the competitiveness of individual firms.

With these pre-requisites in mind, arguably the best method of measuring competitiveness is Total Factor Productivity which is the residual in any growth model after everything else has been taken into account.[25] It measures the efficiency of factor inputs (for example, employee hours or capital intensity) in delivering a particular level of output. It is often seen as a measurement of business efficiency: because it is a residual, it has a large component that can only be attributed to systemic factors such as innovation potential or skills. And at the level of macroeconomic performance, it similarly measures the intangible aspects of productivity that stem from business competitiveness in international and national markets, again, like human resources utilisation, propensity to patent, investment activity and business start-up rates. It represents a useful proxy, therefore, for the capacity of an economy to provide a strong competitive environment within which its businesses can be competitive.[26]

To summarise, then, wealth creation is not something that necessarily undermines principles of equality and fairness. The propensity of a country to create wealth is, however, an important measure of national and company-level competitiveness. Taking this perspective, we can explain the paradoxes of the last 16 years in Germany: why is there poor macroeconomic performance alongside a robust microeconomic base in business? The simple answer is that the institutional linkages at an economic (rather than political or societal) level in Germany have continued to generate wealth despite the traumas of reunification and globalisation. If we understand competitiveness in this way, then we can see where both the strengths and the weaknesses of the economy lie, and it is to this that the discussion now turns.

IS GERMANY COMPETITIVE?

By focusing on high-level macro-indicators, such as unemployment and real wage costs, we are missing the essence of Germany's economic strength. Instead, the model presented here rests on an assumption that we need to look below the surface to the interdependence between factors in the micro-economy that influence Germany's capacity to create wealth.

The index rankings presented below are based on a model that measures competitiveness through Total Factor Productivity, or wealth creation.[27] The total index is a multiple regression constructed from four sub-indices (formed from panel regressions) as follows:[28]

- *Macroeconomic stability:* Dependent variable: real Gross Domestic Product (GDP) volatility. Independent variables: inflation volatility, short-term interest rate volatility, real GDP, unemployment growth.
- *Enterprise*: Dependent variable: Total Entrepreneurial Activity (TEA).[29] Independent variables: years of schooling, capital gains tax, cost and time to start up, the Milken Index of access to capital, venture capital investment per capita.
- *Innovation*: Dependent variable: patents (European and US patenting office). Independent variables: Gross Domestic Expenditure on R&D (GERD) and Business Expenditure on R&D (BERD), years of schooling, full-time equivalent researchers per head of population, journal citations per researcher, technology cooperation.
- *Business investment*: Dependent variable: business investment share of total investment. Independent variables: access to credit, product market regulation, real wages, real GDP volatility, real GDP per capita, tax compliance costs, long-term interest rates.

The index results for the 26 countries included in Deloitte's study rank Germany's competitive position as fifth overall in 2005.[30] There are low rankings for some of the sub-indices, for example, fifteenth for enterprise and sixteenth for investment. Germany ranks fourth for macroeconomic stability (since volatility in the economy has been low over a 20 year period) and sixth for innovation.

A final competitiveness ranking is produced from the effect that all these factors have on Total Factor Productivity growth. So, in the case of Germany, although rankings for enterprise and investment are relatively low, they are working with a stable (if somewhat negative) macro-environment and higher levels of innovation to produce above-expectations Total Factor Productivity growth.

Further, if we use the assumptions that underpin the model, in other words that performance in each of these areas will continue along the same trajectory as the last 20 years, then Germany's position by 2010 will slip from fifth to sixth. Before this is heralded as the final nail in the coffin of the post-war German economic miracle, it is worth noting that the UK's ranking will fall from sixth to twelfth and France's from twelfth to fifteenth. This is illustrated in Figure 1, which shows the rankings over the period since 1984.

There are two points that should be drawn out of this chart. First, the forecast rankings are based on a *ceteris paribus* assumption that the conditions that existed in the last year for which full data were available, 2004, will still prevail in 2010. In other words, if there are no policy changes, no changes in global economic environments and no additional growth created by an economy then the rankings hold. At the time of writing, this set of assumptions looks like a worst case scenario for Germany on the following grounds:

- The German economy looks likely to experience a strong recovery in 2006, largely as the result of increased exports but also because of improved investments in

FIGURE 1
COMPETITIVENESS RANKINGS FOR THE G7 ECONOMIES, INDIA, CHINA AND SOUTH KOREA, 1984–2010

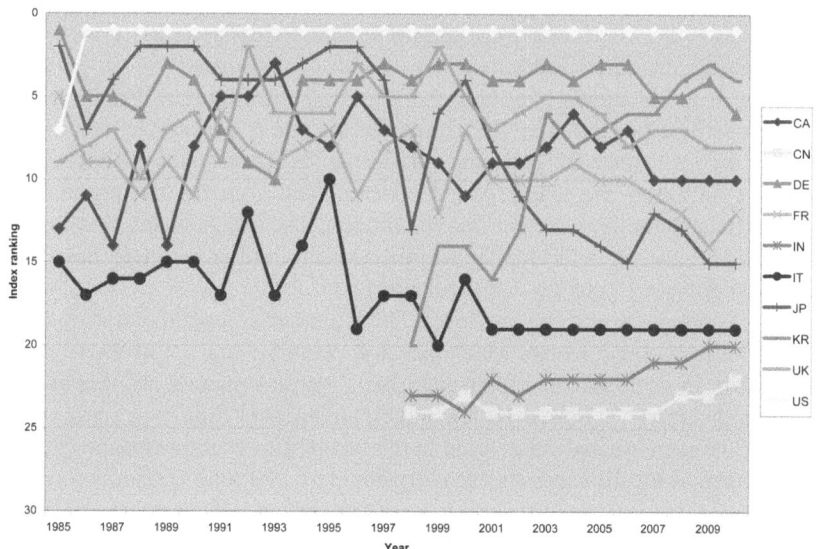

machinery and equipment.[31] The latest Institute for Economic Research (IFO) indicators of consumer and business confidence are improving and unemployment is falling gradually as a result of the Hartz reforms referred to above.
- The *Mittelstand* is demonstrating strong competitive performance and is increasingly a vehicle for private equity investments in Germany. Funds raised for private equity and venture capital have increased.[32]
- There is evidence that although the collapse of the *Neuer Markt* presented Germany and the Germans with a real crisis of confidence in the New Economy, entrepreneurial activity is beginning to increase and confidence is improving.[33] The new economy in Germany is strong, with downward pressure on real wage growth, openness to trade nearly twice as high as other industrialised nations, increased investment overall and improved productivity, especially in manufacturing.[34]
- Spillover effects from the rapid 'New Economy' growth in areas around technology hubs such as Jena have gathered momentum after a shaky start to the twenty-first century.[35] Similarly there is evidence that the initiatives to create regional innovation hubs and networks have been successful and started to generate real growth effects.[36]
- The eastern German innovation base is being fuelled by public R&D grants to a greater extent than in western Germany: more R&D tends to be conducted per 'R&D Euro' spent in public sector grants than in western Germany, and there are greater innovative outputs (for example in products and services) although fewer patents.[37]

Given that the variables comprising the index model are similar to where we are seeing improvements in the German microeconomic conditions, this should lead to improved performance.

Second, it is instructive to look at the other nations covered in Figure 1. The model that underpins the chart captures long-term competitiveness to 'new economy' competitiveness measured in terms of the wealth creation potential of the economy in question. It is remarkable that only the US of all the Group of 7 (G7) economies see its competitive position stay the same over the whole period. Germany performs less badly than the other G7 economies, however, as its real ranking has slipped by just three points over the whole period covered (and arguably by less than that if more positive assumptions are put into the model). The UK fares the worst out of all of the G7 because of deteriorating macroeconomic and investment environments (specifically company taxation and regulation).

Figure 1 contains a warning, however. The increased competitiveness of the emerging economies of South Korea, which put 'new economy' competitiveness structures in place some 25 years ago, and India and China, whose structural changes barely register within this model at present, is remarkable. India and China have some way to go in terms of the systemic indicators used in this model (for example patenting and citations) and their competitiveness is currently largely in the 'old' economy form of low real wage costs. However, as the skills base of both expands and catches up with South Korea, it is likely that the competitive position will improve relative to the forecast.

DEALING WITH THE ELEPHANT

So what has all this told us about *Modell Deutschland*? We have deliberately left discussions about institutional transformation and renewal on one side in favour of establishing how the system as an engine for wealth creation, and hence competitiveness, works. Over the past 16 years since reunification, despite apparent chaos in the macroeconomy, criticism of the institutional structures that underpin the microeconomy has been at least muted, if not non-existent. The analysis here helps us explain why this is the case.

Put simply, what the above discussion suggests is that *Modell Deutschland* cannot, and arguably could never, explain why the German economy remained strong in terms of its business competitiveness. The only period in which Germany has had high growth was in the reconstruction phase of public and private consumption growth in the 1950s and 1960s. Subsequent growth has been led by exports, but not by private consumption, meaning that we need to look to business competitiveness in order to explain any growth in the economy.

Instead, *Modell Deutschland* helps us understand the institutional structure of Germany's economy. These structures, although commonly assumed to be about the relationship between political actors, civil society and corporate governance, are actually most effective in terms of their impact on wealth creation, in the relationships that generate competitiveness in the 'new economy'. What is really interesting, though, is firstly that the new economy strengths have existed for at least the 20 years covered in the model and secondly that any weaknesses are now emerging in two areas: the investment environment and the general 'entrepreneurial' environment (broadly in a German context, this could be deemed the *Mittelstand*).

This interpretation has profound implications for understanding the upturn in economic fortunes in 2005–06. Some of the measures to improve the entrepreneurial climate began with reforms to the labour market that first started with the Hartz Reforms and the broader Agenda 2010. Initiatives like the *Ich-AG* (which promoted self-employment), mini-jobs and benefits' streamlining against very real changes in redundancy law and the way in which unemployment statistics are calculated were bound to begin to have an impact on levels of unemployment after a time lag.[38] Changes to training, initiatives that started in the mid-1990s to promote regional innovation networks and R&D, and small but important changes in the pension system started to create a visible improvement in attitudes towards the competitive environment in Germany during 2005. For example, Germany's Global Entrepreneurship Monitor reports since 2002 have mirrored the lack of confidence in the economy in Germany through the early years of the decade. However, a significant improvement in perception of business opportunities, from 12.5 per cent of the adult population seeing good business opportunities in 2004 to 17.5 per cent in 2005 suggests that the attitudinal rot may have been stopped even before the 2005 election. Policy initiatives already started have begun to have an effect on the climate in Germany and will have an impact on the competitiveness of the economy as time goes by.

Angela Merkel has begun the process of reform slowly and already critics are baying for faster action to inject what they see as much needed dynamism into the economy.[39] Before analysts write off the reforms as they progress, however, two important points are worth bearing in mind:

The underlying drivers of productivity in the economy are strong, as illustrated and, after a time-lag, policy initiatives that started ten years ago are beginning to have an effect. Angela Merkel should wait to see just how robust the recovery is before she acts. This is particularly true if she wishes to accelerate changes in the labour market since many of the measures that exist already should make it more flexible. The health of the labour market and German public opinion are closely interconnected and if optimism becomes muted then this will have an impact.

Endogenous growth relies on market correcting as well as market enabling mechanisms. Germany has historically done extremely well at creating markets (for example the relatively rapid development of biotechnology over the last ten years in Germany has been a product of this success). The model above indicates where the areas of weakness are: the business investment climate and the enterprise environment, particularly in the *Mittelstand*. The improvements in the private equity market are positive and the government has announced a big programme of support for transitioning *Mittelstand* companies to the innovative drivers of new economy growth that they should be. Any policy that supports the *Mittelstand* should not forget its interdependence with the innovation system in Germany, however: the institutions of technology transfer (the Fraunhofer Institutes, government-funded research centres and Max Planck Institutes) are as vital as reform to the university system.

Germany has, over the past 20 years covered in the analysis for this study, maintained standards of living in western Germany and improved standards of living in eastern Germany. Although there are still differences in real incomes, there are also differences in productivity between the two regions. Econometric studies suggest that initiatives to support wealth creation through endogenous growth in eastern Germany are having a positive effect, although of course, because of the lower starting point, the time-lag effects are likely to be more pronounced.

Wealth creation through the new economy does not necessarily mean sustained or widening income inequality between eastern and western Germany or even success of the few at the expense of the many. Entrepreneurship takes many forms, including innovation within existing firms (corporate entrepreneurship) and entrepreneurship for community rather than shareholder gain (social entrepreneurship). Evidence from the Global Entrepreneurship Monitor suggests that there are more people starting businesses in Germany than in the UK and that there are nearly twice as many engaged in entrepreneurial activity within their jobs as compared to the UK. These are activities that fall outside the traditional structures of *Modell Deutschland*, in that entrepreneurs tend to leave behind the comfort of the welfare system in order to pursue their own business interests.

A final note on public service and welfare reform: efficiency drives, such as those in the in the UK, are appealing to a right-of-centre administration with an interest in creating as minimal a state as possible. They do not necessarily lead either to improvements in infrastructure or, indeed, maintain *Gerechtigkeit* in terms of access to services as the current debate in the UK illustrates. More instructively, the German administration could look to the role of social entrepreneurship and not for profit organisations in the provision of public services and community regeneration, particularly in the eastern Länder. Social entrepreneurs tend in the UK to be dominant in public sector arenas of health, education and community care. They potentially also have a bigger impact on job creation and productivity than the mainstream entrepreneurs.[40] Models for social entrepreneurship in the public sector exist in both the US and the UK, and the Merkel government would do well to explore these.

CONCLUDING REMARKS: THE ELEPHANT REVISITED

Modell Deutschland has hidden depths that, in the UK, we have traditionally admired if not understood. We have looked at the political aspects of the model, but ignored its economic aspects for too long, yet it is here that the real policy lessons for the UK can be found. The strengths of the model rest in the symbiotic but competitive relationships between the institutional actors within the national system of innovation (broadly institutions of science and technology, technology transfer and innovation, education and skills and investment). These *symbiotic tensions*, where institutions compete and then collaborate to deliver innovation projects, alongside a developing entrepreneurial culture have kept the drivers of wealth creation strong for the last 20 years through a traumatic period of adjustment within Germany and rapidly accelerating technological and organisational change outside of Germany. In contrast, in the UK there has been competition *or* tension but no symbiosis.

Our elephant is now clearly visible and can no longer be ignored. It is not *Modell Deutschland* itself; it is the drivers of competitiveness that should have been the real subject of debate. *Modell Deutschland* cannot help us to understand the relatively low growth endemic to Germany's economic performance since the late 1970s. But if we take competitiveness to be wealth creation itself, then the institutional symbiosis fundamental to *Modell Deutschland*'s unique innovation system is indeed a vehicle that aids our analysis.

As the developed world faces increased competitiveness challenges from India, China and South Korea, as well as from the emerging economies in Eastern Europe, it is the 'high end' productivity drivers that will fuel competitiveness. The need for efficiency in markets, and particularly the public sector, cannot be disputed, but must be supported by high levels of skill, strong research and development and commercialisation of ideas and a supportive investment environment to enable businesses to grow. These are challenges faced just as much by the UK as by Germany and we ignore them at our peril.

NOTES

1. M. Porter and C. Ketels, 'UK Competitiveness: Moving to the Next Stage', *DTI Economics Paper* 3 (Institute of Strategy and Competitiveness, Harvard Business School, 2003).
2. P. Romer, 'Endogenous Technological Change', *Journal of Political Economy* 98 (1990), pp.71–102.
3. See R. Harding, M. Cowling and N. Turner, *The Missing Link: from Productivity to Performance* (London: The Work Foundation, 2002).
4. The interdependency between institutional structures was first defined in Peter Katzenstein's seminal 1987 contribution, *Policy and Politics in Germany: The Growth of a Semisovereign State* (Philadelphia, PA: Temple University Press, 1987).
5. See, for example, P. Katzenstein, 'Semisovereignty in United Germany', in S. Green and W. Paterson (eds.), *Governance in Contemporary Germany: The Semisovereign State Revisited* (Cambridge:

Cambridge University Press, 2005), pp.283–306; R. Harding and W. Paterson (eds.), *The Future of the German Economy: An End to the Miracle?* (Manchester: Manchester University Press, 2000); C. Annesley, *Post-industrial Germany: Services Transformation and Knowledge in Unified Germany* (Manchester: Manchester University Press, 2004); R. Deeg, 'The Comeback of "Modell Deutschland": The New German Political Economy in the EU', *German Politics* 14/3 (2005), pp.332–53; P. Hall and D. Soskice, *Varieties of Capitalism: The Institutional Foundations of Comparative Advantage* (Oxford: Oxford University Press, 2001).
6. Annesley, *Post-industrial Germany*; R. Harding, 'Competition and Collaboration in German R&D', *Industry and Corporate Change* 10/2 (2001), pp.389–417.
7. Harding, 'Competition and Collaboration in German R&D'.
8. H. Siebert, *The German Economy: Beyond the Social Market* (Princeton, NJ: Princeton University Press, 2005); H. Siebert, 'Comment', *World Economy* 29/2 (2006), p.137; W. Streeck and C. Trampush, 'Economic Reform and the Political Economy of the German State', *German Politics* 14/2 (2005), pp.174–95; H. Giersch, K.-H. Paqué and H. Schmieding, *The Fading Miracle: Four Decades of Market Economics in Germany* (Cambridge: Cambridge University Press, 1992); Economist Intelligence Unit, 'Country Profile Germany: Social Market Model Comes under Pressure', 18 May 2004, available at http://www.economist.com (accessed 20 June 2006); F. Scharpf, 'The German Disease', *Prospect* 26 (Jan. 1998), available at http://www.prospect-magazine.co.uk/article_details.php?search_term = german + disease&id = 4383 (accessed 20 June 2006).
9. K. Dyson, 'Economic Policy Management: Catastrophic Equilibrium, Tipping Points and Crisis Interventions', in S. Green and W. Paterson (eds.), *Governance in Contemporary Germany: The Semisovereign State Revisited* (Cambridge: Cambridge University Press, 2005), pp.115–37.
10. K. Dyson and S. Padgett, 'The Politics of Economic Reform in Germany: Global, Rhineland or Hybrid Capitalism?', *Anglo-German Foundation Report* (London: Anglo-German Foundation, 2005).
11. R. Czada, 'The German Political Economy in Flux', in J. Leonhard and L. Funk (eds.), *Ten Years of German Unification: Transfer, Transformation or Incorporation?* (Birmingham: Birmingham University Press, 2002), pp.151–67.
12. R. Harding, 'New Challenges for Innovation Systems: A Cross Country Comparison', *International Journal of Technology Management* 26/2–4 (2003), pp.226–46. See also Harding and Paterson, *The Future of the German Economy*.
13. K. Ohmae, *The End of the Nation State: The Rise of Regional Economies* (London: Harper Collins, 1996); R. Reich, 'Who is Us?', in W. Lazonick and W. Mass (eds.), *Organisational Capability and Competitive Advantage: Debates, Dynamics and Policy* (Aldershot: Edward Elgar, 1995); R. Reich, *The Work of Nations: Preparing Ourselves for Twenty-First Century Capitalism* (New York: Alfred Knopf, 1991).
14. A. Saxenien, *Regional Advantage: Culture and Competition in Silicon Valley and Route 128* (Cambridge, MA: Harvard University Press, 1997); M. Porter, 'Clusters and the New Economy of Competition', *Harvard Business* Review (Nov.–Dec. 2002), pp.70–90; P. Cooke, 'Regionally Asymmetric Knowledge Capabilities and Open Innovation: Exploring "Globalisation 2" – A New Model of Industry Organisation', *Research Policy* 34 (2005), pp. 1128–49; R. Harding, 'Why Invest in Biotechnology and How?', *Anglo-German Foundation Report* (London: Anglo-German Foundation, 2003); R. Harding, 'Trading Places: How Globalisation will Drive Future UK Competitiveness', *Deloitte Research Report* (Deloitte and Touche LLP, 2005).
15. For a full discussion of the role of intangible assets such as skills, capabilities and innovation potential in allowing firms to learn and, hence, adapt, see D. Teece, G. Pisano and A. Sheun, 'Dynamic Capabilities and Strategic Management', *Strategic Management Journal* 18/7 (1997), pp.509–33.
16. R. Nelson (ed.), *National Innovation Systems: A Comparative Analysis* (Oxford: Oxford University Press, 1993).
17. See, for example, P. Aghion and P. Howitt, *Endogenous Growth Theory* (Cambridge, MA: MIT Press, 1997).
18. OECD, *Economic Survey – Germany 2004* (Paris: OECD, 5 Aug. 2004).
19. Deeg, 'The Comeback of "Modell Deutschland"'.
20. This model was first presented as the Deloitte Competitiveness Index in Harding 'Trading Places'.
21. L. Kim and R. Nelson, *Technology, Learning and Innovation: Experiences of Newly Industrialising Economies* (Cambridge: Cambridge University Press, 2000).
22. R. Harding and J. Cantwell, 'The Internationalisation of German Companies' R&D', *National Institute Economic Review* 1/98 (1998), pp.99–115
23. 'Wieviel Steuern braucht der Staat?', *Der Spiegel* 19, 6 May (2006).
24. See, for example, S. Bergheim and J. Hofmann, 'Globale Wachstumszentren 2020: fundierte Langfristprognosen mid Hilfe von Formel-G', *Deutsche Bank Research*, April 2005, available at http://www.db.com (accessed 10 Jan. 2006); P. Romer, 'Endogenous Technological Change',

Journal of Political Economy 98 (1990), pp.71–102; M. Keilbach and D. Audretsch, 'Entrepreneurial Capital – Determinants and Impact on Regional Economic Performance', *Discussion Papers on Entrepreneurship, Growth and Public Policy* No. 37 (Jena: Max Planck Institute for Economics, 2004).
25. See Bergheim and Hofmann, 'Globale Wachstumszentren 2020' for a fuller discussion.
26. Two papers discuss this in more detail: R. Harding, M. Cowling and N. Turner, 'The Missing Link: From Productivity to Performance', *Report of the First Work and Enterprise Panel of Inquiry* (London: The Work Foundation, 2002); Harding and Gentle, *Trading Places*.
27. This index was first presented as the Deloitte Competitiveness Index and published as Harding and Gentle, *Trading Places*. I am indebted to Djordje Djokovic, Nye Hill and Chensheng Lu for their work on the index at its construction stage and their on-going interest in its maintenance.
28. Simultaneous equations were used to test for interdependencies between the sub-indices. The final index is a simultaneous equation Panel Data multiple regression of the four sub-indices + proxies for openness (measured as the balance of trade) and human capital (measured as years of schooling). The index can explain lagged GDP growth.
29. Total Entrepreneurial Activity is the index of early stage entrepreneurial activity produced by the Global Entrepreneurship Monitor (GEM) (http://www.gemconsortium.org). It measures entrepreneurial activity and behaviours across some 40 countries around the world and is the only measure of the cultural propensity to be entrepreneurial or to risk take that allows international comparisons to be made.
30. The countries above are: the US (1), Sweden (2), Finland (3) and Denmark (4). These are broadly in line with other international rankings such as the World Economic Forum's Global Competitiveness Index and IMD's World Economic Rankings.
31. 'The State of the World Economy and the German Economy in the Spring of 2006', Joint Economic Forecast of Six German Research Institutes, 27 April 2006.
32. Bundesverband Deutscher Kapitalbeteiligungsgesellschaften, *2005 – A Positive Year for the German Private Equity Industry* (2006), available at http://www.bvk-ev.de (accessed 23 Feb. 2006).
33. M. Minniti, *Global Entrepreneurship Monitor, 2005 Executive Report* (London Business School and Babson College, GEM, 2006).
34. Deutsche Bank Research: 'New Economy 2.0: Above Potential Growth Continues in 2006/7' (2006), available at http://www.db.com (accessed 27 April 2006). The growth model used for this forecast report is very similar to that used for the index presented above.
35. G. Buenstorf and D. Fornahl, 'B2C – Bubble to Cluster? The Dotcom Boom and Software Entrepreneurship in an East German Region', *Mimeo*, Max Planck Institute of Economics, Evolutionary Economics Group (2006).
36. A. Eickelpasch and M. Fritsch, 'Contests for Cooperation: A New Approach in German Innovation Policy', *Research Policy* 34/8 (2005), pp.1269–82; see also Harding, 'Why Invest in Biotechnology', and D. Audretsch and E. Lehmann, 'Does the Knowledge Spillover Theory of Entrepreneurship Hold for Regions?', *Research Policy* 34/8 (2005), pp.1191–202.
37. D. Czarnitzki and G. Licht, 'Additionality of Public R&D Grants in a Transition Economy: The Case of Eastern Germany', *Economics of Transition* 14/1 (2006), pp.101–31.
38. For a fuller discussion see Funk's contribution to this volume.
39. 'The Slow Walk Upstairs: Angela Merkel's Reforms are Continuing but They Risk Being Too Little Too Late', *The Economist* (2006), available at http://www.economist.com (accessed 10 Sept. 2006).
40. R. Harding and M. Cowling, *Social Entrepreneurship Monitor* (London: London Business School and the Work Foundation, 2004).

Health Policy: Obstacles to Policy Convergence in Britain and Germany

NILS C. BANDELOW

INTRODUCTION

In 1999, the newly elected centre-left governments of Britain and Germany announced similar and in part jointly developed reform projects under the banner of the 'Third Way', a central element of which was the use of the market to attain social democratic goals.[1] One key area of the Third Way, of which others are discussed elsewhere in this volume, was health policy. In this context, 'Third Way' thinking rejected the belief in the perceived 'knightish' behaviour of the health care providers (that is, public-spirited altruism), which remained prevalent among 'traditional' social democrats. Like conservatives and liberals, the 'Third Way' assumes health care providers to be 'knavish', that is in some way self-interested. Additionally, 'Third Way' social democrats agree with the goal of conservatives and liberals on the desirability of enlarging the scope for decision-making by the recipients of health services. However, while 'modern' social democrats agree with the centre-right parties on the use of the market to optimise the health system, they still follow socialist goals like social equality.[2] At the same time, the 'Third Way' lacked any general definition of how 'equality' and other goals could be translated into health policy or of how this translation should deal with the problem of different national health systems.

While the theoretical basis of centre-left health policy is still evolving, there is clear evidence of differences between centre-right and centre-left policies in this area. Even though both sides of the political divide generally agree over the use of the market, centre-left politicians advocate complementary networks of quality control under the responsibility of the central state.[3] 'Third Way' health policy also relied on increasing international benchmarking and the transfer of strategies that have proven to be successful in other countries.[4]

Despite the lack of clarity about the specific instruments of centre-left health policy to achieve 'equality', both the general ideology and the promise that policies will rely on international best practice allow us to hypothesise that there would be some degree of convergence in Britain and Germany. Policy convergence can affect both policy output and policy outcome. Although there is a large amount of research about the convergence of British and German health policy outcomes, the research has not yet systematically applied the concept of convergence to the health policy strategies of the recent centre-left governments in these countries. This contribution begins by reviewing the available evidence about the convergence and divergence of health policy outcomes. Next, the strategies of the Blair and Schröder governments are analysed to show how the 'Third Way' was translated into health policies in each country. The empirical part then addresses policy convergence and presents indications of cross-national transfer of health policy between Britain and Germany respectively. Lastly, the discussion reviews the obstacles which will continue to hinder convergence between the health policies of Britain and Germany.

SIMULTANEOUS CONVERGENCE AND DIVERGENCE OF HEALTH POLICY OUTCOME

The question of the convergence or divergence of policy outcomes has become increasingly significant in health policy research in recent years.[5] Policy convergence is defined as reduced differences. It must be distinguished from analogy, which is defined as developments in the same direction. There are many theoretical reasons to assume an increase of policy convergence between modern democracies.[6] However, health policy has not produced as many empirical studies as other policy fields such as social policy, tax policy or environmental policy.[7]

Notwithstanding the politically derived expectation of convergence, one can also find theoretical arguments to support an expectation of divergence between Britain and Germany. The British National Health Service (NHS) and German Statutory Health Insurance (SHI) belong to different types of health systems. The NHS as a Beveridge-type system is primarily financed by taxes. The state takes direct responsibility for the organisation and supply of health services. The German Bismarck-type system, on the other hand, is primarily financed by contributions deducted from wages equally shared by employers and employees, although not those sections of the workforce which can afford private insurance. Responsibility for the delivery of health services is organised by self-administration and corporatism. Additionally, the British NHS is part of a 'liberal' welfare state which was originally intended to deliver a basic level of social protection. The German 'conservative' welfare state, on the other hand, was developed to secure the social status of different groups of employees and their families in case of unemployment, illness, old age or accidents.[8] If one looks at the policy outcomes of the 1980s and early 1990s, one can find evidence for the hypothesis that there is much more convergence between countries with similar health systems than between those with the Beveridge- and Bismarck-type systems.[9]

Researchers have so far not found much evidence for unequivocal convergence of British and German health policy outcomes.[10] Even analogy could not be observed in

TABLE 1
EXPENDITURE ON HEALTH AS A PERCENTAGE OF GDP

Year	UK	Germany	EU-15
1996	7.0	10.9	8.2
1997	6.8	10.7	8.0
1998	6.9	10.6	8.0
1999	7.2	10.6	8.1
2000	7.3	10.6	8.1
2001	7.5	10.8	8.3
2002	7.7	10.9	8.5

Source: OECD Health Data 2005.

every respect. Tables 1 and 2 illustrate these results. The total expenditure on health as a percentage of Gross Domestic Product (GDP) shows convergence but no analogy. By contrast, the development of public expenditure on health as a percentage of the total expenditure on health gives evidence for neither convergence nor analogy.

However, the explanatory power of this data is limited. In particular, the data in Table 2 cannot be easily compared, because public expenditure in Britain mainly consists of taxes, while the contributions to the German SHI are also classified as 'public expenditure' by the Organisation for Economic Co-operation and Development (OECD). We must therefore also look at policy output to obtain a more accurate picture about the development of health policy in these two countries.

By focusing on policy processes, the notion of 'policy transfer' comes into play. The concept was originally developed to analyse the transfer of institutions and policies between the states of the USA in the late 1960s and early 1970s.[11] In the 1990s, it became the core of an analytical framework.[12] The framework presents several theses about the probability of policy transfer and the conditions for successful transfer. It is claimed, for example, that different institutional settings hamper transfer. Therefore one might not expect successful health policy transfer between Britain and Germany. However, both countries have already transferred health policy instruments from the USA, although the American health system differs substantially from both the British NHS and the German SHI.[13] Additionally, the political systems may create hurdles for policy transfer. Although both countries are parliamentary democracies,

TABLE 2
PUBLIC EXPENDITURE ON HEALTH AS A PERCENTAGE OF THE
TOTAL EXPENDITURE ON HEALTH

Year	UK	Germany	EU-15*
1996	82.9	80.6	74.8
1997	80.4	79.0	74.8
1998	80.4	78.6	74.6
1999	80.6	78.5	74.2
2000	80.9	78.6	74.3
2001	83.0	78.4	75.0
2002	83.4	78.6	74.6

*No data available for Belgium.
Source: OECD Health Data 2005.

the German 'semisovereign' state with its many veto players is usually considered resistant to any changes that are more than incremental.[14]

There are even more arguments against the adoption of any common health policy project by the 'Third Way' Social Democrats who gained power in Britain (1997) and Germany (1998) at almost the same time. Despite their ideological proximity, both governments started with opposite perceptions of the main health policy problems which had to be tackled in their respective countries. New Labour's health policy started with the results from the 'internal market' that the Conservatives had introduced in 1991. At the end of the Conservative government, more than half of the population in England and Wales was covered by one of the then 19,000 fund-holding GP practices.[15] The institution of GP fund-holders, who manage the NHS budget of their patients and buy health services and goods from other providers, was considered by Labour to be neither efficient nor fair. Additionally, the UK government was soon confronted with the problem of underfunding. In Germany, on the other hand, health policy has traditionally been seen as a central element of employment policy. Both the government of SPD (Sozialdemokratische Partei Deutschlands) and Greens (Bündnis 90/Die Grünen) and the parties of the former coalition of CDU (Christlich Demokratische Union Deutschlands), CSU (Christlich-Soziale Union in Bayern) and FDP (Freie Demokratische Partei) had been faced with the problem that rising health costs usually translated into an increase of non-wage labour costs, which in turn acted as a brake on economic growth and employment. In short, while there has been long-term pressure in Britain towards an increase in the quality and quantity of its health system, German policymakers have been faced with the overwhelming need to reduce costs.

Although policy transfer can be used as a useful heuristic tool to describe policy developments, there are several problems in using it as a theory.[16] The most important problem is the failure of existing empirical applications to deliver any undisputed evidence for a causal connection between policy transfer and policy change. Policy transfer always competes with other possible causes such as power change. It is therefore very difficult to prove causal links between transfer and convergence. Consequently, the term policy transfer will only be used here to describe explicit references to foreign lessons. It will not be claimed that these references are the major or even the only cause for the policy output. A reference to another country thus only gives an indication of the prestige of that other country's policies within the national policy sub-system that referred to them.

NEW LABOUR'S HEALTH POLICY AND NON-CONVERGENCE WITH GERMANY

The health policy of the Blair government has been influenced by several factors. Initially, the incoming government aimed to disassociate itself from its Conservative predecessor. Additionally, health policy was heavily influenced by the conflict between competing wings of the Labour Party, which have led to a continuous evolution of health policies. Drawing on lessons from other states did not play a major role in developing health policy during the first months after New Labour won the election of May 1997. Nonetheless, the subsequent reforms did use lessons drawn from other countries and also led to some convergence with the German health system.

During the electoral campaign of 1997, health policy was a major issue and played a key part in New Labour's comprehensive victory over John Major's Conservative government. In consequence, the Department of Health (DoH) was initially entrusted to an 'Old Labour' stalwart, Frank Dobson. But it was only during his term of office, which lasted until October 1999, that policy would be defined by the party's left wing. Thus, as a first step, the government reversed the 1991 health reforms which had created the internal or 'quasi' market. Only a few months after the election, the DoH published its white paper *The New NHS*; this paved the way for the 1999 Health Act, which abolished the internal market. Even though fund-holding GPs were eliminated, the main idea of the 1991 reform, market contracts between purchasers and providers of health care, was maintained. Fund-holding GPs were replaced by Primary Care Groups and from 2000 onwards by Primary Care Trusts (PCTs). PCTs include all GPs in a geographical area covering populations ranging from 50,000 to 250,000. These groups of GPs and community nurses received full responsibility for local operational management. Table 3 shows these and other reforms in chronological order.

In April 1999, the government introduced another instrument which would become very important for the German reform discussion: the National Institute for Clinical Excellence ('NICE'), which joined with the Health Development Agency on 1 April 2005 to become the 'National Institute for Health and Clinical Excellence'. NICE was founded to provide patients, professionals and the public with information and to establish 'best practice' by teams of experts. The main tasks of the Institute were to appraise new drugs and technologies for use in the NHS and to produce guidelines for public health, health technologies and clinical practice. These guidelines have been implemented by the Commission for Health Improvement (CHImp) as the other main part of a national system of quality control for all NHS services.

In autumn 1999, there was a fundamental change in the direction of British health policy. The catalyst of this change was media reporting of a range of individual cases, which together served to highlight the perceived underfunding of the NHS; as a result,

TABLE 3
MAJOR BRITISH HEALTH POLICIES AND POLITICS, 1997–2005

Date	Health policies and politics
May 1997	New Labour wins general election
	Frank Dobson appointed as Health Secretary
December 1997	White paper *The New NHS. Modern. Dependable* published
April 1999	Health Act passed.
October 1999	Alan Milburn appointed as Health Secretary
July 2000	NHS Plan A Plan for Investment – a Plan for Reform published
February 2001	Health and Social Care Act passed
June 2001	New Labour wins second general election
July 2001	White paper *Shifting the Balance of Power* published
April 2002	Strategy paper *Delivering the NHS Plan – Next Steps on Investment, Next Steps on Reform* published
June 2002	National Health Service Reform and Health Care Provisions Act published
June 2003	John Reid appointed as Health Secretary
December 2003	Strategy paper Building the Best: Choice, Responsiveness, and Equity in the NHS published
June 2004	*NHS Improvement Plan* published
May 2005	New Labour wins third general election with reduced majority
	Patricia Hewitt appointed as Health Secretary

Source: Author's compilation.

public satisfaction fell significantly.[17] The party leadership reacted by forcing Frank Dobson to resign as Health Secretary; Dobson in turn, after a failed attempt to become Mayor of London, became one of the government's fiercest critics over its health policy. For under Dobson's successor Alan Milburn, who came to the job as a leading 'Blairite', the agenda changed dramatically. Certainly, the government announced significant increases in NHS funding, but these were to go hand-in-hand with the 'modernisation' of structures. The new NHS plan of July 2000 promised a 6.3 per cent increase in funding over five years and an improvement in both the quantity and quality of all main health services. The government tried to improve the services by the introduction of public–private partnerships in health care delivery to supplement and to compete with the traditional NHS organisations. It also aimed to improve integrated services, decentralise health care management, and strengthen patient rights. The plan did refer to Germany several times – but interestingly always in a negative sense, with the German (and French) social insurance system described as inefficient and unfair. Even though Germany and France have health systems with nearly unrestricted patient choice, the plan referred to Sweden and Denmark whenever discussing more choice, especially for inpatient care. Additionally, and curiously, the United States served as a major model for the reform agenda,[18] even though a recent World Health Organisation report had ranked the US health system last among industrialised countries.[19]

In February 2001, the Health and Social Care Act translated the 2000 NHS plan into legislation. The Act introduced new options for integrated services by PCTs or NHS Trusts by making further provisions for partnership arrangements between care trusts. Though the Act introduced competition on the supply side of health care services in particular, the subsequent years have been marked by proposals to bring back competition on both sides of a rebuilt internal market. The white paper *Shifting the Balance of Power* (July 2001) developed the PCTs as the leading local organisations on the demand side of health services and NHS Trusts as the leading local organisations on the supply side. In April 2004, a government plan set the agenda for foundation hospitals and a further improvement of patient choice.

Policy-makers in the DoH also showed their willingness to learn from the experiences of other countries. Market-based solutions are used in Germany, as in many other OECD countries, in an attempt to improve efficiency, and, correspondingly, the NHS Plan of June 2004 now referred to the German health care system in a positive sense. Germany was named as an example of the successful introduction of payment-by-results schemes for hospital financing which is to be implemented by 2008. Currently, payment-by-results is a British version of a DRG (Diagnosis Related Groups) system which has been adopted by Germany and many other countries.

Another strategy of British health care policy in the new Millennium which makes the NHS apparently more similar to German health insurance is decentralisation. However, NHS decentralisation differs significantly from German health care federalism. In contrast to Germany, decentralisation is not connected to self-government in the UK. British regions lack the combination of joint decision-making and legal autonomy of the German Länder. Decentralisation in the NHS includes two elements. First, health care provision was one of the competencies passed on to the newly devolved administrations in Scotland and Wales. Secondly, the National Health Service Reform and Health Care Provisions Act 2002 decentralised the structure within the English NHS by creating 28 Strategic Health Authorities (SHAs) to support PCTs and NHS Trusts in delivering the NHS plan. The SHAs develop plans for improving local health services and are responsible for oversight and improvement of the local health services' quality and capacity.

After Alan Milburn had left the government for personal reasons in June 2003, his successors John Reid (June 2003–May 2005) and Patricia Hewitt (since May 2005) have carried on the reforms of increasing funding, including private providers, expanding patient choice, decentralising administration, improving quality assurance, and rebuilding the internal market (see Table 3). In particular, the Labour government formalised its commitment to increase NHS spending from the 1997 level of 6.8 per cent of gross domestic product (GDP) to 9.4 per cent in 2007–08.[20] On the demand side, the 300 PCTs have now begun to manage around 75 per cent of NHS funding. Additionally, after April 2005 the Labour government implemented what may be seen as the first steps to the re-introduction of the GP fund-holding scheme. The DoH gave PCTs the right to devolve indicative budgets to GP practices. Similar to the years 1991–97, the GP practices could fix their own contracts with other providers and could make surplus gains to re-invest in their services. As in the earlier system, the GPs could decide to take part in the scheme or not. In contrast to the original internal market, the PCTs remain legally responsible and the system is open even to small practices.[21]

On the supply side, Labour also continued to build a second internal market with private providers and published performance information. An independent health care inspectorate awards each NHS provider an annual rating from zero to three stars. The ratings determine the degree of operational freedom the NHS providers are allowed, and they are related to (small) financial bonuses. Providers with top ratings may also become independent non-profit 'NHS foundation trusts'. The managers of these trusts then have more freedom to decide how to pay their staff and how to meet the performance standards. By January 2005, 57 hospitals had gained the necessary ratings; 25 of them took the opportunity to become foundation trusts. These foundation hospitals have the opportunity to pay their staff higher wages and thereby to attract better personnel.

Thus, the most recent reforms by New Labour follow a direction similar to the health policy of the Conservatives. Both parties wanted to increase patient choice and provider competition.[22] The major difference is that the Labour government introduced a net of state authorities to provide quality control and to steer the results of competition. Even though Labour prefers the market rather than the state to handle 'knavish' providers and improve consumer choice, Labour's trust in the market has not quite reached the level of the Conservatives.

Germany was never a major model for the British health reforms between 1997 and 2005. There were only minor steps to more convergence of the policy outputs and outcomes. Although the increased funding reduced the difference to Germany, decentralisation and increasing the autonomy of the providers was not meant to lead to real convergence, nor did it actually do so.

GERMANY'S HEALTH POLICY AND INTERNAL FORCES

As in Britain, German health policy has been mainly driven by internal forces and not by transnational learning. The SPD–Green government's health policy underwent changes that were in fact quite similar to the developments of British health policy. As in Britain, the incoming government started with a struggle between the competing wings of the Social Democrats. Even after 'Third Way' supporters gained control of health policy, Britain became a model only for the general ideology of health reform, but there was no convergence of concrete policy instruments.

It is particularly interesting to note that the SPD–Green government, upon taking office, was confronted with health policy problems that were the opposite to the UK's. In contrast to the UK, Germans showed general satisfaction with the quality and quantity of their health services. Instead, there was the problem of rising costs, leading to rising contribution rates and ultimately higher non-wage labour costs. The range of possible solutions essentially revolved around two poles: either the introduction of radical structural reforms to increase the efficiency of the health system, or the adoption of incremental changes to fine-tune the existing model. Yet even though the main parties all agreed on the need for structural reforms, they all found it difficult to break the established mode of only incremental changes to health care in Germany. The main reason for this lies in the extraordinary ability of health care providers to act as highly effective veto players. Thus, and despite some loss of influence since the early 1990s, the medical profession continues to be represented by a powerful network of associations.[23] On the one hand, these consist of corporatist organisations like the Associations of Doctors for Statutory Health Insurance (*Kassenärztliche Vereinigungen*) which are intricately involved in the formulation and implementation of health policies. On the other hand, professional associations and unions such as the *Hartmannbund* and the *Marburger Bund* have proved themselves extremely adept at exerting pressure on elected politicians by using the threat of strikes and public resistance. Pharmacists too are well organised in similar organisations, even though they have not been quite as influential as physicians. Meanwhile, the pharmaceutical industry, and in particular the association of research-based pharmaceutical companies (*Verband Forschender Arzneimittelhersteller*), while not part of the corporatist network itself, has strong links to leading politicians of all parties and has therefore been able to prevent several reforms. Hospitals are the third large group of health service providers and their owners, Länder, municipalities, welfare organisations and private providers, also have powerful interest groups, joined together in a single peak association (*Deutsche Krankenhausgesellschaft*). Its negotiating strength is further bolstered by the knowledge that it can rely on the active political support of one of its main constituencies, the Länder governments.

On the opposite side to the providers, the health insurance funds have also increased their influence. Their peak associations not only represent the (partially competing) interest of different funds, but also the unions and (in most funds) employers' associations that are part of their structure because of the principle of self-government. To make the network of interest groups even more unmanageable, private insurance is organised in another influential association (*PKV, Verband der privaten Krankenversicherung*). Only patient associations have not yet gained major influence.[24]

This formidable network of producer interests has helped ensure that policy changes in Germany have so far tended to be incremental, revolving mainly around the federal government limiting the global size of certain elements of the budget, as well as shifting the financial responsibility for individual areas of expenditure onto patients.[25] Essentially, therefore, the new SPD–Green government came to office in September 1998 against the backdrop of over 20 years of cost containment policies, many of which had been at the (financial) expense of patients.

As in the case of New Labour, the left wing of the SPD had a major influence on health policy during the first few months after reaching office. The 'Act Reinforcing Solidarity in the Statutory Health Insurance Scheme', which came into force in 1999, reversed some budget-shifting which had been enacted by the Kohl government in 1997. In particular, it cut some patient co-payments. Concurrently, the new government again took up the idea of budget-setting. Budget-setting can be seen as an element that originally was typical of NHS systems. The idea of introducing special budgets for outpatient services, hospitals and pharmaceutics was not new in Germany, and the policy-makers did not refer to Britain when introducing it. By cutting health expenditure overall, though, the government at least brought Germany closer to Britain.

But this initial course was dropped following the resignation of Oskar Lafontaine, the leading light of the SPD's left wing, as party leader and Federal Finance Minister in March 1999. The government had already lost its majority in the Bundesrat the previous month, thereby making any future reforms subject to the opposition's agreement. In consequence, the 'managed economy' coalition became dominant in health policy.[26] Table 4 shows the main developments in German health policy from 1998 to 2005.

The defeat of the left-wing 'traditionalists' also made the UK more attractive as a model for Germany. While Lafontaine wanted to tie Germany more closely to France, Chancellor Schröder, who succeeded Lafontaine as SPD party leader, used the opportunity to bring Germany closer to the UK.[27] He also attempted to introduce some structural reforms, for instance in the Health Insurance Reform Act 2000. But perhaps inevitably, most of them – such as the reform of payment systems or the introduction of a positive list of medicines to be paid by the statutory health insurance – failed either before or after they had officially become enacted. During this time, the Federal Health Minister was Andrea Fischer, who, as a member of the Green Party, had the handicap of not having any allies at all among the sector's powerful interest groups. In January 2001, Fischer resigned from government over the discovery of BSE (Bovine spongiform encephalopathy, 'mad cow disease') in German cattle, following which the Greens were happy to hand over the Health Ministry to the SPD, who installed Ulla Schmidt as Minister, a post she has held ever since.

Like Andrea Fischer, Ulla Schmidt did not get off to a good start. Her initial decisions were highly influenced by several interest groups, in particular the large pharmaceutical companies, who profited from the Pharmaceuticals Budget Settlement Act and other decisions. Yet these initial decisions intensified the financial problems of the SHI. The slowing economy compounded the situation: after 2000, the already growing gap between GDP and gross wages, which were subject to SHI contributions, widened further as gross wages and salaries actually fell.[28]

TABLE 4
MAJOR GERMAN HEALTH POLICIES AND POLITICS 1998–2005

Date	Health policies and politics
September 1998	SPD and Green Party win federal election
	Andrea Fischer (Green Party) appointed as Federal Health Minister
December 1998	Act Reinforcing Solidarity in the Statutory Health Insurance passed
February 1999	SPD and Green state governments lose majority in the Bundesrat following election in Hesse
March 999	Oskar Lafontaine resigns as SPD party leader and Federal Finance Minister
June 1999	Blair–Schröder paper published
December 1999	Health Insurance Reform Act 2000 passed
January 2001	Ulla Schmidt (SPD) replaces Andrea Fischer as Federal Health Minister
December 2001	Pharmaceuticals Budget Settlement Act passed
September 2002	SPD and Greens win second federal election with narrow majority
December 2002	Act Safeguarding the Contribution Rate passed
March 2003	Agenda 2010 speech of Gerhard Schröder
November 2003	SHI Modernisation Act passed
March 2004	Schröder steps down SPD party leader, to be succeeded by Franz Müntefering
December 2004	Financing of Dentures Adjustment Act passed
May 2005	Schröder announces early federal elections after the SPD–Green coalition loses the state election in North Rhine-Westphalia
September 2005	SPD–Green federal government replaced by Grand Coalition after federal election

Source: J. Steffen, *Sozialpolitische Chronik. Stand Januar 2005* (Bremen: Arbeiterkammer, 2005), available at http://www.arbeitnehmerkammer.de/sozialpolitik/doku/02_politik/chronik/chronik_gkv_spv.pdf (accessed 24 Aug. 2005); Author's supplements and compilation.

Immediately after winning re-election in September 2002, the SPD–Green government took the unusual step, in a system of traditional self-regulation, of fixing in law the contribution rates, as well as reducing some benefits of the SHI. Further pressure to enforce major reforms arose after the SPD lost power in Schröder's home state of Lower Saxony in the February 2003 election. In his famous 'Agenda 2010' speech of March 2003, Schröder reacted by promising coherent reforms of the labour market and social policies. In the field of health policy, Schröder announced a further budget-shift to reduce non-wage labour costs. But the SPD and Greens' weakness in the Bundesrat meant that any solution could only be negotiated in an informal 'grand coalition' with the CDU/CSU. In July 2003, the governmental parties and the CDU/CSU negotiated a common proposal for a health care reform. The SHI Modernisation Act was passed in November 2003 to become law in January 2004.

Given the cross-party consensus which underpinned it, one might have expected the SHI Modernisation Act to introduce some major changes to the disadvantage of interest groups, as a similar informal grand coalition had indeed done in 1992. Even though the Health Minister at that time, Horst Seehofer, again took part in the negotiations, the various interest groups were on this occasion able to defend their positions to much greater effect. The result was a further privatisation of health costs by abolishing several benefits and increasing patient co-payments, including a flat-rate user charge of €10 for every first contact with any doctor within three months. The Act also ended the long-enshrined principle of equality between the employer's and employee's contributions, by introducing a special premium of 0.5 per cent of wages to be paid by employees alone.

Nonetheless, some individual changes show distinct similarities to the British reforms. For example, the Act obliged all insurers to offer a family doctor scheme. Patients who opt for these schemes obtain financial benefits. As in the UK, these patients must see their GP before they may access secondary care. This system was supported by the SPD, which officially referred not to Britain but to a similar reform that had been introduced (and meanwhile abolished) in the Netherlands.[29] Again similarly to the UK, the Act improves the integration of inpatient and outpatient care by creating financial incentives for new forms of health care provision. The reform also restricted the service guarantee of the Associations of Panel Doctors, which prevents competition in outpatient care. It can thus be seen as a first step towards introducing internal markets in German health care, following the British example.

A further similarity to the UK is the strengthening of patient rights. Since January 2004, patient associations have been allowed to take part in the Federal Commission, which is the major arena of self-regulation in the German health system, bringing together the associations of statutory health insurers and providers. However, patient associations still have no right to vote in the commission.

Since June 2004, the Federal Commission has been supported by the independent Institute for Quality and Efficiency in the Health Care System. This institute was intended by the Social Democrats to be the most explicit transfer from Britain, as it would be the German version of the British NICE. Like NICE, the German institute evaluates the quality and usefulness of services and medicines and is supposed to develop neutral information for patients and continuing education for physicians.[30] Nonetheless, large pharmaceutical firms and the CDU succeeded in making the institute a part of the self-regulatory framework rather than a state authority.[31] As NICE is under direct governmental control, its German counterpart cannot actually be considered as an example of full transfer from the UK.

Soon after the 2003 SHI Modernisation Act had been passed, the federal coalition was gripped by a series of political crises (see Table 4). In March 2004, Schröder resigned as SPD party leader. He chose Franz Müntefering as his successor in the hope that he would be able to meet the dual task of supporting the federal government's reform agenda and while still winning back the left wing of the party. To aid this, the party leadership signalled its readiness to make some minor concessions to the leftwingers, principally by withdrawing some elements of the Modernisation Act. Originally, the reform had planned to remove dentures from the SHI range of services altogether; in December 2004 dentures were brought back, although they remain financed by the patient alone through an increase of the special employee's contribution to 0.9 per cent.

Since the autumn of 2003, the overriding conflict in German health policy has been about the future financing of the health system. In August 2003, an expert commission working on behalf of the Health Secretary presented two competing reform plans. The SPD, the Green Party, and the PDS favoured the idea of a 'citizen insurance' (*Bürgerversicherung*) in order to extend the contribution-based insurance to the entire population (as in Austria and other Bismarck-type health systems) and includes non-wage income in the basis of the contributions. The CDU/CSU and FDP, on the other hand, preferred a flat-rate health premium (*Kopfpauschale*), limited only to those people currently covered by SHI. Ultimately, the compromise agreed by the Grand Coalition in 2006 envisages a hybrid model, with every adult required to pay €109 monthly (up to 7 per cent of their income), while employers would contribute 6.5 per cent of wages up to the contribution ceiling. The latter rate will be fixed, thereby protecting the employers from any future increase in the contribution rate.

It is still too early to predict all the results of the recent government changes on German health policy because there will be many political and economic hurdles to realising all the proposals. Both the *Bürgerversicherung* and the *Kopfpauschale* plans show some similarities, such as the goal of reducing the employers' contributions. Additionally, both plans retain the non-contributory insurance of children. The main difference between the two schemes is that the SPD and Green Party (and even more so the PDS) wanted to retain and even increase the redistribution between higher and lower wage-earners within the health system, whereas the CDU/CSU (and even more so the FDP) plan to eliminate this redistribution from the health care system. Instead, the parties have argued in favour of redistribution through the tax system, but it is still unclear how this would be achieved.

SUMMARY AND OUTLOOK: OBSTACLES AGAINST HEALTH POLICY CONVERGENCE IN BRITAIN AND GERMANY

At the beginning of the centre-left reform project in Britain and Germany in 1997/98, both countries claimed reform strategies which were, broadly speaking, similar. The policy-makers of both countries developed even closer relations and presented joint papers to find common answers to the challenges of globalisation, demographic evolution and technological progress. However, the 'Third Way' did not lead to similar reform strategies. While some of the chosen strategies have led to some convergence, other decisions even increased the differences between the two countries.

The lack of convergence corresponds to the rarity of explicit positive references to each other's health systems. Each government referred to positive experiences of the other country to legitimise policy reforms only once. The British government used the German DRGs to justify the introduction of a 'payment-by-results' system. Nonetheless, the reference can only be found in the official presentation of the reform plan and did not dominate the discussion. The German Social Democrats used the British 'NICE' to legitimate their (failed) plan to bring the German institute of quality supervision under direct state control.

Interestingly, neither in Germany nor in Britain did the reference lead to a real cross-national transfer of the chosen instrument. On the contrary, both countries used each other's experiences as negative references. As Turner and Green note in the introduction to this collection, the term *englische Verhältnisse* continues to be used in a pejorative sense in Germany by referring to perceived long waiting times and low-quality services in the NHS. By contrast, the UK has concentrated on the impression of German unemployment and *Reformstau* (gridlock). In both countries, such justifications have been used to legitimise moves away from common policies. Thus, health policy confirms Radaelli's observation on the diffusion of EU policies to the member states: even the use of similar reform strategies need not lead to convergence.[32] Rather, the comparison of

German and British health policy gives evidence for the concept of path dependency, which has been transferred from economics to politics by historical institutionalists.[33] In both countries, key points in time that have proved to be 'critical junctures' can easily be identified. In Britain, these are the foundation of the NHS and introduction of quasi-markets, which certainly determined the reform options of the Blair government. In Germany, health policy has so far been determined by three 'critical junctures': the introduction of the SHI by Bismarck, the re-establishment of the system after 1945 and the extension of the system to east Germany without major changes after German unification.[34] Therefore the Labour and SPD–Green governments not only had different starting points, they also had to deal with different reform paths, the direction of which had already been determined by the actions of the previous government. Thus, health policy outputs and outcomes in Germany and Britain remain dominated by national political institutions, interests and ideas.

NOTES

1. See A. Giddens, *The Third Way: Renewal of Social Democracy* (Oxford: Polity Press, 2000); A. Giddens, *The Third Way and its Critics* (Oxford: Polity Press, 2000).
2. J. Le Grand, *Motivation, Agency, and Public Policy. Of Knights and Knaves, Pawns and Queens* (Oxford: Oxford University Press, 2003).
3. See for example S. Stevens, 'Reform Strategies for the English NHS', *Health Affairs* 23/3 (2004), pp.37–44, here pp.38–40.
4. See R. Heinze, *Die Berliner Räterepublik. Viel Rat – wenig Tat?* (Wiesbaden: Westdeutscher Verlag, 2002).
5. See for example the contributions to E. Mossialos and J. Le Grand (eds.), *Health Care and Cost Containment in the European Union* (Aldershot: Ashgate, 1999).
6. C. Kerr, *The Future of Industrial Societies: Convergence or Continuing Diversity?* (Cambridge, MA: Harvard University Press, 1983); C. Bennett, 'What Is Policy Convergence and What Causes It?', *British Journal of Political Science* 21/2 (1991), pp.215–33; R. Seeliger, 'Konvergenz oder Divergenz? Sonderabfallpolitik in Deutschland, Kanada und den USA 1970 bis 1996' (PhD Thesis, University of Tübingen, 2001); K. Holzinger and C. Knill, 'Causes and Conditions of Cross-National Policy Convergence', *Journal of European Public Policy* 12/5 (2005), pp.775–96; E. Turner and S. Green, 'Understanding Policy Convergence in Britain and Germany: Towards a Framework for Analysis', introduction to this volume.
7. S. Heichel, J. Pape and T. Sommerer, 'Is there Convergence in Convergence Research? An Overview of Empirical Studies on Policy Convergence', *Journal of European Public Policy* 12/5 (2005), pp.817–40, here pp.820–23, see also Turner and Green, 'Understanding Policy Convergence in Britain and Germany'.
8. G. Esping-Andersen, *Three Worlds of Welfare Capitalism* (Princeton, NJ: Princeton University Press, 1990).
9. A. Comas-Herrera: 'Is there Convergence in the Health Expenditures of the EU Member States?', in Mossialos and Le Grand (eds.), *Health Care and Cost Containment in the European Union*, pp.197–218.
10. Comas-Herrera, 'Is there Convergence in the Health Expenditures of the EU Member States?'; C. Wendt, S. Grimmeisen and H. Rothgang, 'Convergence or Divergence in OECD Health Care Systems?', Paper presented at the Annual Conference of Research Committee 19 of the International Sociological Association (Paris, 2 Sept. 2004), available at http://www.sfb597.uni-bremen.de/ (accessed 6 Sept. 2005); H. Rothgang, M. Cacae, S. Grimmeisen and C. Wendt, 'The Changing Role of the State in Healthcare Systems', *European Review* 13 (2005), pp.187–212.
11. D. Beer, *Ideen auf Reisen* (Baden-Baden: Nomos, 2006).
12. R. Rose, *Lesson Drawing in Public Policy: A Guide to Learning Across Time and Space* (Chathan, New Jersey: Chatham House, 1993); D. Dolowitz and D. Marsh, 'Who learns What from Whom: A Review of the Policy-Transfer Literature', *Political Studies* 44 (1996), pp.343–57; D. Dolowitz and D. Marsh, 'Learning from Abroad: The Role of Policy-Transfer in Contemporary Policy-Making', *Governance* 13 (2000), pp.5–24; M. Evans and J. Davies, 'Understanding Policy-Transfer. A Multi-Level, Multi-Disciplinary Perspective', *Public Administration* 77 (1999), pp.361–85; D. Stone, 'Learning

Lessons and Transferring Policy Across Time, Space and Disciplines', *Politics* 19 (1999), pp.51–9; D. Hough, W. Paterson and J. Sloam (eds.), *Policy-Transfer and Programmatic Change in the Communist-Successor Parties of East Central Europe* (London: Routledge, 2005); C. Knill, 'Introduction: Cross-National Policy Convergence: Concepts, Approaches and Explanatory Factors', *Journal of European Public Policy* 12/5 (2005), pp.764–74; K. Holzinger, H. Jörgens and C. Knill (eds.), *Transfer, Diffusion und Konvergenz von Politiken* (Wiesbaden: VS-Verlag für Sozialwissenschaften, 2007, in print).

13. R. Freeman, *Policy-Transfer in the Health Sector*, available at http://www.pol.ed.ac.uk/freeman/workingpapers/policytransfer_health.pdf (accessed at 21 Aug. 2005); F. O'Neill, 'Health: The "Internal Market" and Reform of the National Health Service', in D. Dolowitz (ed.), *Policy Transfer and British Social Policy. Learning from the USA?* (Buckingham: Open University Press, 2000), pp.59–76.
14. P. Katzenstein, *Policy and Politics in West Germany. The Growth of a Semisovereign State* (Philadelphia, PA: Temple University Press), pp.183–4; P. Katzenstein, 'Conclusion: Semisovereignty in United Germany', in S. Green and W. Paterson (eds.), *Governance in Contemporary Germany. The Semisovereign State Revisited* (Cambridge: Cambridge University Press, 2005), pp.283–306; M. Seeleib-Kaiser, 'The Welfare State: Incremental Transformation', in S. Padgett, W. Paterson and G. Smith (eds.), *Developments in German Politics 3* (Basingstoke: Palgrave, 2003), pp.143–60; G. Tsebelis, *Veto Players: How Political Institutions Work* (Princeton NJ: Princeton University Press, 2002).
15. G. Fattore, 'Cost Containment and Health Care Reforms in the British NHS', in Mossialos and Le Grand (eds.), *Health Care and Cost Containment in the European Union*, p.762; R. Robinson and A. Dixon, *Health Care Systems in Transition: United Kingdom* (Copenhagen: WHO Regional Office for Europe, 1999), p.18; Le Grand, *Motivation, Agency, and Public Policy*, p.99.
16. O. James and M. Lodge, 'The Limitations of "Policy-Transfer" and "Lesson Drawing" for Public Policy Research', *Political Studies Review* 1/1 (2003), pp.179–93.
17. G. Rivett, *NHS History*, available at http://www.nhshistory.net (accessed 23 Sept. 2005).
18. M. Evans and P. Cerny, '"New Labour"', Globalisierung und Sozialpolitik', in S. Lütz and R. Czada (eds.), *Wohlfahrtsstaat – Transformation und Perspektiven* (Wiesbaden: VS Verlag für Sozialwissenschaft, 2004), p.218; Rivett, *NHS History*; C. Ham, 'Lost in Translation? Health Systems in the US and UK', *Social Policy and Administration* 39/2 (2005), pp.192–209.
19. J. Iglehart, 'Foreign Lessons: Is There Value Added?', *Health Affairs* 20/3 (2001), pp.6–7.
20. Stevens, 'Reform Strategies for the English NHS', pp.38–40.
21. Bertelsmann-Stiftung, 'Health Policy Monitor, United Kingdom', available at http://www.hpm.org (accessed 23 Aug. 2005).
22. Le Grand, *Motivation, Agency, and Public Policy*.
23. N. Bandelow, 'Akteure und Interessen in der Gesundheitspolitik: Vom Korporatismus zum Pluralismus', *Politische Bildung* 37/2 (2004), pp.49–63.
24. N. Bandelow, *Gesundheitspolitik: Der Staat in der Hand einzelner Interessengruppen* (Opladen: Leske + Budrich, 1998).
25. E. Mossialos and J. Le Grand, 'Cost Containment in the EU: An Overview', in Mossialos and Le Grand (eds.), *Health Care and Cost Containment in the European Union*, pp.1–154, at pp.73–4.
26. See K. Dyson, 'Economic Policy Management: Catastrophic Equilibrium, Tipping Points and Crisis Interventions', in Green and Paterson (eds.), *Governance in Contemporary Germany*, pp.115–37, at p.135.
27. W. Paterson, 'Germany and Europe', in S. Padgett, W. Paterson and G. Smith (eds.), *Developments in German Politics 3* (Basingstoke: Palgrave, 2003), pp.206–26, at p.212.
28. Deutsche Bundesbank, 'Finanzielle Entwicklung und Perspektiven der gesetzlichen Krankenversicherung', *Monatsberichte der Deutschen Bundesbank* 56/7 (2004), pp.15–32, here p.21.
29. P. Groenewegen and S. Greß, 'Der Hausarzt in den Niederlanden – Auslaufmodell oder Reformperspektive für die GKV?', *Jahrbuch für Kritische Medizin* 38 (2003), pp.73–91.
30. A. Riesberg, S. Weinbrenner and R. Busse Reinhold, 'Gesundheitspolitik im europäischen Vergleich. Was kann Deutschland lernen?', *Aus Politik und Zeitgeschichte* B 33–34 (2003), pp.29–38, here p.34.
31. C. Pick, *Current Themes in UK Health Care: How are They Approached in Germany?*, available at http://www.agf.org.uk/pubs/pdfs/1445web.pdf (accessed 26 Aug. 2005).
32. C. Radaelli, 'Diffusion Without Convergence: How Political Context Shapes the Adoption of Regulatory Impact Assessment', *Journal of European Public Policy* 12/5 (2005), pp.924–43.
33. P. Pierson, 'Increasing Returns, Path Dependence, and the Study of Politics', *American Political Science Review* 94/2 (2000), pp.251–67.
34. N. Bandelow, 'Gesundheitspolitik in der Bundesrepublik Deutschland: Zielkonflikte und Politikwechsel trotz Blockaden', in M. Schmidt and R. Zohlnhöfer (eds.), *Regieren in der Bundesrepublik Deutschland: Innen- und Außenpolitik seit 1949* (Wiesbaden: VS Verlag für Sozialwissenschaften, 2006), pp.159–76.

Environmental Policy in the United Kingdom and Germany

CHARLES LEES

INTRODUCTION

This study examines developments within environmental policy making in the United Kingdom and the Federal Republic of Germany and is examined along three dimensions: (i) the historical context; (ii) policy instruments and discourses; and (iii) policy outcomes. In empirical terms it asks, first, can we identify patterns of convergence and/or divergence along these three dimensions between the two countries and, second, to what extent does the European integration process impact upon these patterns? The second question is particularly useful in a comparative context because it also serves to enhance our understanding of the scope and scale of the processes of Europeanisation and policy transfer within the United Kingdom, Germany and, by inference, further afield. In theoretical terms it uses an historical institutionalist framework within which to build the analysis.

The historical institutionalist approach is useful because it provides a macro-level theoretical lens which makes it possible to both embed and problematise the meso-level concepts of 'Europeanisation' and 'policy transfer'. The mechanics of these two concepts are expanded upon elsewhere in this volume. However, let us clarify the study's use of the concept of Europeanisation at this point. There is a lively debate within the literature as to whether Europeanisation is a 'top-down' or 'bottom-up' process and this debate also touches on the role of intervening variables (nation-specific norms, standard operating procedures) in the process.[1] It is beyond the scope of this essay to engage with these debates. It is, however, useful to point out that although reference is made to a bottom-up conception of Europeanisation – for instance, with regard to the uploading to the European Union level of German regulatory practices in the 1980s – the study gives more weight to a top-down conception of the process. There are two reasons for this. First, because the top-down approach explicitly places member states as the 'receivers' of Europeanisation, it provides a better framework for concentrating on a comparison of policy practices in the United Kingdom and Germany. Second, the top-down approach complements the historical institutionalist framework in that it requires some degree of institutional 'misfit' at the member state level to exert the adaptational pressures for Europeanisation to occur. Again, this allows us to concentrate upon institutional settings in the United Kingdom and Germany. At the same time, however, the study is responsive to criticisms of the top-down approach found in the literature and places significant weight on intervening variables that determine the scope and scale of Europeanisation.[2] This emphasis on intervening variables in the process of Europeanisation ties in with debates surrounding the nature of policy transfer and the more recent and less developed idea of 'policy resistance'.[3] But in order to engage with these concepts, the study first sets out the historical context of environmental policy making in the United Kingdom and Germany.

THE HISTORICAL CONTEXT

Environmental policy is a paradigmatic example of a 'trans-boundary' policy domain. Be it degradation of wetlands, rivers and other water resources, or air pollution and global warming, many environmental problems are not – and cannot – be confined within national borders. It is no surprise, therefore, that there is a tension between the trans-boundary nature of such problems and the dominant mode of governance, which remains based around the institutions of the nation state.[4]

It is a given in the historical institutionalist literature that when institutions are in equilibrium they are characterised by the phenomenon of 'path-dependence'.[5] The day-to-day operation of path-dependent institutions is shaped by established norms and standard operating procedures, many of which were laid down at a very early stage in these institutions' history. Any institutional change or development that takes place in this context is incremental. Path-dependence is not a universal phenomenon, however, and institutions can also evolve through a series of 'punctuated equilibria', in which 'rapid bursts of change [are] followed by long periods of stasis'.[6] Throughout this process, however, the policy choices made and standard operating procedures established around the time of institutional formation shape the scope and scale of subsequent developments. Sometimes, as with the abandonment of Keynesian economic policy in the United Kingdom after 1976, certain institutions are able to leap free of the shackles of prior practice and achieve what amounts to a 'paradigm shift' in the substance of policy making.[7] In most cases, however, we see a more prosaic process in which standard operating procedures often inhibit anything more than incremental change. This leads to two possible ideal types of outcome. In one, successful institutions are able to work with the grain of existing procedures, build upon past successes and enhance existing institutional capacity. In the other, poorly performing institutions are unable to achieve a paradigm shift and the subsequent inability to successfully adapt can then lead to further institutional underperformance and policy failure. Most institutions, of course, fall between these two ideal types but, where failure is clearly evident, the ability of institutions to break the cycle is dependent on the configuration of policy goals and discourses within them – and the more contingent phenomenon of whether key institutional agents are able or willing to do so. This is looked at in more depth later.

So where does this leave the development of environmental policy in the United Kingdom and Germany? The historical institutionalist approach requires that current practices in a given policy area are best explained through a reasonably detailed analysis of its development over time. And as we shall see, such an analysis of the institutional development and performance of environmental policy making in the two countries clearly demonstrates (i) significant variance in institutional performance between the two countries; (ii) the persistence of standard operating procedures in both countries; but also indicates (iii) a capacity for learning and adaptation.[8] Nevertheless, and despite the activist role assumed by the European Union within the policy domain, we can identify nation-specific standard operating procedures that persist to the present. So, let us look at the historical development of each country in turn, before examining the role of the European Union.

The United Kingdom Context

In the United Kingdom it is possible to identify the emergence of an environmental policy domain from the early nineteenth century onwards, thus making it the first industrial democracy in which an identifiable environmental policy domain was to develop. As the first country to industrialise, the United Kingdom underwent a process of political–economic, demographic and physical change that was unprecedented in human history. This process was particularly notable in England and Wales, where industrialisation prompted high levels of both population growth and population transfer. Thus, in the 100 years from the early nineteenth to early twentieth centuries the population of England and Wales grew from 8.9 million to 32.5 million and in the first 50 years of the nineteenth century over 4 million people migrated to towns and cities. As a result, by the mid-nineteenth century over 50 per cent of the population lived in urban areas.[9] The resulting urban squalor prompted a number of environmental reforms, albeit embedded within a wider policy concern for public health, physical and sometimes even moral, improvement, rather than one explicitly predicated on the idea of environmental sustainability. Given that Victorian Britain was the exemplar of a strong unitary state, the standard operating procedures established at this time were consistent with a pattern in which a strong central government took limited measures to empower sub-national levels of government in order to impose what were intended to be broadly uniform (albeit pragmatic and minimalist) standards prescribed by the centre.

As environmental concerns were contingent on the wider set of concerns noted above, it is to be expected that early initiatives were either (i) focused on relatively narrow policy problems; or (ii) nested in legislation that was primarily focused on other – albeit related – policy concerns. Early examples of the former focused on, for instance, hydrogen chloride emissions from alkali works, starting with the 1863 Alkali Act and followed by a number of associated pieces of legislation in the latter half of the nineteenth century. By contrast, a more holistic approach to tackling environmental issues could be found in the wider public health policy domain, as well as in private philanthropic initiatives associated with it. Government initiatives of this kind included legislation prompted by the 1840 Select Committee on the Health of Towns and the 1845 Royal Commission on the State of Large Towns, such as the 1848 Public Health Act, the 1851 Shaftesbury Act, the 1868 Torrens Act, and the 1875 Cross Act. Private initiatives were predicated on the perceived link between living conditions and labour productivity and focused on the creation of new model towns such as Birmingham's Bournville – created by the local Cadbury family – and similar creations elsewhere such as Port Sunlight in the Wirral, and Saltaire near Bradford.

By the end of the nineteenth century we can identify an emerging set of policy discourses and associated norms, buttressed by an institutional architecture and array of standard operating procedures that were to persist into the last decades of the twentieth century and, arguably, were only first seriously challenged under the impact of the *acquis communautaire*. In terms of discourses and norms, we can identify the persistence of a highly empirical problem-solving approach to environmental issues. This manifested itself in two ways. First, as far as we can identify a stand-alone domain of environmental policy, United Kingdom environmental initiatives eschewed the *explicit* incorporation of abstract concepts such as the German norm of *Stand der Technik* ('Best Available Technology') as *a priori* requirements within the policy discourse in favour of focusing on specific problems as and when they emerged and/or were identified as such. This 'tactical rather than strategic' style of policy making can be seen in the Alkali Act noted above, but was still identifiable a century later in the 1956 Clean Air Act.[10] The Act, which sought to control industrial and domestic emissions in *specific* urban areas, was enacted in response to the 'Great Smog' of December 1952, which is estimated to have killed around 4,000 Londoners.[11] To be sure, the Clean Air Act was effective in tackling the specificities of the smog problem of the 1950s, but it was enacted before the exponential growth of automobile ownership that was to take place in the 1960s and 1970s. Thus, it was an effective 'firefighting' measure at the time and brought about long-term improvements. But its failure to enshrine abstract policy principles meant that it was of little use in tackling subsequent emissions problems associated with increased car use. Having said that, however, it would be wrong to exaggerate the legacy of British empiricism and we can see the development of a number of *implicit* abstract principles that would continue to underpin environmental legislation. Thus, as Bell points out, the 1874 Alakali Act effectively introduced the 'Best Practical Means' principle that has become accepted as a distinctive underlying component of United Kingdom environmental legislation.[12] Best Practical Means and other standard-setting philosophies are returned to later in this study.

The second manifestation of this empiricist approach was the ongoing practice, discussed above, of nesting environmental measures within a wider and/or cross-cutting policy agenda. Examples of this include the 1909 Housing, Town Planning etc Act, which granted powers to sub-national tiers of government to regulate suburban growth, and the 1919 Housing and Town Planning Act, which widened the policy remit established in the 1909 Act, the 1947 Town and Country Planning Act, which further extended the policy remit to include the planning of green spaces, reservoirs, security of water supply and sewage disposal, and the 1949 National Parks and Access to the Countryside Act, which established national parks in England and Wales and designated a number of Areas of Natural Beauty.

As noted above, these policy discourses and associated norms were buttressed by an institutional architecture and set of standard operating procedures that persisted well into the late twentieth century. As Carter and Lowe observe, 'government structures ... relating to environmental protection have been (and largely remain) an accretion of agencies, procedures and policies'.[13] The key institutional features have historically been those of fragmentation and the apparently arbitrary division of policy competences across ministries, quasi-autonomous non-governmental organisations (quangos) and associated agencies. Thus, as Baldock observed in the 1980s, England was the only nation that had sought to make the kind of distinction between policy competences seen in the roles of the Countryside Commission (responsible for *landscape* preservation) and English Nature (responsible for *nature* conservation).[14]

Apparently nonsensical divisions of competences within policy domains are not limited to the United Kingdom's management of environmental policy, of course. Yet one cannot escape the sense that this persistent institutional pathology undermines the advantages associated with the feature that has traditionally defined the United Kingdom's structure of government – the strong unitary state. A discussion of the relative strengths and weaknesses of unitary and federal states is beyond the scope of this study, but even the most enthusiastic federalist would not deny that one *potential* advantage of the unitary state structure is its steering capacity and relative lack of veto players. However, when – as was the case in 1969 – up to ten separate ministries were involved in United Kingdom environmental policy making, we cannot escape the conclusion that this one specific advantage over federal states such as Germany was effectively being squandered.[15] And this was recognised by policy makers, who in 1970 unified many of the previously disparate policy competences within the newly created Department of Environment. The remit and title of the Department has changed over the years with successive governments but, at the time of writing (May 2006), the Ministry of Environment, Food and Rural Affairs portfolio is a cabinet post and is occupied by David Milliband.

Amongst the Department's responsibilities at present are the management of the Environment Agency and, from October 2006, a new unified quango (made up of English Nature and the Countryside Commission) called Natural England. This gradual consolidation of competences over time has, however, been matched by an additional degree of fragmentation associated with the process of devolution and constitutional change following Labour's 1997 general election victory. Thus, in Scotland, the Scottish Executive manages environmental policy and there is a separate Environment Protection Agency. In Wales there is a Minister for Environment, Planning, and Countryside. But in Northern Ireland the suspension of devolved government means that environmental policy is still effectively being run from London.

The German Context

The institutional development of German environmental policy is at least as path-dependent as that of the United Kingdom, although the emergence of a distinct environmental policy domain did not take place until later in the nineteenth century. As noted earlier, the pattern established in the United Kingdom was one in which a strong central government passed legislation intended to both impose standards across the territory of the unitary state and empower sub-national levels of government to work within prescribed parameters in order to further these goals. By contrast, and in keeping with the kind of standard operating procedures associated with federal states, the first institutional feature of note in Germany was that of independent Land involvement, dating back to local ordinances such as the Prussian *Gewerbeordnungen*.

In the late nineteenth century, the newly united Germany was engaged in a process of economic and military catch-up with the United Kingdom; and in such an atmosphere of national competition, industrial growth and the wider social welfare were considered to be coterminous.[16] As a result, legislation was limited in scope and focused on individual emissions. Air pollution control authorities issued 'technical instructions' (*Technische Anleitungen*) to individual emitters and, from 1895 onwards, these technical instructions enforced corrective measures commensurate with standards of Best Available Technology. The early establishment of Best Available Technology standards is consistent with the German tradition of formulating public policy within the parameters established by abstract principles. And, as we shall see, the focus on individual emitters and the use of Best Available Technology standards are operating procedures that persist today and were uploaded to the European Union level. Individual Land responsibility for pollution control was less appropriate for the management of wetlands and waterways, in which it is notoriously difficult to establish responsibility for individual acts of pollution and enforce subsequent measures against emitters.[17] In response to this problem of institutional misfit, Land governments set up a number of partnership agreements (*Genossenschaften*) to manage pollution problems affecting adjacent Länder on, for instance, the Rhine, Wuppe, Lippe and Ruhr rivers.[18] Nevertheless, established standard operating procedures remained embedded in wider practices of horizontal co-operation between sub-national tiers of government.

These practices were so well embedded that, by the end of the 1950s, there was still no meaningful role for the federal level of government and most of the regulatory devices in use had been in place since the start of the First World War. But under pressure from a range of societal actors, the federal level began to involve itself. Initial federal legislation, such as the Water Household Act of 1957 and the Clean Air Maintenance Law of 1959, was limited in scope and ambition but the federal government slowly began to assume a more activist role. Building on a template established in the SPD-run state of North Rhine-Westphalia, the federal government issued its own technical instructions (TAs) and set out air quality standards for dust, chlorine, sulphur dioxide, nitrogen dioxide and hydrogen sulphide, which were coupled to Best Available Technology requirements.[19] The establishment of the SPD–FDP coalition in 1969 increased the impetus for federal involvement and it was at this point that Germany began to undergo a phase of 'activist policy design' that was close to the idea of a paradigm shift discussed earlier in this study.[20] The Brandt government framed its new environmental policy programme around existing Best Available Technology standards, but also encouraged the codification of three normative principles – the 'Precautionary' principle, the 'Polluter Pays' principle and the 'Co-operation' principle – that were also subsequently to be uploaded to the European Union level. These three abstractions informed a raft of new legislation, including the Air Traffic Noise Act (1971), the Leaded Petrol Act (1972), the Waste Disposal Act (1972), the DDT Act (1972), the Federal Air Quality Protection Act (1974), and the (1974) Technical Instruction for the Maintenance of Air Purity.[21] In addition, the Federal Agency for the Environment (*Umweltbundesamt*) was set up in 1974. The agency became an effective enforcer of environmental standards and diffuser of best practice. However, it was and remained essentially a technocratic institution and it would be another 12 years before a fully-fledged Environment Ministry was established in the wake of the Chernobyl disaster – 16 years later than its British equivalent.[22]

The economic crises of the mid-to-late 1970s led to a shift in government priorities and, as a result, the environmental agenda was temporarily eclipsed by what appeared to be the more pressing needs of economic retrenchment. However, the late 1970s and early 1980s saw a revival of environmental interest amongst the political class and the beginning of a period of cross-party consensus on the need for an activist policy agenda. Subsequent initiatives included the 1982 Ordinance on Large Combustion Plants (*Grossfeurungsanlagenverordnung*), the 1983 Air Pollution Control Law in July 1983 – that became the model for the subsequent European Communities Directive on Large Combustion Plants – the setting up in 1986 of the Federal Ministry for Environment, Nature Protection and Reactor Safety (*Bundesministerium für Umwelt, Naturschutz und Reaktorsicherheit*) and the 1987 Commission of Enquiry on Preventative Measures to Protect the Earth's Atmosphere (*Enquete-Kommission Vorsage zum Schutz der Erdatmosphäre*).

By the mid-1990s, however, Germany's leadership role in the field of environmental policy had come under pressure on three fronts. First, the economic costs of managing the process of German unification had led to a resurgence of worries about German economic competitiveness amongst elites and had served to erode what had effectively been a decade-long cross-party consensus on environmental policy. This manifested itself both within the Bundestag and, with the accession of five relatively poor eastern Länder, in the Bundesrat. Second, and in response to the economic pressures noted above, the preferences of an enlarged and more socially diverse electorate had shifted away from post-materialist concerns such as environmental protection back towards materialist concerns such as job creation and economic growth. This further constrained the scope of environmental policy innovation elites were prepared to endorse and increased the opportunities for partisan conflict over the issue. Third, not only did the relative lack of domestic consensus on environmental protection at both the elite and mass levels make it harder to *articulate* German interests in the environmental policy domain at the European Union level, but Germany's ongoing economic difficulties also made it harder to *pursue* these interests through the use of side-payments to other member states.[23] Nevertheless, if taken in the round, the Federal Republic today still retains an enviable record in most areas of environmental policy – despite its lower profile compared with the 1980s and early 1990s.

The Impact of the European Union

From the 1980s onwards the development of environmental policy making in both the United Kingdom and Germany took place within the context of an increasingly assertive EU-level policy agenda. But, although there was a common impact on both countries, the effects of this impact were somewhat different. In other words, as in other policy areas, the scope and scale of the Europeanisation of environmental policy making was partly dependent on the level of institutional misfit between the two member states and the European Union.[24] This level of misfit can be conceived as taking place along three dimensions.

The first dimension relates to established standard operating procedures directly associated with the policy domain. Although the dichotomy between environmental 'leaders' and 'laggards' is problematised in the literature, it is clear that those member states that were perceived (or perceived themselves) to be leaders in this regard sought to impose standards as close as possible to their own upon other member states through the medium of the European Union.[25] As a result, at least in the initial period of Europeanisation, the adaptive pressures exerted on the United Kingdom (as a perceived 'laggard') were stronger than those felt by Germany (widely regarded at the time as a 'leader'). Before the 1980s, environmental policy was originally very much a 'Cinderella' policy area at the European level and inasmuch as environmental concerns had any leverage it was as a tangential element to stated Community objectives such as those embodied in European Economic Community Treaty Articles 2 (quality of life, harmonious economic development, balanced expansion), 100 (dismantling barriers to the Common Market) and 235 (allowing Council of Ministers to take action in areas not covered by treaties). From 1973 onwards, the European Community also issued Environmental Action Plans, but it was the Single European Act and the Maastricht Treaty that enabled the European Union to carve out a distinct set of environmental policy objectives and principles.

During the 1980s in particular, a 'German' regulatory culture was uploaded to the European level and subsequent legislation was thus predicated on the precautionary, Polluter Pays, and Best Available Technology principles. These abstractions were absorbed and adapted by British policy makers but, nevertheless, the 1980s saw a number of instances in which the United Kingdom came under both horizontal pressure from other 'leader' states and vertical pressure from the European Union level. This led to the United Kingdom using its veto, for instance with regard to a planned European Communities Directive on Vehicle Emissions and a later proposal to adopt a common carbon dioxide and energy tax. More recently, however, European Union environmental policy (in line with other policy domains) has moved towards a mix of economic instruments and so-called 'soft law' that is closer to United Kingdom practices and preferences.[26] By contrast, the increasing emphasis on soft law approaches served to restrict the ability to upload German environmental practices up to the European Union level and, at the same time, Germany itself has come under increasing pressure to adapt its own standard operating procedures. In particular, Germany's reluctance to embrace economic instruments has been criticised.[27] This is discussed at greater length later in the study.

The second dimension of misfit is related to the wider governance structures in the two states. At the European Union level, the institutional architecture of environmental policy is very close to the kind of multi-level governance ideal-types posited in the literature.[28] Thus, the Single European Act in particular provided the impetus for the European Commission to take an active role, yet we find a clear fragmentation of competences between the Environment, Industry, and Agriculture Directorates General. At the same time, the European Parliament has used this policy domain as a means with which to widen its policy scope, to the extent, as Weale observes, that the European Parliament enjoys 'more influence ... than ... far more established national parliaments' in this area of policy making.[29] Moreover, the European Court of Justice has often ruled in favour of the environmental lobby, for instance in the 1988 'Danish Bottle' case, which led to a ruling that environmental protection may override the free movement of goods within the European Union. The European Union also has a European

Environmental Agency – modelled on its German equivalent – which acts as a decentralised information-gathering and advisory body, often in concert with the Europe-wide 'European Information and Observation Network'. Finally, although environmental lobbying at the European Union level is relatively weak, the Commission has – as in other policy areas – sought to enhance its legitimacy by effectively by-passing national governments and dealing directly with societal actors at the sub-national level.

It is clear that the existence of multi-level governance dynamics generated at the European Union level has differential (and slightly paradoxical) effects on the two member states. On the one hand, and as already noted, internal environmental policy making in the United Kingdom is distinguished by its incremental and fragmented nature. As a result, multi-level governance dynamics are already commonplace in United Kingdom domestic policy making, albeit 'in the shadow of hierarchy'.[30] At the same time, however, the United Kingdom still regards itself as a strong unitary actor in its interaction with the European Union. As a result, where multi-level dynamics have generated EU-level links with *sub*-national levels of governance, this was perceived as undermining the 'gate keeper' status of central government, and was not particularly welcomed. By contrast, the standard operating procedures associated with German federalism – such as bargaining and consensus-building at multiple levels of governance – meant that European Union interventions did not present such a problem for 'national' policy makers who were less accustomed to the gate-keeper role enjoyed by their United Kingdom equivalents.[31]

The third dimension along which Europeanisation exerted differential adaptational pressures was the simple one of political salience and its impact upon party political competition. As Wurzel observes, the framing of European Union environmental policy making within a 'quality of life' discourse has been used strategically 'to increase the political legitimacy of the European Union, especially at times of high public environmental awareness'.[32] However, levels of public awareness, the salience it is accorded, the priority it is given over other concerns, and the means with which it is represented within party systems varies across member states. In Germany, for reasons that are beyond the scope of this study, public awareness is high, the issue is given relatively high salience and priority, and Germany's 'multi-member proportional' electoral system allows for the efficient representation of environmental issues, not least through the vehicle of the German Greens, who have been instrumental in bringing issues of environmental protection into the political mainstream.[33] By contrast, in the United Kingdom – and especially in the 1980s – public awareness was lower, prioritisation was very low, and the 'first-past-the-post' plurality system prevented the effective representation of such issues by shutting out the Green Party, for instance.[34] At the time of writing, the use of environmentalism as a campaign issue by the Conservative Party has – temporarily anyway – led to higher levels of public awareness, issue salience and prioritisation, at least in terms of rhetoric. In addition, the introduction of proportional representation for European Parliament elections in the United Kingdom, combined with some success for the Greens in local elections in cities such as Brighton and Sheffield, has enhanced the representation of environmental issues within the party system. It remains to be seen if this is a long-term development, which would

POLICY CONVERGENCE IN THE UK AND GERMANY 173

surely ease adaptational pressures on the United Kingdom, or if eventually the *status quo ante* will be restored.

POLICY INSTRUMENTS AND DISCOURSES

In this section we compare and contrast the 'styles' of environmental policy making in the United Kingdom and Germany, with an emphasis on the instruments used by policy makers and the types of policy discourses in which these instruments are selected and justified. Let us turn first to the use of policy instruments.

There are three broad categories of policy instrument. First, there are the classic command-and-control regulatory instruments. In addition, however, internationally we have seen the emergence in the last few decades of two additional types of so-called 'new' environmental policy instruments. The first of these are voluntary agreements, ranging from informal methods (e.g. eco-labelling, encouraging re-cycling, and other life-style changes) to more formal instruments such as the International Standards Organisation (ISO 14001), which provides environmental management system benchmarks. The second type of these new instruments are market-based instruments, which can be further divided into two categories: first, rights-based mechanisms, such as tradable permits and quotas, and, second, 'green' or 'eco' taxes.

Policy Instruments and Discourses in the United Kingdom

As already noted, environmental policy making in the United Kingdom has traditionally been characterised by a piecemeal approach, in which a unitary state has overseen the activities of subordinate tiers of sub-national government, as well as a fragmented mosaic of national-level ministries, agencies, and quangos. The style of policy making has been embedded in the British tradition of empiricism and problem-solving and where abstract policy principles have existed, these have been as much implied as made explicit. Whilst all this is true, of course, it would be a mistake to overstate such nation-specific characteristics. Thus, whilst there are clear differences between national policy-making styles and standard operating procedures, the *reductio ad absurdum* of such an analytical position – of national policy styles that are effectively prisoners of path-dependence, with little or no capacity to learn or adapt – is not particularly helpful. As touched upon earlier in this study, the environmental policy community in the United Kingdom has clearly learned and adapted in recent years. Let us now examine the mix of policy instruments and discourses that characterise United Kingdom environmental policy making today.

As described in the previous section, the United Kingdom has a long history of environmental regulation, dating back to the mid-nineteenth century. At the same time, however, although we often refer to regulatory instruments as 'command-and-control' measures, the capacity of United Kingdom policy makers to do so was constrained by a distinctive approach to the mechanics of regulation. Carter and Lowe identify the key distinguishing feature of United Kingdom regulatory culture as the prioritisation of administrative rather than judicial procedures.[35] Thus, established standard operating procedures have tended to be 'informal, accommodative and technocratic rather than formal, confrontational and legalistic ... there has been an avoidance of, *indeed a distaste for* legislatively prescribed standards and quality objectives.... [and] when laws are broken, in the vast majority of cases, officials prefer not to prosecute'.[36] In hindsight, and under pressure from both the Commission and other member states, this cosy, opaque and – some would argue – ineffectual approach has been supplemented by a more transparent, arms-length and potentially conflictual relationship with potential polluters. Nevertheless, the standard-setting philosophies that underpin United Kingdom environmental regulation remain artefacts of established operating procedures and the discourse of empiricism and problem-solving. As a result, the 'light-touch' philosophy of Environmental Quality Objectives are preferred to prescriptive Uniform Emissions Limits, the pragmatism of Best Practical Means or Best Practical Environmental Option are preferred to Best Available Technology, and scientific proof of existing environmental damage is given greater weight than the requirement to react to the potential for damage codified in the Precautionary Principle.[37]

Given the traditional informality of United Kingdom regulatory practices, it is paradoxical that the United Kingdom's recent embrace of new environmental policy instruments has not involved an enthusiastic embrace of voluntary agreements. Thus, there remain far fewer voluntary agreements in the United Kingdom than in other European Union member states and they tend to be (i) concentrated in the sectors of agriculture, chemicals and energy; (ii) non-binding rather than 'in the shadow of the law'; (iii) relatively recent in origin; and (iv) piecemeal and unilateral rather than part of wider, long-term commitments. The lack of voluntary agreements even includes a reluctance to use eco-labelling, which provides a relatively low cost means of increasing the informational resources available to consumers. As Jordan and Liefferink observe, 'one might have expected to find many more voluntary agreements in a sector ... that has such a long historical tradition of decentralisation, consensus building and negotiation with industry'.[38] On the other hand, one could argue that the traditionally accommodative style of environmental regulation in the United Kingdom has served to not only make voluntary agreements less necessary but also to undermine the analytical distinction between such agreements and regulatory instruments.

By contrast, and after a slow start, the United Kingdom has become one of the leading users of market-based instruments amongst European Union member states. In terms of rights-based instruments, two achievements are of note. First, the Department of Environment, Food and Rural Affairs oversaw the setting up in March 2002 of the United Kingdom Emissions Trading Scheme, in which 33 major companies agreed to reduce their emissions over a four-year period by an estimated 11.88 million tonnes of carbon dioxide equivalent. In addition, up to 6,000 additional companies subject to Climate Change Agreements are able to sign up to the scheme and – if they meet their targets – qualify for a reduction in charges from the Climate Change Levy (see below). Over the first three years of operation, the department estimates a total of 5.9 million of carbon dioxide equivalent was saved through the scheme.[39] The second achievement is the United Kingdom's active role in setting up the European Union Emissions Trading Scheme, which began operation in January 2006. At the time of writing, the European Union's first interim assessment of the scheme had just been released and the United Kingdom's performance under the new scheme was generally regarded as being relatively good, although it did exceed its quota and was forced to buy up allowances from other member states.[40]

In addition to rights-based schemes, the United Kingdom has also been a relatively enthusiastic practitioner of eco-taxes. Here, seven examples are of note: the 1987 unleaded petrol price differential (rescinded in 2001), the 1993 decision to impose Value Added Tax on domestic fuel, the 1993 fuel duty escalator, the 1996 Landfill Tax, and differential vehicle excise duties according to engine size (at the time of writing, a modest sharpening of the differential was recently announced in Chancellor Gordon Brown's 2006 Budget speech), the 2001 Climate Change Levy, and the 2002 Aggregates Tax. Despite early resistance to eco-taxes within the United Kingdom environmental policy community, such instruments have become attractive, not only because they generate revenue for the public purse but also because they have the capacity to permanently change the behaviour of polluters. This is because eco-taxes can capture the marginal environmental costs of production and thus tax the externalities of production and resource depletion. Unlike regulatory instruments, eco-taxes embed a set of incentives that make it rational for firms and individuals to constantly improve their environmental practices. Eco-taxes come with political costs and, as the 2000 fuel protests demonstrate, their continued success depends on both careful design and political calibration over time. Nevertheless, eco-taxes and indeed rights-based mechanisms work with the grain of the norms and practices of the United Kingdom's relatively liberal political economy. But, as we shall see below, Germany's social market economy provides a less benign environment for either variety of market-based instruments.

Policy Instruments and Discourses in Germany

As noted above, the environmental policy community in the Federal Republic remains uneasy about the use of market-based instruments. The reasons for this are discussed later in this section. Voluntary agreements, on the other hand, are a well-established element in the armoury of policy instruments and, unlike the United Kingdom, this includes the enthusiastic use of eco-labelling in which Germany – through the use of the 'Blue Angel' and 'Green Spot' schemes – has been a world leader. The widespread use of voluntary agreements in tandem with a strongly judicialised regulatory culture makes up a distinctly 'German' policy mix.

Between 1972 and 1994, the federal government enacted eight major pieces of environmental legislation. These were: the Waste Disposal Act (1972); the Federal Air Quality Protection Act (1974); the Waste Water Charges Act (1976); the Ordinance on Large Combustion Plants (1982/83); the Waste Avoidance Act (1986); the Environmental Impact Assessment Act (1991); the Environmental Liability Act (1991); and the Waste Management Act (1994). All of these pieces of legislation, as Pehle and Jansen observe, are heavily reliant on either traditional command-and-control measures or, in the case of the water, waste and transport sectors, a mixture of command and control plus voluntary agreements.[41]

During the period in office of the 1998–2005 Red–Green coalition, however, Germany's reliance on regulatory instruments was augmented by the use of economic instruments. The partial shift in the policy mix is best demonstrated by an examination of the instruments used in two main planks of the Red–Green coalition's environmental programme during its period in office: first, the phasing out of nuclear power and, second, the introduction of an eco-tax.

The move to phase out nuclear power was a paradigmatic example of Germany's long-established propensity for voluntary agreements made 'in the shadow of the law'. In particular, path-dependency was evident in the use of 'consensus talks' with the nuclear industry in order to establish a timetable for the closing down of reactors. This was a device very similar to the talks on nuclear energy that took place in Lower Saxony during the 1990–94 Red–Green coalition in that state.[42] The eco-tax, by contrast, was something of a departure from the standard operating procedures of environmental policy making in the Federal Republic. Whereas Germany was an undisputed leader in the use of voluntary and regulatory instruments to pursue environmental ends, the forerunners in the use of eco-taxes were the Scandinavian countries and, to a lesser extent, the Netherlands. Indeed, by the late 1990s, when it came to the use of eco-taxes, Germany had also fallen behind former environmental laggards such as Britain, as already noted, as well as France and Italy.[43]

Germany's laggard status in the use of this specific policy instrument is, on the one hand, surprising – especially given the potential environmental benefits of such instruments. The general benefits of eco-taxes have been described above, but the argument in their favour in Germany was augmented by a general perception at the end of the 1990s that non-wage labour costs in the Federal Republic were too high. Thus, it was argued that a revenue-neutral eco-tax could produce a so-called 'double dividend' in Germany, because it would serve both to improve environmental practices *and*, by shifting the burden of taxation from labour to emissions and resource use, to lower non-wage labour costs.

In practice, however, there are a number of reasons why Germany was relatively late in adopting eco-taxes as a major tool of environmental policy. First, as already discussed, once operating procedures are established it is difficult for institutions to transcend them. Thus, for the German environmental policy community, when a new or persistent environmental problem is identified, the instinct is to reach for the tried-and-tested toolkit of existing instruments. In Germany, this tendency was further aggravated by the fact that internal and external perceptions of existing policy performance were favourable, so there were no major drivers for change in this respect. And by and large this self-regard was justified, although – as is discussed later – in recent years the upward curve of German environmental performance has flattened out. The second reason is that, as noted above, eco-taxes go against the grain of some of the Federal Republic's more prized political–economic orthodoxies. No policy instrument is perfect and eco-taxes have been criticised for, for instance, distorting the market, carrying substantial implementation, administrative, monitoring and transaction costs, and leading to lower revenues over time as agents adjust their behaviour in response to the new market signals.[44] However, the most potent criticism – and one that carried more weight in Germany than the United Kingdom – is that eco-taxes are socially regressive and inevitably punish the poorest members of society, who spend a greater proportion of their household income on energy use. This is consistent with Padgett's findings which demonstrate that, in Germany, voters' preferences on welfare issues significantly restrain the use of policy instruments with socially regressive distributional effects.[45]

Although not socially regressive in the manner of eco-taxes, a general distaste for the instrumentalisation of environmental policy can also be detected in the German environmental policy community's resistance to the use of rights-based mechanisms such as the European Union Emissions Trading Scheme. German performance under the new scheme has recently been subjected to close scrutiny and the German government has been criticised for being too generous in its initial allocation of allowances – resulting in its running a surplus of allowances and contributing to a fall in the effective price of carbon.[46] It remains to be seen if this policy failure was the result of misfit between the national and European levels of governance or of a more cynical overestimation of future emissions in order to generate surplus allowances to be traded across the European Union (and thus provide windfall profits for German industry).

POLICY OUTCOMES

As Jörgens observes, the debate about policy diffusion has tended to focus on the impact of policy instruments on outputs.[47] Ultimately, however, the test of the effectiveness of policy instruments lies in their impact upon policy outcomes. Yet making outcomes the dependent variable in our analysis is no simple task. On the one hand, we can identify countries such as Sweden and the Netherlands that have embraced the full array of new environmental policy instruments – including market-based instruments – and are regarded as environmental leaders. But this does not mean that we can demonstrate with confidence that x (use of new environmental policy instruments) leads to y (enhanced environmental performance).

A comparison of the United Kingdom and Germany such as the one in this study highlights two specific problems in making outcomes the dependent variable. First, the institutional history of the policy sector, and in particular the cumulative impact of standard operating procedures and discourses, serves to constrain the scope of policy alternatives and also introduces a degree of complexity that makes a simple causal narrative $x \rightarrow y$ impossible. Second, nation-specific environmental characteristics create different incentive structures in the two countries. As Wurzel points out, Germany is subject to significantly higher levels of ecological vulnerability than the United Kingdom. Germany shares land borders with nine other states, has rivers (such as the Elbe and the Rhine) that originate outside its territory and are often slow-flowing, and is a major north–south and (since the collapse of communism) east–west transit country. The United Kingdom, by contrast, is situated on two North Sea islands, shares one land border (with the Republic of Ireland), has relatively short fast-flowing rivers that originate within the territory, and is not a significant transit country (apart from air travel). In addition, the effects of strong winds and what Wurzel calls the 'scouring sea' help to disperse air and water pollution.[48] These benign environmental characteristics have meant that the United Kingdom has been slower to react to the problems of managing the environmental commons. The United Kingdom has not been subject to significant trans-boundary pollution from its neighbours and over the years became too reliant on the carrying capacity of the environment. Thus, environmentally damaging policies such as those of 'high chimneys' and 'long sea outfalls' went unchallenged for longer than was practically or politically possible in Germany.

Taken together, these different levels of ecological vulnerability mean that the United Kingdom and Germany start from different baselines in terms of both the (real and perceived) severity of environmental problems and the incentives to tackle them. Yet some degree of rough comparison between the two countries is still possible. As discussed earlier in this study, the United Kingdom is not necessarily the environmental laggard that it was 20 years ago and in many ways it is ahead of Germany in its use of new economic policy instruments, especially market-based instruments. But, unlike the Scandinavian countries and the Netherlands, it still lags behind Germany in terms of outcomes. Thus, Germany still has the highest number of low-emission cars in Europe, the highest proportional use of lead-free petrol, and retains some of the most stringent emission limits. Germany remains a global leader in sewage purification technology, in controlling dioxin emissions, and in research and development in the field of renewable energy sources ('renewables'). Indeed, its capacity for wind-generated electricity now exceeds the United Kingdom's nuclear-generated capacity and it is expected that German photo-voltaic capacity will soon do the same. In addition, Germany continues to take an active role in international initiatives.[49] Amongst these are the 1992 United Nations Conference on Environment and Development Conference in Rio, the Helsinki and Sofia protocols on long-range air pollution, the Vienna Agreement and Montreal Protocol on protecting the ozone layer, and in forging collaborative strategies with its neighbours to protect the North Sea and the Baltic.[50] Germany is under pressure from bodies such as the Organisation for Economic Co-operation and Development to make more use of economic instruments.[51] This is, however, suggested in order to transcend the 'law of diminishing returns' that accompanies policy success rather than as a means to address poor environmental performance.[52]

By contrast, the United Kingdom has embraced market-based instruments but its failure to seriously invest in renewables is now beginning to look like a strategic mistake. With rising oil and gas prices, diminishing and unpredictable supply, and the practical and political constraints on any replacement for the United Kingdom's ageing nuclear plant, it remains to be seen how serious a mistake this really is. What can be deduced from the United Kingdom's relatively poor performance in the field of renewables is that agents will react to market signals within the energy market and, in order to foster renewables, the signals required must be strong enough to offset short-term incentives such as those that underpinned the 'dash for gas' in the 1990s. Yet, in order to do so, a degree of old-fashioned command-and-control regulation is necessary and, in this, Germany remains more effective than the United Kingdom in establishing the incentive structures that make long-term investment in renewables worthwhile. In short, in the United Kingdom there has been an over-reliance upon market forces and insufficient recognition of the consequences of market failure.

Finally, it is worth noting that, although there is a long history of British–German co-operation in such areas as trade liberalisation, defence and security policy, there has been very little evidence of co-operation between the two countries in the field of environmental policy. If one looks back to the 1980s and early 1990s this is not particularly surprising, given the mismatch between the two countries in terms of both environmental performance, the priority given to improving that performance, and indeed attitudes to the political arena – the European Union – in which much of this co-operation might have taken place. However, the relative absence of overt gestures of co-operation in recent years is more intriguing – particularly in the context of the so-called 'Third Way' and 'Neue Mitte' agendas of the late 1990s. Indeed, if one re-reads the Blair–Schröder paper of July 1999 one is struck by the emphasis on 'economic dynamism', the 'unleashing of creativity and innovation', 'catching up with the US' and the establishment of a 'robust and competitive market framework' rather than environmental initiatives.[53] The document does mention the need to pursue a 'tax policy to promote sustainable growth' by shifting the tax burden from income to consumption, but little detail is provided and – given the subsequent ditching of the paper and slow deterioration in relations between the two leaders – we shall never know what they might have intended in this regard. The replacement of Schröder as Federal Chancellor by Angela Merkel in 2005 has led to an improvement in relations between the United Kingdom and Germany and this, combined with the slow convergence in policy instruments noted above, does open the door for co-operation between the two countries on environmental matters in the future. But whether this possible co-operation will serve to facilitate or constrain environmental initiatives at the European Union level is a question best left to future research.

CONCLUSIONS

This study has examined developments within the environmental policy domain in the United Kingdom and the Federal Republic of Germany along the dimensions of: (i) the historical context; (ii) policy instruments and discourses; and (iii) policy outcomes. In addition, it asks if we can identify patterns of convergence and divergence along these three dimensions and to what extent the European integration process impacts upon these patterns. In order to answer these questions, let us look at each of the three dimensions in turn.

In terms of the historical context of environmental policy making in the two countries, we can see variance in institutional policy performance, the persistence of standard operating procedures, and a capacity for learning and adaptation. In the United Kingdom, environmental policy making first emerged within the context of the strong Victorian unitary state. The operating procedures established in its early phase, with central government taking limited measures to empower sub-national levels of government to impose uniform, pragmatic and minimalist standards, persisted well into the twentieth century and were only significantly challenged by growing environmental competences sited at the European Union level. The intellectual style of policy initiatives, from the 1863 Alkali Act through to the 1956 Clean Air Act and beyond, was 'tactical rather than strategic' and eschewed the *explicit* incorporation of abstractions such as Best Available Technology.[54] This tactical approach led to 'an accretion of agencies, procedures and policies' in which the key institutional features were those of fragmentation and the division of policy competences.[55] Even after the foundation of the Department of the Environment in 1970, this fragmentation continued and, since devolution, this pattern has been repeated in Scotland, Wales and Northern Ireland. By contrast, German standard operating procedures were grounded in the principle of independent Land involvement in the policy sector, with individual Länder enjoying powers to enact local ordinances that would become the template for federal legislation, from the Water Household Act of 1957 through the Clean Air Maintenance Law of 1959 to the Ordinance on Large Combustion Plants of 1982.[56] As early as the

1890s, local ordinances enforced corrective measures framed by abstractions such as Best Available Technology and this tendency to abstraction has persisted in ideas such as the Precautionary principle. Prior to the involvement of the federal level, there was a significant degree of horizontal co-operation between Länder through the *Genossenschaften*. But even after the involvement of the federal level, the multi-level character of the policy sector persisted. It took until 1986 to set up a Federal Environment Ministry and the resulting portfolio still shares competences with rival ministries (such as the Economics Ministry) and rival levels of governance. Nevertheless, a high degree of expert and cross-party consensus at all levels of governance in the late 1980s and early 1990s provided the platform for significant uploading of environmental policy to the European Union level.

In terms of policy instruments and discourses, the study demonstrates how nation-specific patterns remain central. Thus, despite some absorption of German-style abstraction, in the United Kingdom we see the persistence of traditions of empiricism and problem-solving, as seen in the emphasis upon Environmental Quality Objectives in the United Kingdom rather than German-style Uniform Emissions Limits, Best Practical Means or Best Practical Environmental Option rather than the wholehearted embrace of Best Available Technology, and a reactive approach to existing environmental damage rather than a proactive approach to potential threats as codified in the Precautionary principle.

Finally, as noted in the previous section, we can discern a strong variance in the environmental outcomes between the two countries; although, for reasons already described, it is of little value trying to ascribe a simplistic causality to the relationship between standard operating procedures and outcomes.

So we have established significant levels of variance across the three dimensions. This study, however, has also identified instances of policy diffusion and adaptation, particularly by the United Kingdom. For instance, the old light-touch 'informal, accommodative' style of regulation has been replaced by a more transparent, arms-length and potentially conflictual regulatory style.[57] Moreover, after early resistance to market-based instruments, the United Kingdom has become an enthusiastic advocate of this type of new environmental policy instruments. Germany, by contrast, has a long history of voluntary agreements but has been far more resistant to market-based instruments. So, in answer to our first question, although all European Union countries have widened their portfolio of policy instruments, one must conclude that there has been only limited convergence between the United Kingdom and Germany. This is not to argue that there cannot be such a process of convergence and Wurzel, in particular, makes a strong case for the combination of United Kingdom-style pragmatism and German abstraction.[58] Nevertheless, at present such a synthesis has not taken place in any meaningful way.

Paradoxically, one of the reasons for this is found in the development of environmental policy competences at the European Union level. As already noted, from the mid-1980s the European Union became increasingly assertive in the development of environmental policy making. However, although in the early years Germany was relatively successful in uploading policy principles to the European Union, from the mid-1990s it increasingly found itself working against the grain of developments at the EU level. By contrast, after an initial period in which the United Kingdom was embattled at the EU level, the degree of 'misfit' between United Kingdom and European Union policy making has eased.[59]

It will be recalled that this misfit took place along three dimensions: (i) established standard operating procedures directly associated with the policy domain; (ii) governance structures; and (iii) political salience and party political competition. And, as has already been discussed, the strength of adaptational pressures varies across these dimensions. In terms of standard operating procedures, the shift at the European Union level towards a mix of economic instruments and so-called 'soft law' is closer to United Kingdom practices and preferences.[60] At the same time, the emergence of multi-level governance within the sector has challenged the gatekeeper status of the United Kingdom core executive. Finally, in terms of political salience and party political competition, it remains to be seen whether the recent (re)emergence of the environment as a key concern in United Kingdom party political discourse represents a substantive shift by the United Kingdom along this dimension. What is clear, however, is that the shift away from command-and-control measures towards market-based instruments – but crucially combined with the soft law approach – provides a challenge to our understanding of the scope and scale of the processes of Europeanisation and policy transfer. In particular, the emphasis on misfit as the *sine qua non* for Europeanisation overemphasises the top-down effects of engagement with the European Union.[61] This study has worked from the premise that intervening variables such as nation-specific standard operating procedures, norms and discourses really do determine the scope and scale of Europeanisation.

Thus, to conclude, it is as much the shift to a soft law approach as it is the emphasis on market-based instruments that has determined the shape of environmental policy making in the United Kingdom and Germany. Soft law approaches still allow policy transfer to take place, but they re-emphasise the role of agency at the national and sub-national level. Moreover, this is a development that impacts upon *all* policy areas in which the European Union has enjoyed a shared competence and not just that of environmental policy. Given this new emphasis on agency at the member state level, it follows that the relatively recent concept of policy resistance will become an increasingly important analytical tool, both in the study of environmental policy, and in the study of the Europeanisation of policy making more broadly defined.[62]

NOTES

1. For instance, See T. Börzel, 'Europeanisation: How the EU Interacts with its Member States', in S. Bulmer and C. Lequesne (eds.), *The Member States of the European Union* (Oxford: Oxford University Press, 2005), pp.45–76; M. Haverland, 'The Impact of the European Union on Environmental Polices', in K. Featherstone and C. Radaelli (eds.), *The Politics of Europeanisation* (Oxford: Oxford University Press, 2003), pp.203–23; A. Jordan and D. Liefferink (eds.), *Environmental Policy in Europe: The Europeanisation of National Environmental Policy* (London: Routledge, 2004).
2. See C. Radaelli, 'Europeanisation: Solution or Problem?', in M. Cini and A. Bourne (eds.), Palgrave Advanced in European Union Studies (Basingstoke: Palgrave, 2005), pp. 56–76.
3. On policy transfer, see D. Dolowitz, and D. Marsh, 'Who Learns What From Whom: A Review of the Policy Transfer Literature', *Political Studies* 44/2 (1996), pp.343–57. On policy resistance, see I. Bache and A. Taylor, 'The Politics of Policy Resistance: Reconstructing Higher Education in Kosovo', *Journal of Public Policy* 23/3 (2003), pp.279–300.

4. B. Jessop, 'Multi-level Governance and Multi-level Metagovernance', in I. Bache and M. Flinders (eds.), *Multi-level Governance* (Oxford: Oxford University Press, 2004), pp.49–75.
5. See P. Pierson, *Politics in Time: History, Institutions and Social Analysis* (Princeton, NJ: Princeton University Press, 2004); D. King, *Actively Seeking Work. The Politics of Unemployment and Welfare Policy in the United States* (Chicago: University of Chicago Press, 1995); T. Skocpol, *Protecting Soldiers and Mothers: The Political Origins of Social Policy in the United States* (Cambridge, MA: Belknap Press, 1992); P. Hall, *The Power of Economic Ideas* (Princeton, NJ: Princeton University Press, 1989); S. Krasner, 'Approaches to the State: Alternative Conceptions and Historical Dynamics', *Comparative Politics* 16/2 (1984), pp.223–46.
6. Krasner, 'Approaches to the State', p.242.
7. See P. Kerr and S. Kettell, 'In Defence of British Politics, the Past, Present, and Future of the Discipline', *British Politics* 1/1 (2006), pp.3–25; R. Heffernan, *Thatcherism and New Labour: Political Change in Britain* (Basingstoke: Palgrave, 2001); C. Hay, *The Political Economy of New Labour* (Manchester: Manchester University Press, 1999); P. Hall, 'Policy Paradigms, Social Learning and the State; The Case of Economic Policymaking in Britain', *Comparative Politics* 25/2 (1993), pp.275–96.
8. R. Wurzel, *Environmental Policy-Making in Britain, Germany and the European Union* (Manchester: Manchester University Press, 2002).
9. Y. Rydin, *Urban and Environmental Planning in the UK* (London: Palgrave Macmillan, 2003), p.11.
10. G. Richardson, with A. Ogus and P. Burrows *Policing Pollution* (Oxford: Clarendon Press, 1982), p.33.
11. E. Ashby and M. Anderson, *The Politics of Clean Air* (Oxford: Clarendon Press, 1981).
12. S. Bell, *Ball and Bell on Environmental Policy*, 4th edition (London: Blackstone Press, 1997).
13. N. Carter and P. Lowe, 'Britain: Coming to Terms with Sustainable Development?', in K. Hanf and A.-I. Jansen (eds.), *Governance and Environmental Quality: Environmental Politics, Policy, and Administration in Western Europe* (Harlow: Addison Wesley Longman, 1998), p.22.
14. D. Baldock, *The Organization of Nature Conservation in Selected EC Countries* (London: Institute for European Environmental Policy, 1987).
15. Carter and Lowe, 'Britain: Coming to Terms with Sustainable Development?'.
16. H. Weidner, *25 Years of Modern Environmental Policy in Germany: Treading a Well-worn Path to the Top of the International Field* (Berlin: Wissenschaftszentrum Berlin für Sozialforschung, FS II 95-301, 1995); K.-G. Wey, *Umweltpolitik in Deutschland: Kurze Geschichte des Umweltschutzes in Deutschland seit 1900* (Opladen: Westdeutscher Verlag, 1982).
17. M. Skou Andersen, *Governance by Green Taxes: Making Pollution Prevention Pay* (Manchester: Manchester University Press, 1994); Wey, *Umweltpolitik in Deutschland*.
18. A. Weale, *The New Politics of Pollution* (Manchester: Manchester University Press, 1992).
19. F. Dreyhaupt, W. Dierschke, L. Kropp, B. Prinz and H. Schade, *Handbuch zur Aufstellung von Luftreinhalteplänen. Entwicklung und Ziele regionaler Luftreinhaltestrategie* (Mainz: TÜV Rheinland GmbH, 1979).
20. E. Müller, 'Sozial-liberale Umweltpolitik. Von der Karriere eines neuen Politikbereichs', *Aus Politik und Zeitgeschichte* B 47-48 (1989), p.23.
21. Weidner, *25 Years of Modern Environmental Policy in Germany*.
22. C. Lees, 'The Law of Diminishing Returns? Environmental Policy in the Federal Republic of Germany', in S. Green and W. Paterson (eds.), *Governance in Contemporary Germany: The Semisovereign State Revisited* (Cambridge: Cambridge University Press, 2005), pp.212–38.
23. Ibid.; see also C. Lees, *Party Politics in Germany: A Comparative Politics Approach* (Basingstoke: Palgrave, 2005).
24. T. Börzel, 'The Europeanisation of National Policy', in S. Bulmer and C. Lequesne (eds.), *The Member States of the European Union* (Oxford: Oxford University Press, 2005).
25. See Wurzel, *Environmental Policy-Making*; also A. Héritier, C. Knill and S. Mingers, in collaboration with B. Rhodes, *Ringing the Changes. Regulatory Competition and the Transformation of the State. Britain, France, Germany* (Berlin: Walter de Gruyter, 1996).
26. B. Flynn, 'Subsidiarity and the Rise of Soft Law', OP-40, Human Capital and Mobility Network, University of Essex, Colchester, Essex, 1997.
27. Lees, 'The Law of Diminishing Returns?'
28. A. Jordan and D. Liefferink, 'The Europeanisation of Public Policy', in Featherstone and Radaelli (eds.), *The Politics of Europeanisation*.
29. A. Weale, 'European Environmental Policy by Stealth: The Disfunctionality of Functionalism', *Environment and Planning, Government and Policy* 17/1 (1999), pp.37–51, here p.37.
30. Jessop, 'Multi-level Governance'; also I. Bache and M. Flinders, 'Multi-level Governance and British Politics', in Bache and Flinders (eds.), *Multi-level Governance*, pp.93–107.
31. For a more detailed discussion on this theme, see C. Lees, 'Reconstituting European Social Democracy: Germany's Pivotal Role', *German Politics* 9/2 (2000), pp.71–88.

32. Wurzel, *Environmental Policy-Making*, p.6.
33. Paterson provides a compelling account of how, in the mid-1980s, Joschka Fischer and the Hesse Greens forced issues of environmental protection onto the political agenda. See W. Grant, W. Paterson and C. Whitson, *Government and the Chemical Industry: A Comparative Study of Britain and West Germany* (Oxford: Clarendon Press, 1988); T. Scharf, *The German Greens: Challenging the Consensus* (Providence: Berg, 1994); A. Markovits and P. Gorski, *The German Left: Red, Green and Beyond* (Cambridge: Polity Press, 1993); K. von Beyme, *Das politische System der Bundesrepublik Deutschland nach der Vereinigung* (München: Piper, 1991).
34. Lees, *Party Politics in Germany*.
35. Carter and Lowe, 'Britain: Coming to Terms with Sustainable Development?'
36. Ibid., p.25 (emphasis added).
37. Wurzel, *Environmental Policy-Making*; also Héritier *et al.*, *Ringing the Changes*.
38. Jordan and Liefferink, 'The Europeanisation of Public Policy', p.194.
39. See http://www.defra.gov.uk (accessed 14 May 2006).
40. See http://www.euractiv.com (accessed 29 May 2006).
41. H. Pehle and A.-I. Jansen, 'Germany: The Engine in European Environmental Policy?' in Hanf and Jansen (eds.), *Governance and Environmental Quality*, p.96.
42. C. Lees, *The Red–Green Coalition in Germany: Politics, Personalities and Power* (Manchester: Manchester University Press, 2000).
43. D. Luckin and S. Lightfoot, 'Environmental Taxation in Contemporary European Politics', *Contemporary Politics* 5/3 (1999), pp.243–61.
44. M. Strübin, 'Ecological Tax Reform in Germany', *German Politics* 6/2 (1997), pp.170–71.
45. S. Padgett, 'Welfare Bias in the Party System: A Neo-Downsian Explanation for Gridlock in Economic Reform', *German Politics* 12/2 (2004), pp.360–83.
46. See http://www.euractiv.com (accessed 29 May 2006).
47. II. Jörgens, 'The Diffusion of Environmental Policy Innovations – Findings from an International Workshop', *Environmental Politics* 10/2 (2001), pp.122–7, here p.125.
48. Wurzel, *Environmental Policy-Making*, pp.7–8.
49. For a Habermasian analysis of Germany's role in this regard, see L. Jaggard, *German Climate Change Policy: Best Practice in International Relations?* (Berlin: Wissenschaftszentrum Berlin für Sozialforschung, 2005).
50. Lees, 'The Law of Diminishing Returns?'; Weidner, *25 Years of Modern Environmental Policy in Germany*.
51. OECD, *OECD Environmental Performance Reviews: Germany* (Paris: OECD, 1993), pp.208–9.
52. Lees, 'The Law of Diminishing Returns?'
53. SPD, *Der Weg nach vorne für Europas Sozialdemonkraten. Ein Vorschlag von Gerhard Schröder und Tony Blair* (Berlin: SPD Parteivorstand, 1999).
54. Richardson, *et al. Pricing Pollution*, p.33.
55. Carter and Lowe, 'Britain: Coming to Terms with Sustainable Development?', p.22.
56. Dreyhaupt *et al.*, *Handbuch zur Aufstellung von Luftreinhalteplänen*.
57. Carter and Lowe, 'Britain: Coming to Terms with Sustainable Development?', p.25.
58. Wurzel, *Environmental Policy-Making*.
59. Börzel, 'The Europeanisation of National Policy'.
60. Flynn, 'Subsidiarity and the Rise of Soft Law'.
61. Featherstone and Radaelli (eds.), *The Politics of Europeanisation*.
62. Bache and Taylor, 'The Politics of Policy Resistance'.

Conclusions

EDWARD C. PAGE

The issues of policy convergence and, more specifically, policy learning, have recently come to occupy a central position in the study of comparative policy research. Yet policy learning has been with us for a long time. At the beginning of the twentieth century the German historian Otto Hintze argued that constitutional and administrative change in Europe ceased to be explicable solely through conditions he described as *bodenständig* – literally conditions arising from the soil.[1] To him, they were the result of the more-or-less conscious influence of currents of thought, if not outright borrowing, at the start of the nineteenth century. Thus, German municipal reform in the nineteenth century was shaped by perceptions of English local self-government, and later on in the nineteenth century there is evidence that German conditions fed their way back into the wave of municipal reform in Britain after the 1880s. Germany and Britain have therefore long been influential in supplying some of the key models and concepts that have shaped the development of public policies and the institutions that generate them. The significance of policy and institutional developments in these two countries, not only for each other but also for the rest of Europe and beyond, makes the question of how they have influenced each other especially interesting and important for the comparative study of public policy.

The essays in this volume have developed their own forms of analysis, using different kinds of evidence and different forms of argument, to explore this central question of cross-national policy influence. They have generally, however, stuck to the central questions set out by the editors in their introduction. The main purpose of this piece is to revisit the framework set out by Turner and Green and suggest some answers to the questions they pose.

WEIGHING UP THE FORCES FOR CONVERGENCE AND DIVERGENCE

What do the cases tell us about the processes of convergence? Turner and Green's introduction lists a series of forces promoting convergence and another series that promotes divergence. If we think of this as analogous to the application of forces in physics, what is the resulting movement from these potentially countervailing forces?

Overall, the resultant force seems to be predominantly continued divergence. In only one major policy area, that of immigration (see Green's essay in this volume), do the forces for convergence appear to be powerful enough to swamp the forces for divergence. Germany and the UK, starting with radically different approaches and goals in relation to immigration have, under pressure of new forms of immigration, asylum and the recasting of policy in the light of anti-terrorism, have 'notably [converged] in a number of goals in immigration policy as well as in a range of specific policy instruments adopted' (p. 95). While Bulmer's broad discussion takes in a range of EU-related issues, on one of the central policy issues, air liberalisation, there is also clear evidence of the EU performing a significant role in transferring policies from one jurisdiction to another through 'uploading' the liberalisation preferences of the UK and the Netherlands into EU policy that eventually bound other member states. However, the picture for the other policy areas, though at times offering evidence of pressures for convergence, shows that continued divergence persists.

In the case of party strategy (Hough and Sloam) the collaboration between the SPD and New Labour that came in part from the latter's 1997 victory produced rather limited results once differing party contexts and changing agendas had come into play, as well as quite simply the shine disappearing from the 'Third Way' brand. On decentralisation (Jeffery) the pressures for equity in welfare states have produced radically different approaches to decentralisation despite some apparently convergent trends towards decentralisation and centralisation in the UK and Germany through devolution and federal reform respectively. Foreign and security policy (Longhurst and Miskimmon) remains characterised by different 'starting points and long-term goals' (p. 79). While employment policy (Funk) has witnessed the conscious promotion of cross-national convergence, not only through the EU but also through the Blair–Schröder paper, the results were that 'convergence ... has remained low' (p. 116). Elsewhere, Harding's paper concentrates on *Modell Deutschland* and understanding the nature of this beast in its own terms; the implication is that it remains a distinctive approach to the issue of competitiveness even if its survival may be in doubt. Health policy (Bandelow) has produced little evidence of convergence and, somewhat surprisingly given the EU involvement in environmental policy and the 'uploading' of environmental policy goals, the mechanisms and discourses of environmental policy did not converge strongly and 'nation-specific patterns remain central' (p. 150).

Why do national patterns appear to be so persistent despite the apparently strong pressures towards convergence? Turner and Green's introductory discussion of convergence offers the possibility of exploring this question further. Their exposition of the pressures for convergence and divergence allow an analytical separation of the forces in operation in each of the case studies examined here and allows us to discuss what particular mechanisms pushed convergent forms of change as well as the character of the forces ranged against them. Without wanting to repeat their informative discussion, the forces for convergence they described can be listed as: a) some form of obligation (while this was two separate categories reflecting conditionality and coercion, because they refer to similar, albeit analytically distinct, mechanisms I treat them here as one); b) competition between states and economies; c) common problem pressures (discussed further below) and d) the desire for legitimacy. Ranged against these, but not their direct counterparts; the forces for divergence, or the maintenance of differences, are also fourfold: a) varieties of capitalism; b) differential effects of globalisation; c) the resistance of national institutions and d) the sustained power of the state.

As several of the essays in this volume have suggested, the different forces of convergence and divergence are often interlinked. Europeanisation, for example, as a form of coercion or legitimacy links with changes in domestic policy and institutions and globalisation (which as a force for convergence can be understood as a form of problem pressure) in the development of liberalisation policies as well as immigration and environmental policy. Moreover, most of the forces of convergence and divergence play at least a minor role in most of the policy cases discussed in the contributions to this collection.

However, if we try and summarise the main emphasis given to different forces in each of the studies (Table 1) two forces stand out: the problem pressure as a force for convergence and the resistance of national institutions as a force for continuing divergence.

In Bulmer's account of liberalisation, common policy pressures played less of a role in promoting convergence, and the uploading/downloading dynamic within the EU was far more prominent. In security policy, the similar problem pressures have sufficiently frequently been perceived so differently that they did not actually constitute particularly powerful forces for convergence. While problem pressures may have led to some modification of *Modell Deutschland*, the main cue for change has come less from common pressures and more from the processes of competition within the European and global economies. In all other cases the common problem pressures, for example of asylum or of changes in employment, have played a large part in pushing towards policy convergence, even if convergence itself, as with the case of environment policy for example, was reinforced by other mechanisms, such as some form of regulatory compulsion.

The forces for divergence are similarly dominated by national institutional resistance, perhaps even more so than the 'problem pressures' are part of the story of the potential for convergence. Such a conclusion reinforces the generally widely accepted notion that 'path dependence' – broadly speaking (and definitions of the term vary) this refers to the inherited sets of institutions and the norms and assumptions that surround them – is crucial for understanding policy change, since past choices, as reflected in existing institutions, limit the current options available to policy makers. Only in security policy did such national institutional resistance seem to have at best only a small role – this was one of the three cases (along with environmental policy and regulatory policy) where something like 'realist' conceptions of state interest played an evident and major role. Even with the policy areas where the EU created some form of legal obligations to convergence, national political and institutional characteristics, the kind of feature that many would describe as that of 'path dependence', have served to inhibit the degree to which real convergence has taken place.

To some degree this conclusion – that problem pressures account for pressures to converge and institutional resistance accounts for persisting differences – might be something of an artefact of how these two forces are set up: 'problem pressures' are relatively indeterminate and can take a variety of forms: whether the specific need to win an election (Hough and Sloam), the desire to satisfy citizen demands for equity (Jeffery) or increasing demands on spending (Bandelow). Indeed the general need to compete in a global economy (Harding) can be construed as 'problem pressure' rather than a separate competition-driven imperative to change. Thus, to some degree, 'problem pressure' might be something of a 'wild card' that overlaps with many of the other forces for convergence. Similarly, institutional resistance, whether because of the specifics of party structures (Hough and Sloam), outright political opposition (Bandelow) or different conceptions of the appropriate forms and mechanisms of policy intervention (Funk; Lees), is a second broad category to be considered a 'wild card'. So while the new institutionalist might claim victory in that 'institutions matter', the multiple meanings of the term 'institution' stack the odds extremely strongly in its favour. Consequently, if path dependence is saying that where they start from defines the choices open to policy makers about where they go, then path dependence is always going to have some influence on policy almost by definition.

TABLE 1
FORCES FOR CONVERGENCE AND DIVERGENCE

Dimension study	Convergence					Divergence		
	Coercion and obligation	Competition	Problem pressure	Legitimacy	Varieties of Capitalism	Globalisation	National institutional resistance	Power of the state
Party strategy (Hough and Sloan)			x			x	x	
Regulatory policy (Bulmer)	x	x					x	x
Decentralisation (Jeffery)			x				x	
Security (Longhurst and Miskimmon)				x				x
Immigration (Green)			x				x	
Employment (Funk)			x				x	
Competitiveness (Harding)		x			x		x	
Health (Bandelow)			x				x	
Environment (Lees)	x		x				x	x

A QUESTION OF ANCHORAGE

Can we go any further than this and ask what precisely leads to the somewhat different results from these two sets of forces? While persistent divergence is a common result, it is not universally so, and some policy areas show convergent tendencies even if true similarity remains far distant. To some degree, a proper answer to this question might require further refinement of the terms 'problem pressure' and 'institutional resistance' – dissecting the different forms both might take and (far more difficult) developing some metric that can assess the transforming power of different problems or the resisting power of different institutions. But such measures are a long way off in social science and calling for 'more research' or 'more refinement' is an unsatisfactory way of concluding any academic investigation, and especially a collection that can with great justification claim to have provided the empirical material to answer key questions about policy convergence.

I would like to propose here that some of the puzzles that remain about the character of convergence and divergence can be addressed using Kurt Weyland's concept of 'heuristics' in policy learning and, above all in this context, the notion of the 'anchor' heuristic. To do this a brief exposition of Weyland's perspective, developed in his work on Latin America is needed.[2]

Policy learning is a difficult and expensive exercise. To look around for lessons, to examine the policies and programmes of other countries in the kind of way outlined by Richard Rose in his practical guide to lesson-drawing,[3] is a costly enterprise in terms of time and money. Moreover, the exercise is intellectually demanding and requires the evaluation of evidence that is often not there and that runs up against the fact that our theoretical understanding of social phenomena might be highly limited. Thus it is not surprising that rigorous lesson-drawing is found only rarely, an expectation confirmed by this collection: in practice, the limited amount of direct policy learning that can be identified is strictly limited. We might have expected far more of such direct bilateral learning in the German and British development of policy after the late 1990s in light of the common commitment to the Third Way and the British influence on the EU's Agenda 2010. Rightly or wrongly, policy makers in Britain, Germany, or anywhere else, tend to use shortcuts that avoid the costly business of lesson drawing. Weyland, in his study of pension reform in Bolivia, refers to these shortcuts as 'heuristics'.[4]

In this, Weyland shows that decision-makers in Bolivia did not search widely for pension policy models to imitate, but chose Chile as a model because advice on how to set up a Chilean-style system was easily available through written guides and consultants ready to help. The choice thus reflected an *availability heuristic* rather than any other kind of search process. Rather than evaluate exhaustively the performance of the Chilean model, Bolivian decision-makers fixed on one or two key facts about how the scheme performed (above all the annual return on investment by Chilean pension managers in one particularly good year) as representative of its success overall. This was the *representativeness heuristic*. The *anchoring heuristic* reflected the government's approach to how the Chilean model should be adapted to Bolivian circumstances: stick as closely as you can to the Chilean model and only give way to pressures for change when they domestically become hard, if not impossible, to resist.

Thus, using the notion of anchorage, the question of how far an 'imported' outside model shapes a particular policy programme depends upon how strongly anchored it is when it is exposed to domestic political forces. The domestic political forces can change the foreign model, though not necessarily (indeed probably rarely) by any conscious processes of policy learning, but through political processes of opposition and compromise or reactive administrative processes of adaptation. Thus, in Weyland's pensions study, the answer to the question of how the policy should be adapted to Bolivian circumstances involved no systematic consideration of how to change the Chilean model but rather rigid adherence to the model until the legislative phase of policy development, when political pressures within the Bolivian political system forced some deviations from it. In this case the deviations concerned 'peripheral aspects' of the reform rather than its core, though there is no necessary reason to expect the policy process to affect only peripheral aspects of borrowed policies.

The notion of 'anchorage' might help us understand some of the variation in the essays in this volume. Anchorage can come about above all because of a strong political commitment to support a particular borrowed policy or, in a European context, because the policy is enshrined in a European law. The political forms of anchorage – 'Third Wayism' and the Blair–Schröder paper – appear to have been, despite appearances at the time, very weak, and became almost imperceptible when faced with the slightest challenge from domestic policy forces[6]. Indeed, in health service reform the 'Third Way', which might have been expected to shape policy development, was so weakly anchored that it led to radically different interpretations of the goals of health reform in both countries. Moreover, where Germany did produce reforms similar to those of Britain the acknowledged debt was to the Netherlands, not Britain. The strongest forms of anchorage tend to be found, unsurprisingly, when policy initiatives are transformed into EU mandates. What it is that is 'anchored' is of crucial importance: in environmental policy the concentration (with some exceptions) has been on anchoring targets and outcomes, leaving philosophies, processes and institutions to remain different.

The fact that immigration policy, although involving EU norm-setting, did not display convergent trends solely because of EU regulation highlights the importance of the other side of the anchoring equation: the character of the domestic political forces that counteract forces for change. It is characteristic that convergence appears to be found in this specific area where the domestic political constituency (consisting of people who have not yet arrived in either country or have only recently done so) is likely to be weak; the constituency is simply not able to overcome strong pressures for convergence by itself. By contrast domestic political forces representing more powerful constituencies, whether of patients, pharmaceutical companies, party members, employers or unions, for example, appear successfully to have countered pressures for convergence where the anchorage is weak.

The strong performance of the 'wild cards' of institutional resistance and path dependence in this evaluation of the forces for convergence and divergence should not surprise us. As with similar concepts before it, such as 'incrementalism' or even inertia,[5] it has always been a safe bet to claim that things will not change substantially very quickly. Convergence or direct mutual policy borrowing is rare in Britain and Germany only in part because the forces of inertia, incrementalism or path dependence are so strong. At least as important, the policy innovations that borrow from the other country have been only very weakly anchored and it is hardly a testament to the forces of path dependence that any potential for radical transformation arising from such attempted innovations tend to disintegrate when exposed to domestic political processes. If path dependence were particularly powerful, we would expect *increasing divergence* to be a perceptible trend, at least in some policy areas, as the constellation of norms, institutions and political forces in each country sets them on divergent trajectories.

Moreover, path dependence cannot explain the type of common experiences of institutional and policy change that Hintze was pointing to over a longer time horizon. For instance, if one compares Germany and Britain at 30-year periods since the end of World War Two, the overall trend is likely not to be towards greater divergence, but rather increasing similarity across broad areas of state activity such as the development of the welfare state, liberalisation, economic management and the environment. That the reasons behind growing similarities over the longer term may not be directly observable in the mechanisms that drive policy over the shorter and medium term helps us to dispense with some of the assertions and assumptions about policy convergence, borrowing and transfer. Yet thinking about the longer term pattern raises the further question: what it is about European nations, and especially Britain and Germany that keeps their paths of development moving sometimes in parallel, sometimes converging but rarely moving further apart, over the long term?

NOTES

1. O. Hintze; 'Staatenbildung und Kommunnalverwaltung', in O. Hintze, Staat und *Verfassung. Gesammelte Abhandlungen zur Allgemeine Verwaltungsgeschichte* Band I, Gerhard Oestreich (edited, and introduced) (Göttingen: Vandenhoeck und Ruprecht, 1962 [1927], p. 216).
2. K. Weyland, 'The Diffusion of Innovations: How Cognitive Heuristics Shaped Bolivian Pension Reform', *Comparative Politics* 38/1 (2005), pp.21–42; also K. Weyland (ed.), *Learning from Foreign Models in Latin American Policy Reform* (Washington, DC: Woodrow Wilson Center Press, 2004).
3. R. Rose, *Learning from Comparative Public Policy – A Practical Guide* (London and New York: Routledge, 2005).
4. Weyland, 'The Diffusion of Innovations'.
5. On incrementalism in Germany, see P. Katzenstein, *Policy and Politics in West Germany: The Growth of a Semisovereign State* (Philadelphia, PA: Temple University Press, 1987).
6. T. Blair and G. Schröder, Europe: The Third Way (The Labour Party: London, 1999).

Index

Page numbers in **Bold** represent Figures

Adenauer, K. 22
adversarial governance 51
Aerospatiale-Matre 40–1
Afghanisation 85–6
Air Berlin 45
Airbus 40
Alkali Act 166, 179
Alliance for Jobs 129
Allied Control Council 23
anchoring heuristic 188
Anglo-Scottish contentions **68**
Armed forces; German 81–2
asylum; liberal universalist model of 101
Asylum application in EU 100
Asylum Policy 108–9

Bandelow, N.C. 150–62
Bank of England 118, 138
banking sector; German 10
Bavarian state government 47
Bennett, C. 3
Best Available Technology 169, 179; Principle 171
Bevan, A. 61
bicarmelism 16
bilateralism; multiple 84
Blair, T. 2, 27, 29, 32, 48, 116–34
Blair-Schröder paper 124, 129–32, 179, 189
Blue Angel scheme 175
Börzel, T. 42
Bournville 167
Britain: Conservative government 119; social citizenship 59–62; Victorian 166
British Airways 45
British citizenship 97
British Dependent Territories Citizenship (BDTC) 97
British Labour Party 61–2
British National Health Service 72, 151, *see also* NHS
British Nationality Act 97
British Overseas Citizenship (BOC) 97
British welfare state programmes 59
Brixton riots 99

Brown, G. 61, 68, 74
BSE (Bovine spongiform encephalopathy) 158
Bulmer, S. 13, 39–54
Bundesbank 122
Bürgerversicherung 160

Calmfors, L. 131
Cameron, D. 74
capitalism: lean-welfare model of 41; varieties of 15, 124
Carter administration 45
centralised government 63
centralism 51
Cerny, P. 41
character of policy transfer 49–50
China 144
Chirac, J. 48
Christian Democrats 31
citizen insurance 160
citizenship: British 97; in the early twenty-first century **72**; and integration policy 106–8; social 58–75
citizenship in Britain; evolution of **72**
Clean Air Act 179
Clean Air Maintenance Law 169, 179
Climate Change Agreements 174
Climate Change Levy 174–5
Clinton, B. 2
Co-operation principle 169
co-ordinated market economies (CMEs) 9
coalition government 16, 51
coercive isomorphism 7
Commission for Health Improvement (CHImp) 154
Common Foreign and Security Policy (CFSP) 81
competition; incentives to 10
competition state model 41
competitiveness 138–47
competitiveness rankings for G7 economies **143**
conditional policy transfer 8
conditionality 8

Conference on Security and Co-operation in Europe (CSCE) 81
consensus/consociational governance 51
Conservative government (Britain) 119
Conservative Party; environmentalism 172
conservative welfare state 151
constitutional court 16
Construcciones Aeronauticas SA (CASA) 40–1
convergence: definition of 40–6; Europeanisation an types of **14**; forces for **187**
convergence of institutional variable **126**
convergence processes; heuristic understanding of **18**
Countryside Commission 168

Daimler-Chrysler Aerospace AG (DASA) 40–1
Danish Bottle case 171
Darling, A. 68
decentralisation 185; of the NHS 155–6
defence spending 90–1
demand management; Keynesian 123
Democrats; Christian 31
dependant migration 104–6
devolution 62–7; in Scotland and Wales; impacts of **65**
dioxin emissions 178
direct coercive transfer 7–8
divergence; forces for 186, **187**
diversity 98
Dolowitz, D. 3–5
domestic policy change; and Europeanisation **44**

easyJet 45
eco-tax 176
economic integration 9
economic interdependence; of national economies 13
economic policy; Keynesian 165
education policy **67**
Employment Protection Legislation (EPI) 128
employment related public policies 116–34
endogenous growth 140, 146
English Nature 168
entrepreneurial propensity 141
entrepreneurship 146

environmental policy 164–81
environmental policy making; Europeanisation of 170
environmentalism; Conservative Party 172
European Aeronautic Defence and Space Company (EADS) 40
European Central Bank 122
European Civil Aviation Conference (ECAC) 45
European Commission 132
European Convention on Human Rights 9
European security 79–92
European Security and Defence Identity (ESDI) 82
European Security and Defence Policy (ESDP) 48, 79
European Union Emissions Trading Scheme 177
European Union (EU) 39–54, 170–3; as security and defence actor 88–90
Europeanisation 12–14, 41–4, 164, 181; domestic policy change **44**; types and mechanisms of convergence **14**

federalism 16, 51, 62–7, 67; competitive 62
fiscal equalisation in Germany; support for **71**
Fischer, A. 158
Fischer, J. 84
foreign policy; European Union common **89**
foreign policy elites; German 81–2
Funk, L. 11, 116–34

G-6 group 104
Garrett, G. 15
Geddes, A. 107
Geneva Convention 9
Genscher, H.D. 82
German banking sector 10
German Democratic Republic 99
German labour market 131
German Länder; economic disparities among **69**
German military deployment overseas **83**
German semisovereignty 22
German Statutory Health Insurance (SHI) 151, *see also* SHI
German unification 80

INDEX

German welfare state 67; nationalising ambition 60
German Wings 45
Germany: conflict between East and West **70**; Green Party 31; Party of Democratic Socialism *see* Party of Democratic Socialism; policy instruments and discourses 175–7; social citizenship 59–62; social democratic politics 26–36; support for fiscal equalisation in **71**
Giddens, A. 2
Global Entrepreneurship Monitor 145–6
globalisation 9, 12–14, 40–1, 139; differing impact of 15–16
government; centralised 63
Green Card scheme 104
Green Party 31
Green, S. 1–19, 95–111
Green Spot scheme 175
Group of Eight (G8) 17, 44
growth; endogenous 140, 146
Guiraudon, V. 107

Haider, J. 107
Harding, R. 138–47
health; expenditure on **152**
health policy 150–62; British **154**; German **159**; New Labour 153–6
health policy convergence; obstacles against 161–2
Hewitt, P. 156
Highly Skilled Migrants Programme (HSMP) 105
Hombach, B. 33
Hough, D. 26–36
Human Rights; European Convention on 9
Hussein, S. 91

Ich-AG 145
immigration 95–111; Highly Skilled Migrants Programme (HSMP) 105
immigration and citizenship **96**
immigration and integration; policy convergence **110**
immigration policy 189
India 144
industrialisation 59
industry; nationalisation of 61
innovation potential 141

Institute for Quality and Efficiency in the Health Care System 160
institutional change 10
institutional racism 99
institutional resilience; national 16–17
institutions; as agents of policy transfer 48–9
integration policy 95–111; and citizenship 106–8
interest rates 138
international laws 8–9
international mediation 44–5
International Monetary Fund (IMF) 132
International Standards Organisation (ISO) 173
Iraq 85–6
isomorphism 3–5; coercive 7

Jeffery, C. 58–75
Jenkins, R. 98
Job Centres 35
Jospin, L. 2
Jump programme 35

Kaiser, K. 80
Katzenstein, P. 22
key indicators in Britain and Germany **4**
Keynes, J.M. 123
Kinnock, N. 30, 61
Knill, C. 5, 40
Koch, R. 11
Kohl, H. 23, 81
Kosovo 85

labour; and dependant migration 104–6
labour market related indicators **117**
Labour Party 23, 26–36, 61–2; social contract 34
Lafontaine, O. 123, 158
Learning and Skills council 102
Lees, C. 164–81
legitimacy pressure 12
lesson-drawing 10–11
liberal market economy (LME) 9, 118
liberal welfare state 151
liberalisation 10, 45, 186
Lisbon Agenda 52
Longhurst, K. 79–92
Lufthansa 45

Macpherson report 99
majoritarian government 51
Mandelson, P. 33
market economies: alternative 118–19; coordinated 118; liberal 118
Marsh, D. 5
Marshall, T.H. 59, 71–3
Merkel, A. 24, 86–7, 145–6, 179
Metropolitan Police 99
migrants; high-skilled 104
migration; dependant 104–6
Milburn, A. 155, 156
Milliband, D. 168
Miskimmon, A. 79–92
Mitchell, J. 64–5
Modell Deutschland 138–47, 185
modernisation 32
Monetary Policy Committee 138
monetary policy frameworks **121**
Morgan, R. 74
multiple bilateralism 84
Müntefering 160

nation states 17
national economies; economic interdependence of 13
National Health Service 60–1
National Health Service Plan 11
National Institute for Clinical Excellence (NICE) 154
national institutional resilience 16–17
nationalisation of industry 61
Nationality Immigration and Asylum Act 106
negative conditionality 8
Netherlands 160
Neue Mitte (New Centre) 30–1, 33, 84
New Deal 35
New Labour 84, 123; health policy 153–6
NHS; decentralisation of 155–6
non-governmental organisation (NGOs); as agents of policy transfer 49
North Atlantic Treaty Organisation (NATO) 44
Notting Hill riots 99

Open Method of Coordination 43, 52
Ordinance on Large Combustion Plants 179
Organisation for Economic Co-operation and Development (OECD) 12, 17, 44

Parti Socialiste 2
party cohesion 16
Party of Democratic Socialism 71, 74–5
Party of European Socialists (PES) 48
Paterson, W. 22–4
path-dependence 165
pharmaceutical companies 157
policy areas in convergence literature **6**
policy convergence: definition of 3–7, 40–6; factors promoting 7–12; notion of 1–3; and policy transfer 28–9
policy convergence and related concepts **5**
policy diffusion 3–5, 177
policy disasters 50
policy instruments and discourses: Germany 175–7; United Kingdom 173–5
policy learning 10; and programmatic convergence 32–6
policy transfer 3–5, 39–54, 153, 164; conditional 8; definition of 46–7; flow chart **53**; forced 7–8; and policy convergence 28–9; sources of 49–50
politicians and civil servants; as agents of policy transfer 48
politics: ownership of 65; territorial 58–75
poll tax 50
Polluter Pays 171; principle 169
Port Sunlight 167
positive conditionality 8
Precautionary Principle 169, 179
Primary Care Groups 154
Primary Care Trusts (PCTs) 154
problem pressures 10–11, 75
problem-solving; transnational 10–11
programmatic convergence; and policy learning 32–6
public expenditure 33
public policies; employment related 116–34
Pulzer, P. 22–4

Race Equality Directive 107
rail privatisation 50
Red-Green coalition 175
regulatory environments **121**
Reid, J. 68, 156
renewable energy sources 178
representativeness heuristic 188
Robbe, R. 90–1
Roper, J. 80
Ryanair 45

INDEX

Safe Country of Origin 109
Saltaire 167
Schily, O. 104, 109
Schmidt, H. 23
Schmidt, U. 158
Schneiderhan, W. 92
Schröder, G. 2, 24, 27, 29, 32, 48, 87, 104
Scottish Constitutional Convention 65
Scottish identity 64
Scottish Office 47–8
Scottish-Anglo contentions **68**
SDP 23, 26–36
security; European 79–92
security policy 1
Seehofer, H. 159
semisovereignty 153; German 22
sewage purification technology 178
SHI Modernisation Act 160
Shifting the Balance of Power (White Paper) 155
Shröder, G. 116–34
Single European Act 171
Sloam, J. 26–36
Smith, J. 30
social citizenship 58–75
social contract 34
Social Democratic Party (SDP) *see* SDP
social democratic politics 26–36
social insurance reforms 59
social justice 34
social market economy; German model of 70
Sodesxho 109
sources of policy transfer 49–50
South Korea 144
SPD 84; Green Coalition 123, 157; Green government 10
Steinbrück, P. 34
Stille Allianz 80
subject of policy transfer 49–50
supranational institutions; as agents of policy transfer 48
Süssmuth Commission 104

tax- eco-tax 176
technological change 40
territorial cleavages 68–71

territorial identity 74–5
territorial policy variation in Britain **66**
territorial politics 58–75
terror; war on 88
terrorism 101
Thatcher, M. 23, 120
think-tanks; as agents of policy transfer 49
Third Reich 59
Third Way 2, 27, 84, 117, 150, 157, 185
Total Factor Productivity 142
trade union 10
transnational business; as agents of policy transfer 49
transnational problem-solving 10–11
Turner, E. 1–19

UN Charter 9
unemployment benefits 128
unemployment, youth 35
unification; German 80
United Kingdom (UK): National Health Service Plan 11; policy instruments and discourses 173–5; renewable energy sources 178; social democratic politics 26–36
United States (US); Carter administration 45

veto players 16
Victorian Britain 166
Vogel, D. 10

Wales; post-devolution 74
war on terror 88
Water Household Act 169, 179
welfare state 58; conservative 151; equity in 185; liberal 151; reform of 33
welfare state programmes; British 59
Welsh identity 64
Welsh political process 65
Westminster; views on the influence of **63**
World Trade Organisation (WTO) 17

youth unemployment 35